带动小农户发展的制度安排、产业选择和价值链建设研究
——基于国际农业发展基金贷款优势特色产业发展示范项目

Research on Institutional Arrangement, Agro-industrial Choice and Value Chain Construction for Promoting Smallholders' Development
——The IFAD Program for Specialized Agribusiness Development in Sichuan and Ningxia

尹昌斌 等 编著

中国农业科学技术出版社

《带动小农户发展的制度安排、产业选择和价值链建设研究——基于国际农业发展基金贷款优势特色产业发展示范项目》

指导委员会

主　任：郭永田

副主任：苏　葳　孙印洪

委　员：郑　苗　史茵茵

编著委员会

主 编 著：尹昌斌　吴洪伟
副主编著：苏　葳　易小燕
参编人员：郑　苗　任　静　杨晓梅　李福夺
　　　　　韦　伟　唐　捷　刘红兵　吴　昊
　　　　　张　奇　袁　芳　吴焜玥　梁　繁
　　　　　赵　涛　曾继红　兰光明　邓德全
　　　　　刘海龙　马少君　雍艳霞　郝丹东
　　　　　梁生藩　王芳芝　李灵露　倪子璇
　　　　　杨紫洪　张泽蔚　周礼君　徐珂怡
　　　　　赵玛璠　尹彦舒

前言

党的二十大报告对新时代农业农村发展作出重大决策部署,强调要全面推进乡村振兴、加快建设农业强国。产业振兴是乡村振兴的基础,农业经营主体能力提升是产业振兴的支撑。小农户仍然是我国农业经营的基础单元,是农民群体的大多数,让广大小农户发展得更好,事关农业农村现代化,是农业强国建设的重要环节。

党中央、国务院高度重视发挥小农户家庭经营在农业发展中的作用。习近平总书记多次强调,"大国小农"是我国的基本国情农情,要注重解决小农户生产经营面临的困难,把他们引入现代农业发展大格局。2019年,中共中央办公厅、国务院办公厅印发《关于促进小农户和现代农业发展有机衔接的意见》,对扶持小农户、提升小农户能力,发展现代农业提出指导意见。2022年中央一号文件强调要"巩固提升脱贫地区特色产业,完善联农带农机制,提高脱贫人口家庭经营性收入"。2024年中央一号文件进一步提出"以小农户为基础、新型农业经营主体为重点、社会化服务为支撑,加快打造适应现代农业发展的高素质生产经营队伍。提升家庭农场和农民专业合作社生产经营水平,增强服务带动小农户能力"。

扶持小农户发展是一个长期过程,需要给予资金支持,提供生产技术指导,解决小农户在生产经营中面临的诸多问题,持续提升小农户发展能力。为借鉴国际组织现代农业发展的理念和经验,推进我国农业农村现代化发展,2018年10月,我国政府向国际农业发展基金(以下简称"国际农发基金")申请8 000万美元贷赠款,开展优势特色产业发展示范项目(IPRAD-SN,以下简称"项目"),旨在通过项目实施,建设和完善农业基础设施,提高小农户和合作社发展能力,建立具有包容性、平等性和可持续性的价值链,促进区域优势特色产业发展,为项目县(区)巩固脱贫成果、促进乡村振兴作出贡献。项目建设周期6年,在四川苍溪县、仪陇县、叙州区、广安区、宣汉县和宁夏兴庆区、利通区、红寺堡区、原州区、彭阳县10个县（区）开展实施，涉及乡镇43个、行政村121个，农户总人口19.9万人，其中贫困村93个、贫困人口3.9万人。建设内容主要包括：（1）基础设施建设及气候智慧型生产基地建设；（2）惠农价值链建设；（3）项目管理与协调能力建设。

为推进农民合作社带动小农户发展制度建设，提升当地优势特色产业选择和发展能力，建立健全农业产业链和价值链，促进传统农业向现代农业转型升级，2022年5月16日，国家项目管理办公室（设在农业农村部农田建设管理司，以下简称"国家项目办"）与中国农业科学院农业资源与农业区划研究所（以下简称"资划所"）签订咨询服务合同，委托开展"带动小农户发展的制度安排、产业选择和价值链建设（GB-21005）"课题研究。课题组在系统梳理项目实施过程中的国家相关制度安排和政策措施，分析项目区优势特色产业基础和条件，针对项目实施主体，设计合作社带动小农户发展的一套调查问卷，采取分层随机抽样方法，一对一、面对面与合作社和农户进行交流，先后开展专题调研4次，获得一手资料和数据，对数据资料进行分析，剖析典型案例，撰写形成调研报告4份，在此基础上编写本著作。

本著作是课题研究成果之一，分上下两篇，上篇为综合报告，梳理我国当前促进小农户发展的战略决策部署、制度安排与支持政策，剖析项目区优势特色产业发展状况及重点产业选择，通过对项目扶持合作社开展调研，总结自身发展及其带动小农户的方式，阐明合作社在产业发展、价值链建设及带动小农户等方面的做法与成效，凝练形成项目扶持合作社带动小农户发展的主要模式；下篇为项目区典型案例，按照项目实施内容和产业类型，选择了粮油、蔬菜、水果、茶、牛羊养殖等优势特色产业发展典型案例共25个。英文对照中文内容翻译，一一对应。

国际农业发展基金贷款优势特色产业发展示范项目（IPRAD-SN）咨询课题"带动小农户发展的制度安排、产业选择与价值链建设（GB-21005）"为课题研究和著作出版提供资助。

编著委员会
2024年12月
北京

目录

上篇　综合报告

第一章　项目实施与课题研究　/3
　　一、项目实施背景与进展成效　/3
　　二、课题研究目的与意义　/4
　　三、课题调研与资料数据收集　/5

第二章　促进小农户发展的制度安排　/8
　　一、国家战略决策部署　/8
　　二、国家制度安排　/9
　　三、地方推进措施　/11

第三章　项目区优势特色产业选择　/14
　　一、四川项目区　/14
　　二、宁夏项目区　/14

第四章　合作社带动小农户发展的做法与成效　/17
　　一、改善基础设施设备，经营类型多元化　/17
　　二、加强价值链建设，提升产业效益　/18
　　三、提供多样化服务，多渠道带动小农户　/20
　　四、小农户参与方式及增收效果　/23

第五章　带动小农户发展的典型模式与推广建议　/29
　　一、带动小农户发展的典型模式　/29
　　二、带动小农户发展模式推广的对策建议　/33

下篇　项目区典型案例

1. 宣汉项目区桂刚种植专业合作社　/40
2. 原州项目区新星土地股份专业合作社　/42
3. 苍溪项目区高成山蔬菜专业合作社　/45
4. 红寺堡项目区周福贵黄花菜种植专业合作社　/48
5. 苍溪项目区五福猕猴桃专业合作社　/51
6. 利通项目区烽火台苹果种植专业合作社　/54
7. 苍溪项目区雍河桃园天麻中药材专业合作社　/57
8. 宣汉项目区寿口岩种植专业合作社　/59
9. 叙州项目区功益茶叶专业合作社　/61
10. 宣汉项目区佳和种植专业合作社　/64
11. 仪陇项目区茂园种植农民专业合作社　/66
12. 原州项目区中河村益农养殖示范基地　/69
13. 彭阳项目区山牛源肉牛科技养殖专业合作社　/71
14. 红寺堡项目区香园村肉羊养殖基地　/73
15. 红寺堡项目区水套村养殖基地　/75
16. 原州项目区宏科农民养殖专业合作社　/77
17. 原州项目区六盘山生态养殖专业合作社　/79
18. 仪陇项目区丰泰养殖农民专业合作社　/81
19. 宣汉项目区江鑫生态养殖专业合作社　/84
20. 叙州项目区顺盈桑蚕养殖专业合作社　/86
21. 苍溪项目区金永丰农机服务专业合作社　/89
22. 利通项目区吴忠市海之峰种植农民专业合作社　/91
23. 仪陇项目区勇旗种养殖农民专业合作社　/93
24. 广安项目区初山农谷种养专业合作社　/95
25. 银川项目区月益农农艺专业合作社　/98

致谢　/100

附件1：调研问卷　/101

附件2：调研照片　/117

Part I Comprehensive Report

Chapter 1 Project Background and Research Overview   / 135

    1. Background and Progress of IPRAD-SN Project   / 135

    2. Research Purpose and Significance   / 137

    3. Survey Methodology and Data Collection   / 139

Chapter 2 Institutional Arrangement for Promoting Smallholders' Development   / 142

    1. National Strategic Deployment   / 142

    2. Institutional Arrangement   / 144

    3. Local Policy Measures   / 148

Chapter 3 Advantageous Agro-industry in Project Areas   / 153

    1. Sichuan Project Area   / 153

    2. Ningxia Project Area   / 154

Chapter 4 Practices and Effectiveness of Cooperatives in Promoting Smallholders' Development   / 157

    1. Improvement of Infrastructures and Diversification of Business Types   / 157

    2. Strengthening the Value Chain and Enhancing Agro-industry Efficiency   / 158

    3. Providing Diversified Services and Supporting Smallholders Through Multiple Channels   / 162

    4. Effectiveness of Smallholders' Participation in Cooperatives   / 165

Chapter 5 Typical Modes and Suggestions for Cooperatives Promoting Smallholders' Development   / 173

    1. Typical Modes for Promoting the Development of Smallholders   / 173

    2. Suggestions for Modes of Application and Promoting Smallholders' Development   / 179

Part II Case Study

1. Guigang Planting Professional Cooperative in Xuanhan / 189
2. Xinxing Land Stock Professional Cooperative in Yuanzhou / 192
3. Gaochengshan Vegetable Professional Cooperative in Cangxi / 195
4. Zhou Fugui Day Lily Planting Professional Cooperative in Hongsibu / 199
5. Wufu Kiwi Fruit Professional Cooperative in Cangxi / 203
6. Fenghuotai Apple Planting Professional Cooperative in Litong / 206
7. Yonghe Taoyuan Gastrodia Elata Chinese Medicinal Materials Professional Cooperative in Cangxi / 210
8. Shoukouyan Planting Professional Cooperative in Xuanhan / 214
9. Gongyi Tea Professional Cooperative in Xuzhou / 217
10. Jiahe Planting Professional Cooperative in Xuanhan / 221
11. Maoyuan Planting Farmers' Professional Cooperative in Yilong / 224
12. Zhonghe Village Yinong Breeding Demonstration Base in Yuanzhou / 227
13. Shanniuyuan Beef Cattle Science and Technology Breeding Professional Cooperative in Pengyang / 230
14. Xiangyuan Village Mutton Sheep Breeding Base in Hongsibu / 232
15. Shuitao Village Breeding Base in Hongsibu / 234
16. Hongke Farmers' Breeding Professional Cooperative in Yuanzhou / 236
17. Liupanshan Ecological Breeding Professional Cooperative in Yuanzhou / 239
18. Fengtai Breeding Farmers' Professional Cooperative in Yilong / 242
19. Jiangxin Ecological Breeding Professional Cooperative in Xuanhan / 245
20. Shunying Silkworm Breeding Professional Cooperative in Xuzhou / 247
21. Jinyongfeng Agricultural Machinery Service Professional Cooperative in Cangxi / 251
22. Wuzhong Haizhifeng Planting Farmers' Professional Cooperative in Litong / 254
23. Yongqi Planting and Breeding Farmers' Professional Cooperative in Yilong / 257
24. Chushannonggu Planting and Breeding Professional Cooperative in Guangan / 260
25. Yueyinong Agronomic Professional Cooperative in Yinchuan / 264

Acknowledgements / 267

Attachment 1: Investigation Questionnaire / 269

Attachment 2: Investigation Photos / 289

上篇　综合报告

第一章　项目实施与课题研究

一、项目实施背景与进展成效

为贯彻落实党中央、国务院关于实施乡村振兴战略，加快农业农村现代化的决策部署，借鉴国际金融组织现代农业发展理念和经验，2018年10月30日，我国政府与国际农业发展基金签订"优势特色产业发展示范项目"（IPRAD-SN，以下简称"项目"）《贷款协定》，投资总额为8 000万美元。

项目由国家项目办（设在农业农村部农田建设管理司）组织实施，在四川苍溪县、宣汉县、广安市广安区、宜宾市叙州区（原宜宾县）、仪陇县与宁夏固原市原州区、彭阳县、吴忠市红寺堡区、利通区和银川市兴庆区的10个县（区）开展实施，涉及43个乡镇、121个行政村，19.9万农村人口，其中贫困村93个、贫困人口3.9万人。

项目建设期6年，总投入约为人民币10.4亿元[①]，其中农发基金投入资金8 000万美元，折合人民币5.2亿元，占总投入的49.8%，由中央财政借统还，其中投入四川27 950万元、投入宁夏23 397万元；地方财政资金投入52 468万元，占总投入的50.2%，其中四川27 449万元、宁夏25 019万元。

项目实施旨在建设和完善基础设施，发展农产品加工及销售，强化对农业价值链的开发，并着力延伸、完善、提升产业价值链，提高小农户和合作社的生产、管理、交易和服务等发展能力，增强小农户和合作社的市场竞争力，为小农户建立起具有包容性的、平等的、可持续的稳定增收价值链，为地区发展作出贡献，探索、创新并形成可复制推广的产业发展机制。项目具体建设内容主要包括以下3个方面。

（一）完善基础设施建设，拓宽小农户与市场连接渠道

对项目区的基础设施加以改善、开发、重建及维护，具体包括排灌系统、水

---

① 按照《贷款协定》当年美元与人民币汇率为1∶6.5。

源工程、人畜安全饮水工程、供电系统、村舍和田间道路等建设内容。截至 2024 年底，公共基础设施累计投资额超过 2.8 亿元，其中农发资金 922 万元，占比 3.29%。基础设施建设改善小农户生产生活条件，为特色农业产业的发展提供基础保障。

（二）气候智慧型生产基地建设，增强小农户应对气候变化能力

气候智慧型生产基地建设通过土地平整等工程措施，实现土地规模化应用，截至 2024 年底，气候智慧型生产基地累计投资 7 909 万元，其中农发资金 6 144 万元，占比 77.68%。节水灌溉、水肥一体化、病虫害远程监控等先进技术的应用，增强小农户应对干旱、洪涝、病虫害等灾害风险的能力，帮助其掌握农业绿色生产技术，提升农业生产效率和农产品质量，带动分散小农户摆脱单一农业生产的束缚，推动产业链向二三产业延伸，以多种途径带动小农户增加收入。

（三）扶持合作社发展，带动小农户能力提升

项目通过扶持合作社发展来带动小农户与产业发展，与有需求的合作社签订商业计划书，使合作社的发展目标更加明确，发展规划更为科学合理。截至 2024 年底，项目共扶持合作社 119 家，其中四川 89 家，宁夏 30 家。合作社对加入合作社的成员进行技术培训并提供就业机会，为提升市场竞争力和议价能力，通过 App 等方式向群众传递合作社田间生产控制过程，通过田间认养、合作社代管的方式实现优质农产品的销售，并通过农超对接、网络销售、农旅融合等方式延伸产业链、提高产业链质量。

二、课题研究目的与意义

项目实施目标人群主要为小农户，让更多的小农户在项目的基础设施建设、价值链建设中获得直接或间接收益，并参与到项目活动中，掌握更多技能，实现能力提升。小农户作为乡村振兴的主体力量，其发展直接关系到农村经济繁荣和社会稳定。"大国小农"是我国基本国情，第三次农业普查数据显示，全国小农户数量占农业经营主体 98% 以上，小农户经营耕地面积约占耕地总面积的 70%[①]。小农户生

---

① 促进小农户和现代农业发展有机衔接，经济日报，2024 年 8 月 27 日第 10 版，http://www.moa.gov.cn/ztzl/ymksn/jjrbbd/202408/t20240827_6461328.htm。

产经营面临包括生产规模有限、土地碎片化严重、机械化普及率低及市场参与度不足等诸多挑战，这些因素制约小农户与现代农业及市场经济体系的有效连接，抑制农业生产力提升。

随着新型农业经营主体组织优势凸显、服务能力持续增强，提升小农户的规模化和专业化水平成为带动小农户对接"大市场"，提高农业生产效率的重要途径。合作社是兼具经济和社会双重属性的互助型经济组织，也是现代农业实现可持续发展的组织方式。中央一号文件多次对合作社的社会地位、组织结构、法律地位进行新的定位，国家也通过修订《中华人民共和国农民专业合作社法》以保障合作社的运行。我国合作社数量也呈现出蓬勃发展的态势。根据农业农村部公布的数据显示，截至2023年底，全国超过109万个组织开展农业社会化服务，服务面积超过21.4亿亩次，服务小农户9 400多万户[①]。合作社通过与小农户之间结成利益联结体，带动小农户更深入地参与到农业产业链和价值链建设中，对激发小农户内生动力具有重要意义。

为及时掌握项目区合作社发展动态，总结合作社带动小农户发展的做法与成效，中国农业科学院农业资源与农业区划研究所课题组开展多次实地调研，与合作社、受益农户进行一对一、面对面访谈（附件1、附件2），收集了大量的一手资料。

三、课题调研与资料数据收集

（一）调研范围及样本选择

为及时掌握项目实施效果，课题组开展专题调研，收集项目实施最新进展与成效。调研范围涉及四川、宁夏10个项目区，调研以项目区受益农户和扶持合作社为对象，受益农户采取分层随机抽样方法，每个项目区（兴庆区除外）抽取3个项目村，每个项目村（兴庆区项目村除外）随机抽取10~15户，共抽取426户（表1-1）；扶持合作社选取2023年6月底前成立并运行的合作社，共选取105家，原因在于考虑项目合作社成立时间先后可能影响带动效果。

---

① 发挥新型农业经营主体带动效应，经济日报，2024年4月25日第8版，http://www.moa.gov.cn/ztzl/ymksn/jjrbbd/202404/t20240425_6454364.htm。

表1-1 调研范围

项目省	项目县（区）	项目村	样本户数	合计
四川	苍溪县	大营村、青盐村、权家村	45	225
	广安区	干埝村、桥梁村、同心村	45	
	叙州区	干溪村、三块石村、宣化社区	45	
	宣汉县	牛背村、高伦村、龙洞村	45	
	仪陇县	高堂沟村、果山村、七星桥村	45	
宁夏	兴庆区	海陶南村、月牙湖村	10	201
	利通区	白寺滩村、烽火墩村、海子井村	40	
	红寺堡区	朝阳村、柳树台村、水套村	49	
	原州区	别庄村、曹泾村、蒋口村	55	
	彭阳县	城阳村、茨湾村、高庄村	47	
合计				426

（二）调研方式与主要内容

调研采取一对一、面对面的方式进行访谈，并实地了解合作社经营产品、服务内容与经营效益（图1-1），考察宁夏设施农业基地，了解生产基地建设成效（图1-2）。

图1-1 合作社经营产品和提供服务

图 1-2 宁夏生产基地建设

调研问卷分为两类：一是农户调研问卷，调研内容涉及农户家庭基本情况、农业经营情况、参与合作社及利益联结方式等；二是专业合作社调研问卷，调研内容涉及合作社成员结构、股权结构、经营管理和价值链建设情况等（附件1）。同时，结合项目中期调研数据（2020年，农户907户，合作社43家），对比分析项目区合作社带动小农户发展的做法与成效。

第二章 促进小农户发展的制度安排

一、国家战略决策部署

党的十九大报告提出实施乡村振兴战略，指出农业农村农民问题是关系国计民生的根本性问题，必须坚持把解决好"三农"问题作为全党工作重中之重。2018年中央一号文件对乡村振兴战略进行了全面顶层设计。2018年2月，中共中央、国务院印发《国家乡村振兴战略规划（2018—2022年）》，对实施乡村振兴战略作出总体决策部署。

为贯彻落实乡村振兴战略，提升小农户发展现代农业能力，2019年中共中央办公厅、国务院办公厅印发《关于促进小农户和现代农业发展有机衔接的意见》，提出坚持小农户家庭经营为基础与多种形式适度规模经营为引领相协调，按照服务小农户、提高小农户、富裕小农户的要求，加快构建扶持小农户发展的政策体系，促进传统小农户向现代小农户转变，实现小农户与现代农业发展有机衔接。

2020年，随着我国脱贫攻坚战取得全面胜利，实现了现行标准下9 899万农村贫困人口全部脱贫，832个贫困县全部摘帽，12.8万个贫困村全部出列，区域性整体贫困得到解决，完成了消除绝对贫困的艰巨任务[①]。中共中央、国务院出台《关于实现巩固拓展脱贫攻坚成果同乡村振兴有效衔接的意见》，提出设立5年过渡期，从集中资源支持脱贫攻坚转向巩固拓展脱贫攻坚成果和全面推进乡村振兴，并提出支持脱贫地区乡村特色产业发展壮大，持续改善脱贫地区基础设施条件等措施，加强脱贫攻坚与乡村振兴有效衔接。

党的二十大报告强调"坚持农业农村优先发展，巩固拓展脱贫攻坚成果，加快建设农业强国，扎实推动乡村产业、人才、文化、生态、组织振兴，全方位夯实粮食安全根基。"2024年中央一号文件进一步提出"锚定建设农业强国目标，以确保国家粮食安全、确保不发生规模性返贫为底线，以提升乡村产业发展水平、提升乡村建设水平、提升乡村治理水平为重点，强化科技和改革双轮驱动，强化农民增收

---

① 习近平：在全国脱贫攻坚总结表彰大会上的讲话，2021年2月。

举措，以加快农业农村现代化更好推进中国式现代化建设。"

二、国家制度安排

党的十八大以来，以习近平同志为核心的党中央坚持把解决好"三农"问题作为全党工作重中之重，把农村改革作为全面深化改革的重要内容，开创性地提出一系列重大改革发展战略、举措，推动"三农"事业取得历史性成就、发生历史性变革。项目实施期间，农村土地制度、农业经营管理制度等方面不断改革创新，为项目顺利推进提供了支撑保障。

（一）农村土地"三权分置"为小农户发展提供制度保障

2016 年，中共中央办公厅、国务院办公厅印发《关于完善农村土地所有权承包权经营权分置办法的意见》，将农村土地承包经营权分为承包权和经营权，实行所有权、承包权、经营权分置并行。土地经营权人对流转土地依法享有在一定期限内占有、耕作并取得相应收益的权利，这是继家庭联产承包责任制后又一重大制度创新。在"三权分置"的制度安排下，进城务工农户拥有稳定的承包权，可以放心流转出土地经营权；想多种土地的农户，可以多种渠道流转入土地经营权，扩大生产经营规模。土地"三权分置"实现了村组集体、承包农户、新型农业经营主体对土地权利的共享，土地所有者、承包者和经营者各有所得、无有所失，集体土地作为要素在生产经营中实现流动，流出土地经营权的农户增加财产性收入，新型农业经营主体实现规模收益。

（二）新型农业经营主体扶持政策为带动小农户发展提供路径选择

2017 年，中共中央办公厅、国务院办公厅印发《关于加快构建政策体系培育新型农业经营主体的意见》，从财政税收、基础设施建设、金融信贷、保险、营销市场、人才培养引进等方面重点部署，强调要全方位通过政策支持培育新型农业经营主体，以规模经营优势对农户进行辐射带动，让农民成为现代农业发展的参与者、受益者。2018 年 1 月，《中共中央 国务院关于实施乡村振兴战略的意见》这一重要文件中提出"统筹兼顾培育新型农业经营主体和扶持小农户，采取有针对性的措施，把小农生产引入现代农业发展轨道。"同年 9 月，中共中央、国务院印发《乡村振兴战略规划（2018—2022 年）》指出"壮大新型农业经营主体，实施新型农业经营主体培育工程，鼓励通过多种形式开展适度规模经营。"2019年2月，中共中央办公厅、国务院办公厅印发《关于促进小农户和现代农业发展有机衔接的意见》，为扶持与提升小农户发展现代农业能力创造了政策保障，更好地发挥小农户在乡村振兴中的主体作用。2020年3月，为提高新型农业经营主体发展质量，农业农村部印发了《新型农业经营主体和服务主体高质量发展规划（2020—2022年）》，规划针对不同类型的农业经营主体细化了具体发展要求，为政策实施提供明确指导，并将带动小农户作为培育内容包含其中，进一步加深二者间的关联性。

（三）农业支持保护制度完善为强农惠农富农提供支撑

2019年11月26日，十九届中央全面深化改革委员会第十一次会议审议通过了《关于完善农业支持保护制度的意见》和《关于加强农业科技社会化服务体系建设的若干意见》，提出建立完善农业支持保护制度，要坚持农业农村优先发展，以实施乡村振兴战略为总抓手，从农业供给侧结构性改革、农业可持续发展、农业投入保障、农业补贴补偿、支农资金使用管理等方面深化改革，逐步构建符合国情、覆盖全面、指向明确、重点突出、措施配套、操作简便的农业支持保护制度，不断增强强农惠农富农政策的精准性、稳定性、实效性（表2-1）。同时指出加强农业科技社会化服务体系建设，要以增加农业科技服务有效供给、加强供需对接为着力点，以提高农业科技服务效能为目标，推进农技推广机构服务创新，强化高校与科研院所服务功能，壮大市场化社会化服务力量，加快构建开放竞争、多元互补、协同高效的农业科技社会化服务体系。

表2-1 促进小农户发展的制度安排

年份	名称	相关内容
2015	财政部印发《农业综合开发扶持农业优势特色产业促进农业产业化发展的指导意见》	以"优化布局、突出优势、精准扶持、提高效益"为主线，以促进农村一二三产业融合发展、农户持续增收为目标，以打造农业优势特色产业集群为着力点。
2016	中共中央办公厅、国务院办公厅印发《关于完善农村土地所有权承包权经营权分置办法的意见》	将农村土地承包经营权分为承包权和经营权，实行所有权、承包权、经营权分置并行，土地经营权人对流转土地依法享有在一定期限内占有、耕作并取得相应收益的权利。
2016	《中共中央 国务院关于稳步推进农村集体产权制度改革的意见》	以明晰产权归属、维护成员权利为目的，以推进集体经营性资产改革为重点，探索集体经济新的实现形式和运行机制。

（续表）

年份	名称	相关内容
2017	中共中央办公厅、国务院办公厅印发《关于加快构建政策体系培育新型农业经营主体的意见》	加快培育新型农业经营主体，形成完备的政策扶持体系，发挥新型农业经营主体在推进农业现代化中的引领作用。
2019	中共中央办公厅、国务院办公厅印发《关于促进小农户和现代农业发展有机衔接的意见》	通过政策支持、服务提升、机制创新等措施，促进小农户与现代农业的有机衔接。
2019	十九届中央全面深化改革委员会第十一次会议审议通过《关于完善农业支持保护制度的意见》《关于加强农业科技社会化服务体系建设的若干意见》	从农业供给侧结构性改革、农业可持续发展、农业投入保障、农业补贴补偿、支农资金使用管理等方面深化改革，逐步构建符合国情、覆盖全面、指向明确、重点突出、措施配套、操作简便的农业支持保护制度。以增加农业科技服务有效供给、加强供需对接为着力点，以提高农业科技服务效能为目标，推进农技推广机构服务创新，强化高校与科研院所服务功能，壮大市场化社会化服务力量。
2021	《中华人民共和国乡村振兴促进法》	全面规定乡村振兴的总体要求、工作原则、主要任务、支持措施等，为乡村振兴提供法律保障。

三、地方推进措施

项目实施期间，四川和宁夏积极制定和推行适合地区农业发展的相关政策（表2-2），对农业转型升级、产业融合发展、品牌建设、小农户与现代农业有机衔接高度重视，在保障粮食安全、提升农业效益、促进农民增收的同时实现农业农村现代化的长远目标。

四川根据《四川省农村扶贫开发纲要（2011—2020年）》总体部署，结合全省实际提出要促进产业结构调整、支持农民专业合作社等新型农业经营主体发展，大力推动农业产业化经营，带动农民持续稳定增收。发展特色产业，发展农业专业合作组织，立足贫困地区资源禀赋，制定和完善产业发展规划，加大支持力度，推动特色农业发展。完善农户的利益联结机制，推广"专业合作组织＋农户""龙头企业＋专业合作组织＋农户"等组织模式。强化与市场对接，延伸产业链，增加农产品附加值，打造优势特色农产品品牌。2021年，四川省委、四川省人民政府发布《关于全面实施乡村振兴战略开启农业农村现代化建设新征程的意见》提出"构建起符合四川实际的现代农业园区梯级发展体系，带动小农户进入现代农业发展轨道，形成乡村一二三产业融合发展新态势。"同年 5 月，四川省委、四川省人民政府发布《关于实现巩固拓展脱贫攻坚成果同乡村振兴有效衔接的实施意见》提出健全巩固拓展脱贫攻坚成果长效机制；提升农村供水保障水平；持续加大对原深度贫困地区和秦巴山腹地所在市经济发展条件差、巩固拓展脱贫攻坚成果任务较重的县（市、区）的支持力度；发展壮大脱贫地区乡村特色产业。同年 7 月，四川省人民政府印发《四川省"十四五"推进农业农村现代化规划》，提出开启全面推进农业农村现代化新征程；坚决守住粮食安全底线，提升重要农副产品供给保障水平；加快发展高质高效现代特色农业，提升产业链供应链现代化水平；加快补齐"10+3"产业体系支撑性短板，构建现代农业园区梯级发展体系。

宁夏于 2018 年出台《打赢脱贫攻坚战三年行动实施方案》提出重点关注培养贫困地区和贫困人口自我发展能力；做优做强优势特色产业。在《宁夏乡村振兴战略规划（2018—2022 年）》和《促进小农户和现代农业发展有机衔接的实施意见》等文件强调发展新型农业经营主体，促进农业产业融合，提升农产品市场竞争力。《宁夏回族自治区农业农村现代化发展"十四五"规划》及《自治区党委 人民政府关于全面推进乡村振兴加快农业农村现代化的实施意见》围绕农业绿色发展、重点产业发展、粮食安全与产业提质增效等核心领域，布局现代农业体系建设。2021 年，宁夏乡村振兴局出台《关于支持乡村振兴重点帮扶县的若干意见》中指出原州区、红寺堡区是国家乡村振兴重点帮扶县，彭阳县是自治区乡村振兴重点帮扶县，这些脱贫基础较为薄弱的地区是"十四五"期间防止返贫致贫、巩固拓展脱贫攻坚成果的重点地区。

表 2-2　地方促进小农户发展的推进政策

年份	名称	相关内容
四川		
2018	《中共四川省委　四川省人民政府关于实施乡村振兴战略开创新时代"三农"全面发展新局面的意见》	明确四川实施乡村振兴战略的总体要求、主要任务和保障措施，强调发展多种形式适度规模经营，培育壮大新型农业经营主体。
2019	《四川省现代农业园区建设考评激励方案》	通过建立现代农业园区，提升农业综合效益和竞争力，促进农业转型升级，带动农户增收，加强与市场的有效联结。

（续表）

年份	名称	相关内容
2021	《四川省"十四五"推进农业农村现代化规划》	坚持农业现代化和农村现代化一体设计、一并推进，统筹考虑区域差异、发展基础等因素，因地制宜研究制定推进农业农村现代化的时间表、任务书和路径图。
2023	《四川省农村一二三产业融合发展行动方案》	实施农产品精深加工、"川字号"农产品市场拓展和农产品品牌提升、农文旅融合发展、经营主体培育壮大、科技赋能提升，推进农村一二三产业融合发展。
2024	《中共四川省委 四川省人民政府关于学习运用"千村示范、万村整治"工程经验在推进乡村振兴上全面发力的意见》	从构建现代农业经营体系、发展新型农村集体经济、探索县域内城乡融合发展改革等方面加快推进。
宁夏		
2017	《关于加快推进宁夏特色优质农产品品牌建设的意见》	加强品牌农业标准化生产、科技创新提升品牌建设、培育品牌农业建设主体、加强宁夏特色农产品区域公用品牌、建立宁夏农产品品牌目录制度、拓展品牌农产品市场销售渠道、加强品牌农产品质量安全监测监管，全面提升现代农业效益，促进农户持续增收。
2019	《宁夏乡村振兴战略规划（2018—2022年）》	提出乡村振兴的具体规划，包括发展合作社和家庭农场等新型农业经营主体，推动农业产业融合，增强农产品市场竞争力。
2020	宁夏回族自治区《关于促进小农户和现代农业发展有机衔接的实施意见》	通过政策引导支持，帮助小农户提升生产能力，鼓励小农户通过合作社、联合社等形式与现代农业经营主体建立稳定利益联结机制。
2021	《宁夏回族自治区农业农村现代化发展"十四五"规划》	创建国家农业绿色发展先行区为载体，聚焦宁夏"九大重点产业""四大提升行动"，加快建设现代农业产业体系、生产体系和经营体系。
2021	《自治区党委 人民政府关于全面推进乡村振兴加快农业农村现代化的实施意见》	保障粮食和重要农产品供给安全、坚决守住耕地红线、提质发展高效种养业、加快发展壮大现代乡村产业等8个方面加快推进农业现代化。

第三章　项目区优势特色产业选择

项目区优势特色产业特征明显，四川粮油、蔬菜、水果产业基础扎实，宁夏冷凉蔬菜、牛、羊等产业优势突出，为项目区产业发展奠定良好基础。

一、四川项目区

四川位于我国西南部，地处长江上游，素有"天府之国"的美誉。全省总面积48.6万平方千米，占全国总面积的5.1%。地跨青藏高原、横断山脉、云贵高原、秦巴山地、四川盆地等几大地理区域，地势西高东低，由西北向东南倾斜。以山地为主，有平原、台地、丘陵、山地4类地貌，可分为川西南山地区、川西北高原地区和四川盆地底部地区。

四川是农业大省，是保障国家重要初级产品供给的战略基地，在全国农业发展中占有重要位置。四川优势特色农业产业包括粮油、水果、茶叶、生猪、蚕桑、中药材等。晚熟柑橘种植面积和产量也位居全国前列，凭借独特的上市时间错位优势，在全国柑橘市场中占据重要地位。四川茶叶种植面积位居全国第二，水果中的柠檬、石榴、枇杷等在全国占有重要地位。四川生猪产业以规模化养殖为主，拥有多个地方品牌，如"川藏黑猪"等。2024年前三季度，四川生猪出栏量达到4 512.9万头，猪肉产量为356.8万吨，均位居全国首位。此外，四川的蔬菜、泡菜、水果加工等产业也具有较高的市场竞争力。

四川项目区选择广元市苍溪县、达州市宣汉县、广安市广安区、宜宾市叙州区、南充市仪陇县作为项目实施区域，各项目县（区）在水果、茶叶、菌菇、花椒、桑蚕、生猪等方面具有较好的产业基础。

二、宁夏项目区

宁夏位于中国西北部的黄河中上游地区，经济欠发达，原贫困人口较为集中。区域内地形南北狭长，地势南高北低，西部高差较大，东部起伏较缓。平原地区位于中部，地势平坦开阔，土壤肥沃，引黄河水灌溉而形成著名的"塞上江南"，主要农业类型为灌溉农业和特色瓜果蔬菜种植。南部六盘山海拔多在2 000米以上，主要农业类型为林业和山地旱作农业。北部属宁夏蒙古高原，海拔在1 000～1 500米，以草原和荒漠为主，气候较为干旱，降水稀少，主要农业类型为草原畜牧业和旱作农业与绿洲农业。

宁夏优势特色主导产业有冷凉蔬菜、枸杞、滩羊、肉牛等。宁夏的冷凉蔬菜因高品质和安全性而闻名，冷凉蔬菜种植面积保持在300万亩（1亩≈667平方米）以上，产量稳定在730万吨以上。其中宁夏菜心种植面积超过27万亩，销售额达到36亿元以上。"宁夏菜心"已成为国家农产品地理标志产品，并通过冷链运输供应粤港澳大湾区市场。宁夏的滩羊是国内外知名的肉类产品，特别是在高端餐饮市场中占有重要地位。此外，宁夏已经注册"固原黄牛"和"泾源黄牛肉"两个国家地理标志保护产品品牌，以及"西海固"区域公用品牌，并培育了"穆和春""臻回味"等一批企业品牌。

宁夏项目区选择固原市原州区和彭阳县、吴忠市红寺堡区和利通区、银川市兴庆区作为项目实施区域。各项目县（区）以农业生产为主，但农业生产基础条件较为薄弱，部分地区缺水较为严重，产业发展滞后。

基于四川、宁夏资源条件和优势产业基础，农发基金项目选择具有代表性的项目区及产业，重点涉及粮油、蔬菜、水果、中药材等种植业和生猪、牛羊鸡等养殖业（各项目区产业选择见表3-1）。通过项目扶持，一方面，加强产业发展的基础设施建设，改善交通运输条件，为获得更多市场机会奠定基础；另一方面，促进科技赋能产业发展，运用现代化农业设施设备和技术模式，如自动化节水灌溉、无人机播种、病虫害绿色防控等，加强经营主体技术培训，掌握生产技能，提升产业价值链。

表3-1 各项目区产业选择

项目省	项目县（区）	扶持产业
四川	苍溪	红心猕猴桃、苍溪梨、蔬菜、农机服务、粮油、花椒、柠檬、柑橘、中药材
	仪陇	水果、食用菌、肉牛、蔬菜、粮油、生猪、水产品
	宣汉	休闲农业、茶叶、花椒、粮油、中药材、水果、生猪、蔬菜、肉牛
	广安	水果、花椒、休闲农业、粮油
	叙州	桑蚕、茶叶、蔬菜、生猪、中药材、花卉

（续表）

项目省	项目县（区）	扶持产业
宁夏	红寺堡	粮油、水果、黄花菜、中药材、滩羊
	原州	肉鸡、蛋鸡、粮油、肉牛
	利通	粮油、饲草、肉牛
	彭阳	中药材、肉牛、蛋鸡、牧草、水果、蜜蜂
	兴庆	水果、蔬菜、肉牛

第四章　合作社带动小农户发展的做法与成效

以合作社为载体，带动小农户发展是项目实施的一项重要任务和内容。课题基于2023年调查收集的105家项目扶持合作社数据资料，分析合作社生产经营状况及产业发展情况，总结合作社带动小农户发展模式，并通过调查数据分析小农户增收及满意度状况。

一、改善基础设施设备，经营类型多元化

合作社通过项目资金支持，改善合作社办公环境，增强基础设施设备。105家合作社办公面积增加14 279平方米，加工厂房面积增加78 791平方米，仓储面积增加40 980平方米；合作社加工设备增加933台（套），仓储设备增加141台（套），物流设备增加52台（套）（表4-1）。

表4-1　合作社基础设施设备增加情况

项目区	基础设施面积/平方米			设备/台（套）		
	办公	加工厂房	仓储	加工	仓储	物流
四川	12 435	68 350	28 620	715	122	43
宁夏	1 844	10 441	12 360	218	19	9
合计	14 279	78 791	40 980	933	141	52

合作社经营类型多样化，其业务范围包括种植、养殖、种养结合、农机服务和农旅结合等5类（图4-1）。其中，种植合作社有52家，占比49.5%；养殖合作社有9家，占比8.6%；种养结合类合作社有31家，占比29.5%；农旅结合类合作社有9家，占比8.6%；农机服务类合作社有4家，占比3.8%。

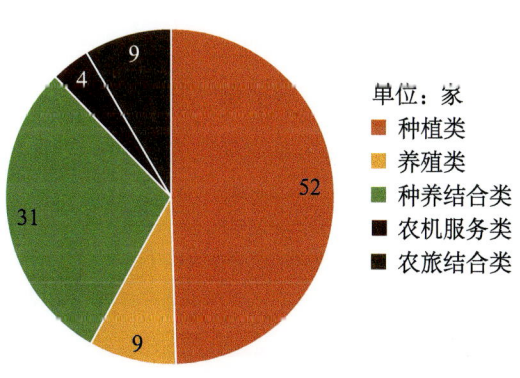

图4-1　不同类型的合作社数量

二、加强价值链建设，提升产业效益

（一）健全内部管理，推进规范化运营

通过项目扶持，105家合作社均制定了合作社管理制度，每年召开两次成员大会、三次理事会。68家聘请专职会计，未聘请专职会计的合作社通过聘用专业会计或财务公司管账；63家合作社能够独立撰写商业计划书（表4-2）。

表4-2　合作社内部管理情况　　　　　　　　　　　　　　　单位：家

项目区	制定管理制度	拥有专职会计	独立撰写商业计划书
四川	89	55	55
宁夏	16	13	8
合计	105	68	63

（二）拓展延伸产业链，提升价值链

（1）引进新品种、新技术。合作社在生产基础设施改善的情况下，着力引进新品种、新技术。截至2023年底，合作社借助项目扶持引进新品种379个，投资金额1 388.3万元；引进新技术111项，投资金额265.3万元（表4-3）。

表4-3　引进新品种、新技术的数量和金额

项目区	新品种/个	新品种投资/万元	新技术/项	新技术投资/万元
四川	364	1 378.2	105	262.8
宁夏	15	10.1	6	2.5
合计	379	1 388.3	111	265.3

（2）发展特色产业。合作社经营产业涉及粮油、水果、蔬菜、茶叶、牛、羊等当地特色产业。调研数据显示，2023年，合作社特色产业销售总额①达13 286.2万元，其中合作社代收代销的销售额6 433.4万元，占合作社销售总额的48.4%。就产业类型而言，养殖业销售总额2 292.1万元，其中合作社代收代销售额352万元，占合作社销售总额的15.4%；种植业销售总额10 994.0万元，其中合作社代收代销销售额6 081.4万元，占合作社销售总额的55.3%（表4-4）。

---

① 合作社的销售总额由自主生产销售额与代收代销销售额构成。

表 4-4　合作社销售额及占比

产业类型	销售总额/万元	自主生产销售额/万元	占比/%	代收代销售额/万元	占比/%
种植业	10 994.0	4 912.7	44.7	6 081.4	55.3
养殖业	2 292.1	1 940.1	84.6	352	15.4
合计	13 286.2	6 852.8	51.6	6 433.4	48.4

（3）延伸产业链。随着项目的深入推进，合作社在经营农业产业的同时向农产品加工、餐饮、旅馆等服务业发展，延伸产业链。经营农产品加工业务的合作社比例从2020年的39.5%增长到2023年的43.8%；经营餐饮、旅馆等服务的合作社比例从2020年的4.6%增长至2023年的10.5%（表4-5）。

表 4-5　产业链延伸的合作社数量和比例

业务类型	2020年①		2023年	
	数量/家	比例/%	数量/家	比例/%
农产品加工	17	39.5	46	43.8
餐饮、旅馆等服务	2	4.6	11	10.5

注：①2020年中期调查合作社共43家，其中四川调查27家，宁夏调查16家。②2023年共调查合作社105家，其中四川调查89家，宁夏调查16家。

（4）注重品牌建设。品牌建设是合作社提升市场竞争力的重要渠道。2023年，105家合作社中有69家示范性合作社，占比65.7%，其中，10家国家级示范性合作社，16家省级示范性合作社，20家市级示范性合作社，23家县级示范性合作社。47家合作社有农产品品牌，68家合作社有农产品"三品一标"（无公害农产品、绿色农产品、有机农产品、农产品地理标志），49家合作社有商标注册证。

通过项目扶持，合作社不仅提升了产业经营管理能力，而且不断推动产品品牌建设。与中期情况相比，项目区扶持的合作社在农产品品牌、"三品一标"与注册商标方面均有提升。建立农产品品牌的合作社比例由27.9%增加到44.8%，增长16.9个百分点；拥有"三品一标"的合作社比例由34.9%增加到64.8%，增长29.9个百分点（图4-2）。

（5）经营效益有所显现。随着特色产业不断发展，合作社经营效益逐渐显现。2023年，合作社中开始盈利的有59家，占调研总数的56.2%。其中，四川共有89家合作社，四川盈利合作社50家，盈利比例由中期的51.8%增长至56.2%；宁夏共有16家合作社，宁夏盈利合作社9家，盈利合作社比例较中期有所下降，

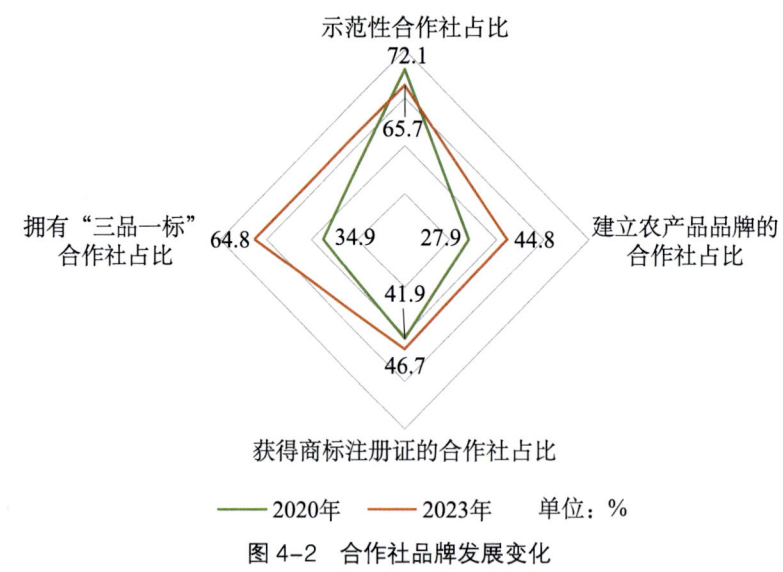

图 4-2 合作社品牌发展变化

可能是 2023 年受市场价格波动影响，牛、羊肉价格普遍下降，合作社收益受损（表 4-6）。

表 4-6 盈利合作社情况对比

项目区	2020 年[①]		2023 年[②]	
	数量/家	比例/%	数量/家	比例/%
四川	14	51.8	50	56.2
宁夏	11	68.7	9	56.3
合计	25	58.1	59	56.2

注：① 2020 年中期调查合作社共 43 家，其中四川调查 27 家，宁夏调查 16 家；② 2023 年共调查合作社 105 家，其中四川 89 家，宁夏 16 家。

三、提供多样化服务，多渠道带动小农户

（一）明确分工，建立利益联结

带动小农户发展的首要环节是让小农户加入合作社。合作社成员以小农户为主，2023 年调研的 105 家合作社共带动小农户 8 708 户，占合作社成员的 97.4%。四川项目区调研的合作社中小农户有 7 951 户，占 97.9%；宁夏项目区调研的合作社中小农户有 757 户，占 92.5%。

小农户在合作社管理层中占主要地位，理事会中 82.9% 为小农户。四川项目区

合作社理事会中小农户有362户，占81.7%；宁夏项目区合作社理事会中小农户有70户，占89.7%。

合作社对小农户投入的土地、资金进行折股量化，以此加强与小农户的利益联结。以土地入股的成员，合作社按照当地土地流转价格折算成资金进行折股量化，并按照股权分配盈余，成员获得分红收益。

（二）提供就业，加强互动合作

2023年，调研的105家合作社为农户提供了5 638个就业岗位，提供就业岗位的多少取决于扶持的合作社数量、产业类型、生产规模等。在合作社提供的就业岗位中，约20.0%是长期岗位，80.0%是临时岗位（表4-7）。

表4-7 合作社提供就业岗位类型

项目区	就业岗位/个	长期岗位比例/%	临时岗位比例/%
四川	4 933	21.6	78.4
宁夏	705	8.6	91.4
合计	5 638	20.0	80.0

（三）开展培训，提升生产技能

合作社在提供技术培训方面发挥重要作用。调研的105家合作社共组织培训402次，培训对象以小农户为主，共培训小农户8 299人。四川89家合作社共培训小农户7 309人，宁夏16家合作社共培训小农户990人（表4-8）。

表4-8 合作社培训次数和人数

项目区	次数/次	人数/人
四川	362	7 309
宁夏	40	990
合计	402	8 299

合作社是推广应用农业绿色生产技术的重要主体。2023年，调研的合作社中，有81家合作社在生产过程中应用绿色生产技术，占比77.1%。其中，75家应用有机肥替代化肥技术，66家应用节水灌溉/水肥一体化技术，66家应用绿色生物农药技术（表4-9）。

表 4-9　应用绿色生产技术的合作社数量

单位：家

项目区	有机肥替代化肥	节水灌溉/水肥一体化	绿色生物农药	秸秆还田
四川	50	44	45	26
宁夏	25	22	21	15
合计	75	66	66	41

（四）提供服务，确保产品质量

合作社向周边区域的农户提供产前、产中、产后各种类型的农业服务，将农户的种植、养殖、加工等环节有机结合起来，实现农户节本增收。2023年调研合作社中，有80家合作社提供病虫害防控等农业生产技术服务，占比76.2%，有60家合作社提供种子、化肥、农药、饲料等农资服务，57家提供农产品销售服务，39家提供代耕代收等农机服务，34家提供产品加工、包装等服务。与2020年相比，合作社提供的社会化服务中增加了产品存储服务与产品运输服务，有36家提供产品存储服务，32家提供产品运输服务（图4-3）。

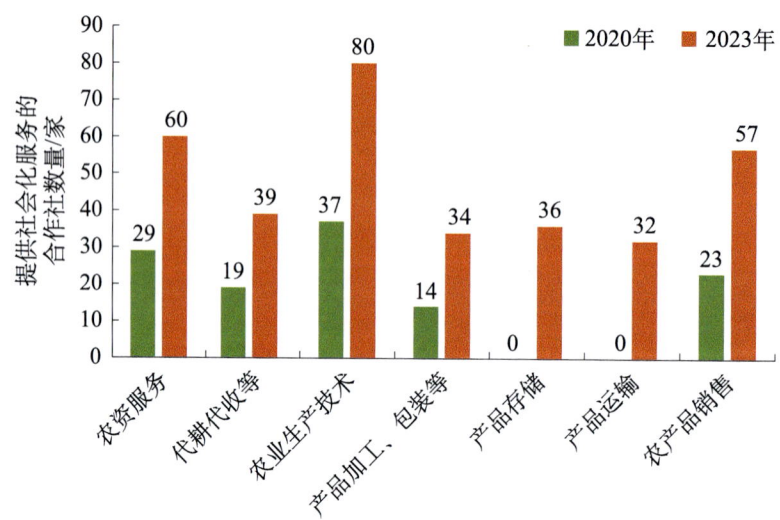

图 4-3　合作社社会化服务提供情况对比

四川项目区合作社侧重产前、产中服务，有61.8%提供农资服务，37.1%提供代耕代收服务，82%提供农业生产技术服务。宁夏项目区合作社侧重产后服务，有25.0%提供产品加工、包装等服务，32.6%提供产品存储服务，31.3%提供产品运输服务，56.3%提供产品销售服务（图4-4）。

第四章 合作社带动小农户发展的做法与成效

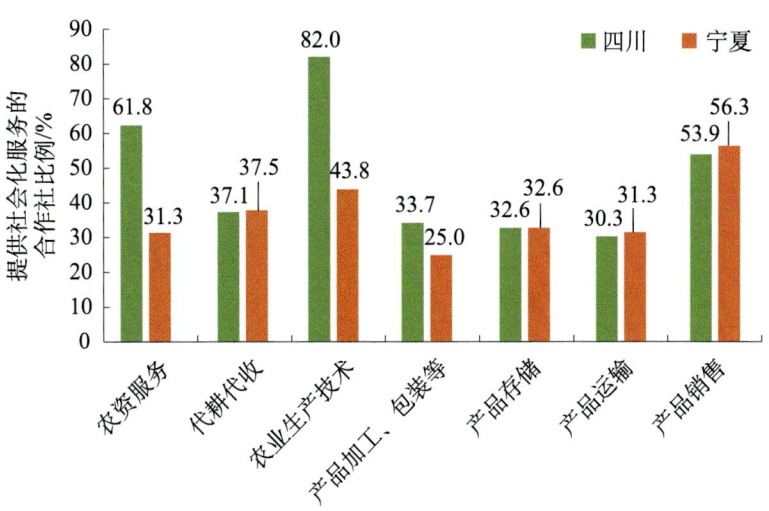

图 4-4 不同项目区合作社提供的社会化服务

四、小农户参与方式及增收效果

（一）以土地等资产入股，加入合作社

调研的 426 户农户中，有 239 户加入项目扶持的合作社，占比超过 50%。其中，有 221 户享有合作社股权，占比超过 90%，以土地出资的农户占 63.8%（表 4-10）。

表 4-10 农户加入合作社出资方式　　　　　　　　　　　　　单位：户

项目区	土地	资金	土地和资金
四川	76	39	3
宁夏	60	36	2
合计	136	75	5

（二）参与合作社培训，学习应用生产技术

农户积极参与合作社组织的培训，对培训效果较为满意。调研的农户中，有 231 人参加了合作社组织的培训，其中合作社成员 223 人。农户每年参加培训约 3 次，农户认为合作社培训效果较好（表 4-11）。

23

表 4-11 参加培训的人数

项目区	培训人数/人	成员人数/人	培训次数/次	培训效果/分
四川	123	115	4	1.6
宁夏	108	108	2	1.2
合计	231	223	3	1.4

注：培训效果打分分值代表：1=非常好；2=较好；3=一般；4=较差；5=非常差。

参加技术培训后，农户积极应用绿色生产技术。调研的农户中，229 户采纳水肥一体化、有机肥替代化肥等绿色生产技术。其中四川项目区有 187 户采纳绿色生产技术，宁夏项目区有 42 户采纳绿色生产技术（表 4-12）。

表 4-12 绿色生产技术的采纳农户数量和比例

项目区	数量/户	比例/%
四川	187	83.1
宁夏	42	20.9
合计	229	53.7

从不同生产技术看，有 154 户采纳秸秆还田或综合利用技术，139 户采纳有机肥替代化肥技术，129 户采纳病虫害绿色防控技术，121 户采纳休耕轮作、间作、套作、深翻深耕等保护性耕作技术（图 4-5）。

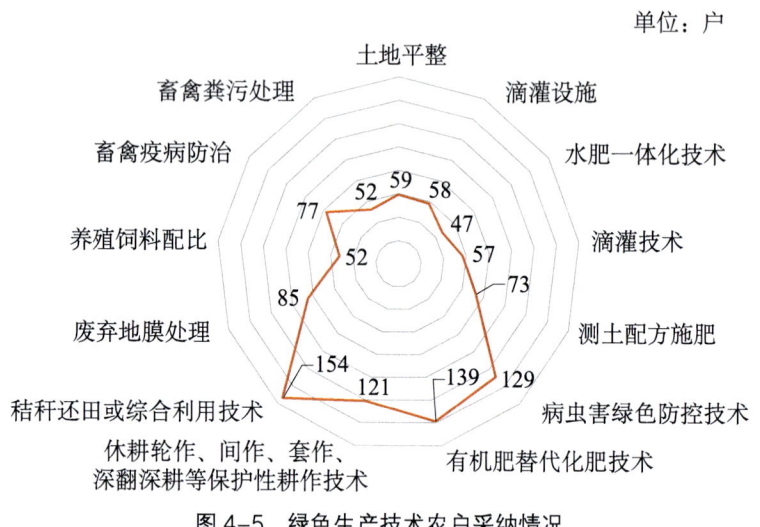

图 4-5 绿色生产技术农户采纳情况

（三）采用合作社服务，促进产业提质增效

农业社会化服务有效降低了农户生产成本，为特色产业链的延伸与产业功能拓展提供了有力的支撑。调研农户中,农户采用合作社提供的社会化服务较为普遍,218 户采用合作社提供的社会化服务,其中四川 98 户,宁夏 120 户(表 4-13)。

表 4-13 采用合作社提供的社会化服务的农户数量和比例

项目区	数量 / 户	比例 /%
四川	98	43.6
宁夏	120	59.7
合计	218	51.2

从社会化服务类型看,农户采用的社会化服务主要集中于产前、产中服务。有 143 户采用农机服务,98 户采用农资采购服务。合作社产后服务也逐渐加强,有 64 户采用存储与加工服务,26 户采用运输服务,23 户采用产品销售服务(图 4-6)。

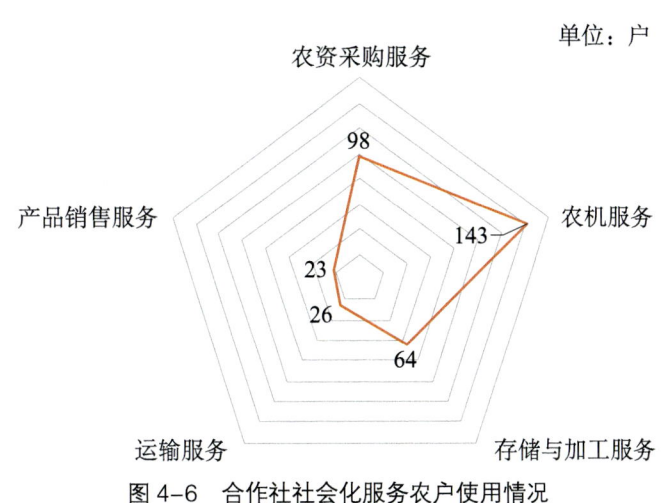

图 4-6 合作社社会化服务农户使用情况

(四)小农户增收效果及满意度反馈

合作社成员家庭收入显著增加。调研的合作社成员中,家庭年收入为 5.9 万元[①],其中,工资性收入 3.6 万元,农业经营收入 1.7 万元,财产性收入 0.03 万元,其他收入 0.6 万元(表 4-14、图 4-7)。与非成员相比,合作社成员家庭收入高 13.5%。其中,工资性收入高 0.8%,农业经营收入高 41.2%。该结果表明,农户加入合作社后,实现了多渠道增收。

---

① 收入均指毛收入,项目区小农户经营性收入以农业为主,此处只统计农业经营收入情况,其他收入包含转移性收入、个体工商户经营收入、儿女赡养接济等。

表 4-14　项目区合作社成员收入构成　　　　　　　　　单位：万元

项目区	工资性收入	农业经营收入	财产性收入	其他收入	总收入
四川	4.5	1.3	0.03	1.0	6.8
宁夏	2.6	2.2	0.03	0.2	5.0
平均	3.6	1.7	0.03	0.6	5.9

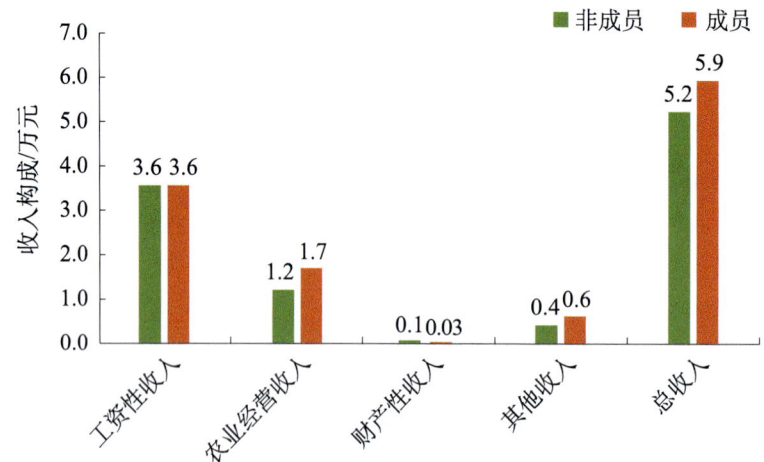

图 4-7　成员和非成员收入对比

　　四川与宁夏项目区合作社成员收入结构存在差异。四川项目区合作社成员工资性收入占家庭收入的 66.0%，农业经营收入占比 18.6%；宁夏项目区合作社成员工资性收入占家庭收入的 51.8%，农业经营收入占比 43%。同时，在农业收入中四川项目区 62.9% 为水果种植收入，宁夏项目区 41% 为粮食种植收入，32.1% 为养殖收入（图 4-8、图 4-9）。

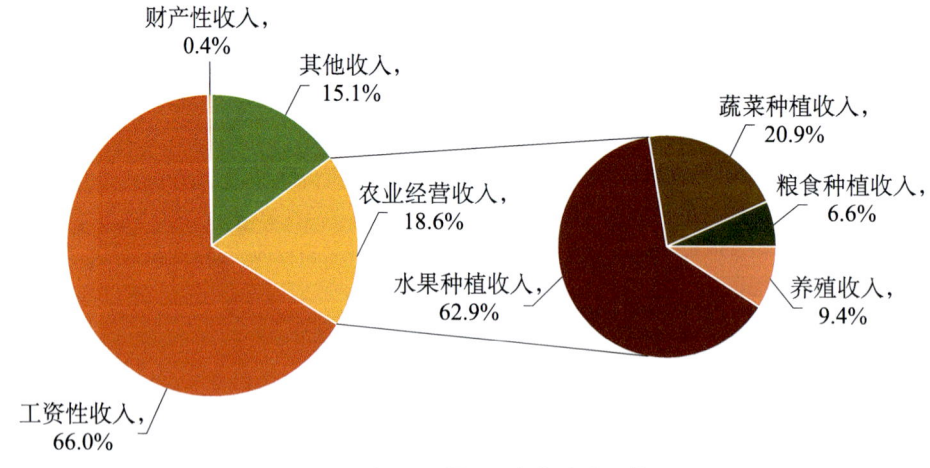

图 4-8　2023 年四川项目区合作社成员收入结构

第四章 合作社带动小农户发展的做法与成效

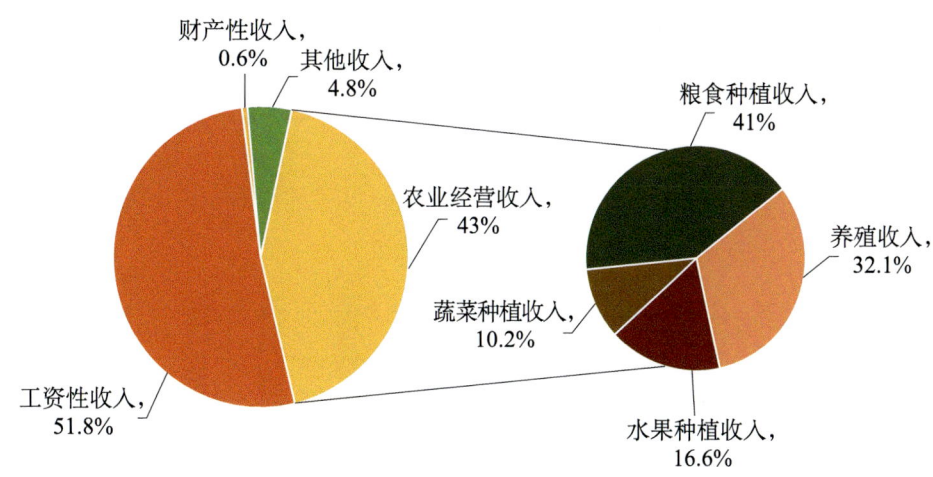

图 4-9 2023 年宁夏项目区合作社成员收入结构

分红收入是小农户增收的重要组成部分。2023 年，宁夏 9 家盈利合作社中有 5 家进行收益分红，受益小农户有 264 户，平均每户分红 446 元；四川 50 家盈利合作社中有 25 家进行收益分红，受益小农户有 2 218 户，平均每户分红 1 556 元。

根据合作社成员反馈数据，认为加入合作社从多方面受益。239 份成员问卷中，有 155 户认为加入合作社最大的好处是有入股分红，34 户认为加入合作社最大的好处是有就业机会、增加务工收入，32 户认为加入合作社最大的好处是能学到相关生产技术或经营管理经验（图 4-10）。

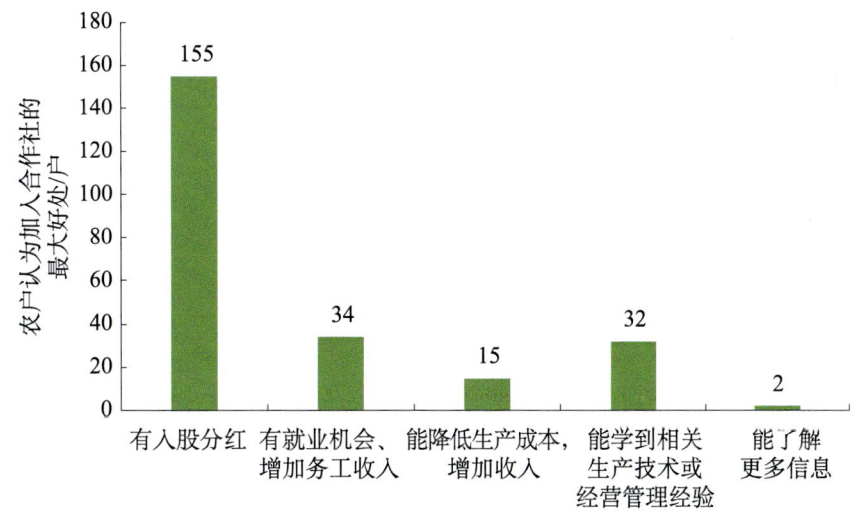

图 4-10 合作社成员受益反馈情况分析

根据受访人的感知划分为 5 个等级：非常满意赋值为 5，比较满意赋值为 4，一般满意赋值为 3，不太满意赋值为 2，非常不满意赋值为 1。其中，对畜禽疫病防治、养殖饲料配比、秸秆还田或综合利用以及休耕轮作、间作、套作、深翻深耕等保护性耕作技术的满意度在4.9分及以上，对有机肥替代化肥技术和滴灌技术满意度在4.5分以上（图4-11）。

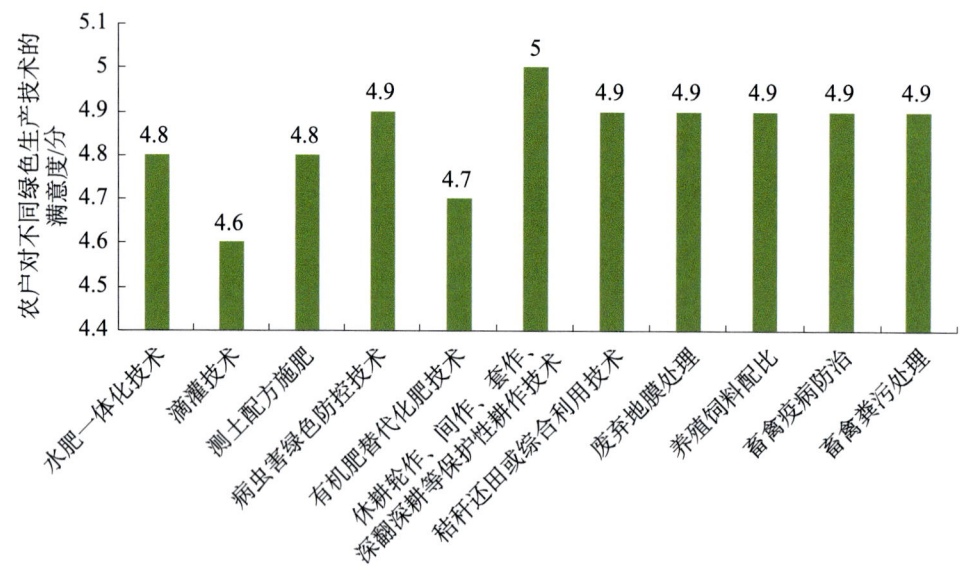

图4-11 合作社成员对绿色生产技术的满意度

注：满意度范围为1~5分，5分为最满意，下同。

合作社成员对合作社提供的农业生产性服务也非常满意。其中，农机服务和农资采购服务满意度为4.9分，运输服务、存储与加工服务和产品销售服务满意度均为4.8分（图4-12）。

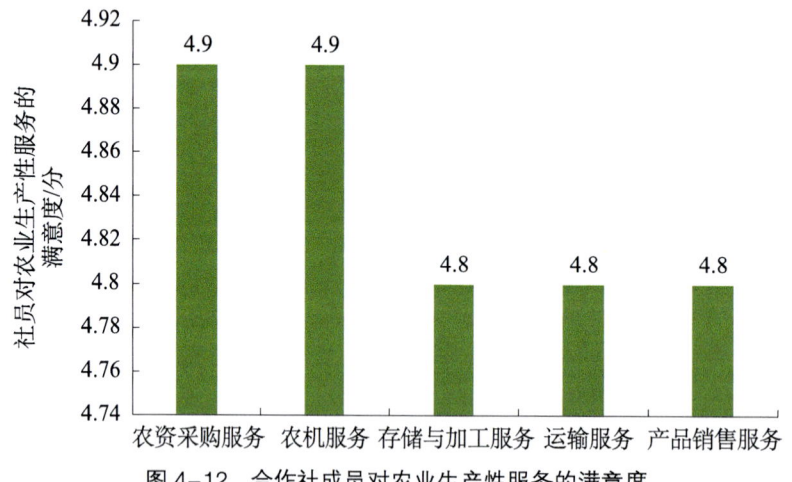

图4-12 合作社成员对农业生产性服务的满意度

第五章 带动小农户发展的典型模式与推广建议

项目实施以来,各项目区探索形成多种多样的带动小农户发展模式。课题组结合前期调研资料,总结形成5种带动小农户发展的典型模式,包括"合作社+小农户""合作社+农业企业+小农户""村集体+生产基地+小农户""村集体+合作社+生产基地+小农户""新农人+小农户"。为持续发挥项目影响与效益,进一步增强小农户发展能力,提出合作社带动小农户发展运行模式的推广建议。

一、带动小农户发展的典型模式

(一)"合作社+小农户"模式

"合作社+小农户"是合作社带动小农户发展的最直接模式。调查的105家合作社中有36家,占比34.3%。该模式下,合作社利用资金支持自身发展,进行基础设施以及气候智慧型生产基地建设,并为小农户提供加工、包装、存储、运输和销售等社会化服务,为小农户提供就业岗位,合作社与小农户之间形成优势互补、互利共赢的利益联结(图5-1)。

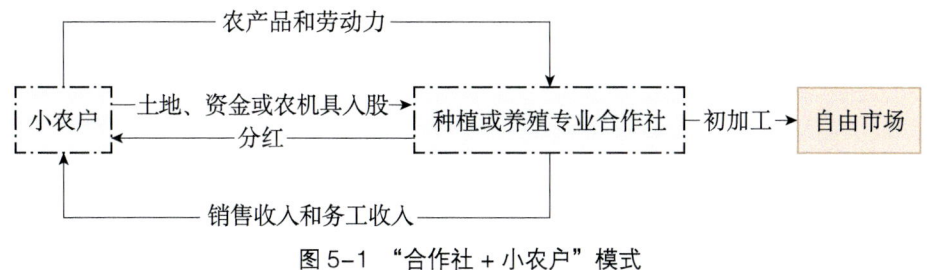

图5-1 "合作社+小农户"模式

该模式小农户受益方式主要有两个方面,一是农产品销售收入与务工收入,小农户将农产品和劳动力转让给合作社,以获取代收代销收入和务工收入,合作社承担全部的生产风险和市场风险;二是分红收入,小农户以土地、资金或农机具等形式入股合作社,合作社遵循"利益共享、风险共担"的原则以当年盈余按股分红,小农户获得分红收益。

(二)"合作社 + 农业企业 + 小农户"模式

"合作社 + 农业企业 + 小农户"是合作社经营带动小农户的典型模式。调查的105家合作社中,共有68家合作社与农业企业联合发展,占比64.8%。该模式下合作社与企业签订合作经营合同,为社员提供产前、产中、产后全方位的社会化服务,避免小农户在农业生产、市场销售中"单打独斗"的状态,与小农户结成"风险共担,成本分摊,利益共享"的利益联结机制(图5-2)。

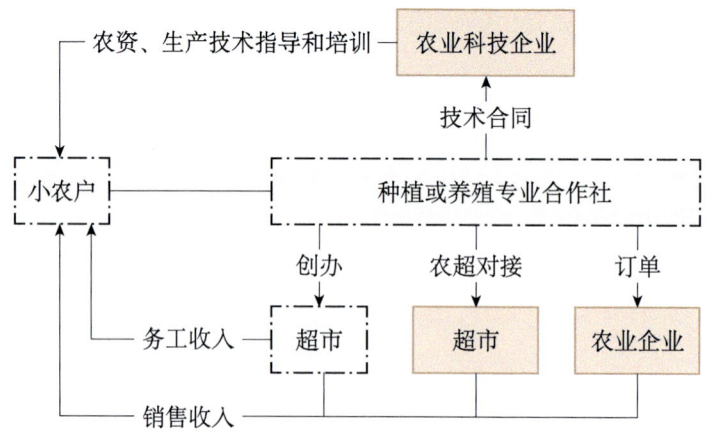

图5-2 "合作社 + 农业企业 + 小农户"模式

在生产阶段,合作社购买农业科技企业的化肥与绿色生物农药,农业科技企业定期为小农户提供生产技术指导和培训,预防大规模病虫害的发生,为合作社的生产提供技术支撑与保障,通过生产技术培训提高小农户生产管理能力。

在销售阶段,农业企业成为合作社主要的下游合作方,合作社负责种植管理、协调合作社成员等相关工作,小农户负责按照合作社要求种植,企业负责产品的加工、包装和市场营销。合作社与农业企业的订单式农业合作协议稳定合作社下游销售渠道,减少市场波动带来的经济损失,消除小农户"种出来卖不掉"的后顾之忧,让小农户收入更有保障。

"合作社 + 超市 + 小农户"经营模式与企业合作类似。该模式需满足进入超市的基本条件,如农产品通过农残等相关检测,可成为农超对接的主体。合作社以基地化、品质化、标准化、安全化的模式生产产品,超市直接上门收购符合标准的产品,减少农产品从生产地进入超市的中间环节,促进"菜园子"与"菜篮子"的有效衔接。由于蔬菜等农产品季节时效性强,合作社与超市需要时刻保持沟通,及时反映基地情况,同时了解超市销售需求。合作社与超市直接对接,减少中间商获利环节，提高小农户的销售收入。

项目实施中也有合作社利用扶持资金自行创办超市，建立超市销售分拣系统，开拓网络销售、社区直销、快递配送等销售途径，消费者既可以线下购买，也可以线上下单配送到家。合作社实现生产基地到线下门店和送货上门的全覆盖，惠及周边消费者，也为小农户提供更多的就业机会。

（三）"村集体＋生产基地＋小农户"模式

这种模式是村集体利用项目扶持资金建设生产基地发展特色产业，需要村集体具有管理能力的村干部统筹协调各方利益，有效组织和动员小农户，充分利用村庄资源优势发展特色产业。村集体中部分种植养殖能手受土地面积限制，生产规模难以扩大，生产基地的建设为他们提供扩大生产的条件。种植大户可租赁生产基地的土地以扩大生产经营规模，提升种植大户生产积极性（图5-3）。

小农户将土地统一流转给村集体，并在生产基地务工，生产基地的发展为村集体创造更多的集体经济收益。村集体与小农户成为利益关联体，小农户提供劳动力保证生产基地正常运作，生产基地的利润分红与务工工资提高了小农户收入。

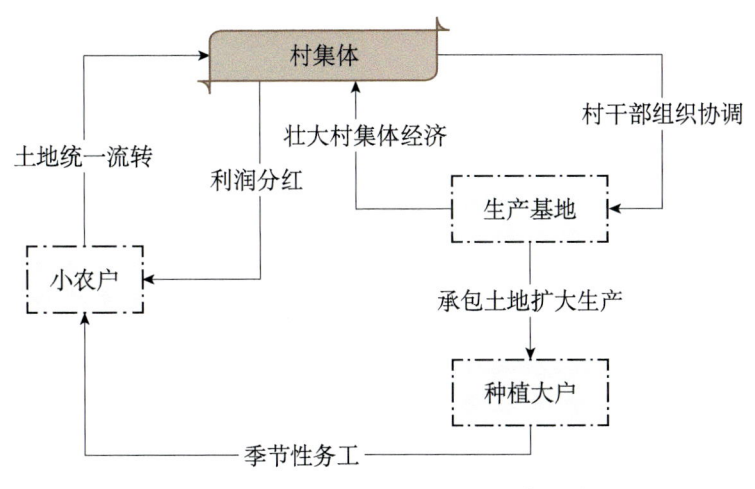

图5-3 "村集体＋生产基地＋小农户"模式

（四）"村集体＋合作社＋生产基地＋小农户"模式

该模式是在村中能手或者村干部的带动下形成的，以村集体土地服务合作社为基础，将小农户手中承包的土地通过租赁的形式流转集中到一起，统一对土地进行规划而来，并成立种植或养殖专业合作社，进一步发展特色产业（图5-4）。

项目扶持后,村集体合作社借助扶持资金对现有生产基地进行扩建,小农户可以通过土地或资金方式加入合作社,保障小农户参与主动性和积极性。合作社对生产的各个环节统一管理。同时,合作社与农业企业建立合作关系,为小农户提供销售服务,降低小农户与市场交易成本和风险,保障小农户的收入,带动当地小农户发展。

村集体领导的合作社应更侧重发挥村集体整合资源和组织协调的作用,整村利用生产基地发展特色产业,以发展规模化为主。小农户是否加入合作社,很大程度受其社会关系的影响,村干部在带动小农户加入合作社方面起到重要作用。村集体的角色也从小农户与政府之间的沟通桥梁转变为小农户进行农业生产经营活动的引导者,并且小农户仍可以保持其生产经营的自主性。

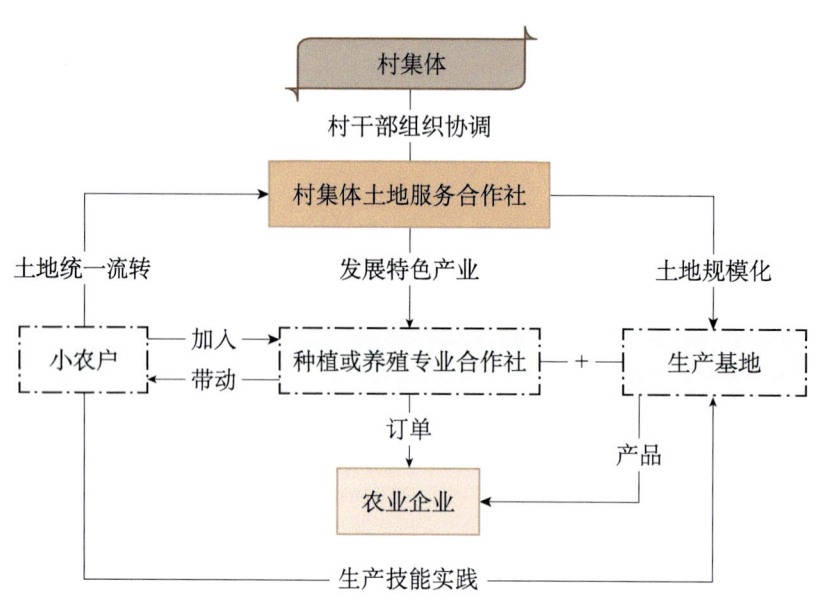

图5-4 "村集体+合作社+生产基地+小农户"模式

(五)"新农人+小农户"模式

"新农人+小农户"是项目实施过程中探索形成的一种新型带动模式,调查的105家合作社中有43家,占比40.9%。该模式下,合作社理事会成员是返乡创业的年轻人,也是合作社发起者、引领者。他们具有较高的文化水平、较好的组织管理能力与广泛的社交网络以及产业发展资源。该模式对合作社管理较为规范,通过制定合理的产业发展计划,完善的内部管理机制,如《合作社章程》《成员代表大会制度》等多项管理制度,明确成员股权、制定利益分配方案,确保每一位成员能通过利润分红和劳务收入等方式直接受益,部分合作社还为曾经的建档立卡贫困成员提供特定分红(图 5-5)。

新农人们借助合作社,发展地区特色产业,并在特色产业价值链中带动小农户。生产经营中新农人借助自身的人力资本与物质资本,将农业与其他产业结合,构建多样化、开放性的合作社经营模式。在销售渠道方面,合作社有通过开展农超对接、单位食堂配送等销售渠道;也有通过发展休闲农业,吸引消费者前来游玩与消费。新农人通过不同经营方式提高合作社的综合效益,也为小农户提供更多的就业岗位。

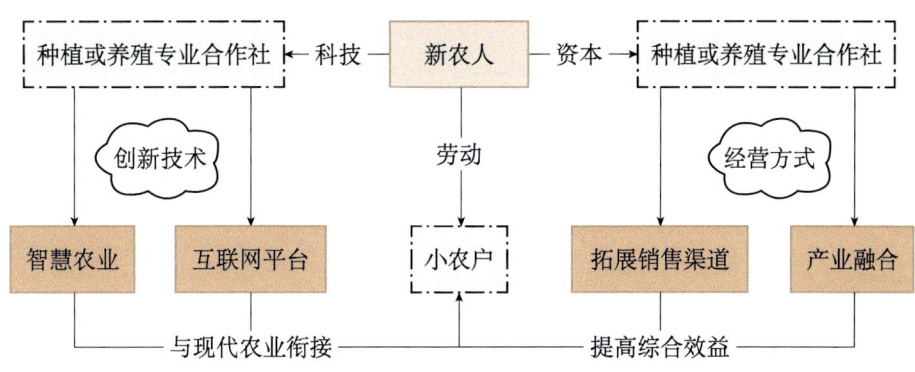

图 5-5 "新农人 + 小农户"模式

还有一部分新农人深耕农业科技,在互联网、人工智能、云计算等数字技术的嵌入下,新农人们利用科技力量为合作社提质增效。他们有利用互联网 5G 通信技术建立智慧农业产业园区,将智能化应用于农业生产之中;也有利用电商、微信公众号等互联网平台开展农产品营销,提升品牌知名度。这类新农人利用科技实现农业高质量可持续发展,提升小农户现代技术的应用能力,带动小农户与现代农业实现衔接。

二、带动小农户发展模式推广的对策建议

以上几种模式与小农户建立了较为紧密的利益联结机制,取得显著成效,促进小农户就业和增收,对小农户发展发挥了重要作用。同时,研究也发现合作社在管理规范、品牌建设、盈利能力方面还有一定提升空间,在与小农户利益联结和收益分配上存在优化路径。

(一)加强合作社规范化管理,促进合作社高质量发展

提升农民专业合作社的规范化水平是实现高质量发展的关键。2019 年,中央农

办联合农业农村部等 11 部门印发《关于开展农民合作社规范提升行动的若干意见》（中农发〔2019〕18 号），提出从组织机构、财务管理等方面提升合作社规范化水平。本项目扶持合作社是经过商业计划竞标遴选出来的，合作社管理相对规范，但调研数据也反映出有 35.2% 的合作社没有专职会计，商业计划书大多委托第三方完成，能够独立完成商业计划书的合作社仅占 60%。

规范化的合作社能够确保运营的稳定性和可持续性，降低运营风险，提高运营效率。为此，建议合作社进一步规范化管理：一是建立健全的内部管理制度，包括财务管理、生产管理、营销管理等，并确保制度的执行和监督；二是合作社需要完善组织架构，明确各部门的职责和权限，建立科学合理的决策机制，确保决策的科学性和民主性；三是健全合作社成员账户保障，普通成员的利益诉求在于盈余返还，需要准确记录成员的真实出资与交易量，合作社承担的财政项目可获得的财政补贴必须量化到每一个人的成员账户，设置完善的成员账户是保障合作社依法依规分配盈余的关键；四是合作社需加强人才培养和引进，提升员工的专业素质和管理能力，为合作社的规范化发展提供人才保障。

（二）加大政策支持力度，提升合作社服务能力

开展农业社会化服务是合作社带动小农户的重要抓手。调研发现项目扶持合作社提供的农业生产性服务大多集中于产前阶段，产后加工、包装等服务仅有 34 家合作社提供，产品存储服务有 36 家合作社提供，产品运输服务有 32 家合作社提供。

为此，建议通过政策引导、资金扶持等方式，激发合作社的服务能力。一是政府应制定科学合理的政策措施，为合作社的发展创造良好的外部环境。例如，提供税收优惠、财政补贴等政策支持，加大对合作社的金融支持力度，建立合作社发展的公共服务体系，加强对合作社的宣传和推广等，有效激发合作社的创新活力，提高合作社自主发展能力，推动合作社的高质量发展。二是政府应建立完善的监管机制，确保政策的执行和监督，严肃处理违反法律法规和政策的合作社，维护公平竞争的市场环境。通过政府的引导支持和监管，促进农民专业合作社高质量发展，推动农业产业转型升级和农民持续增收。

（三）完善利益联结机制，激发合作社带动小农户的内生动力

建立合作社的初衷就是要与当地小农户合作共赢、共同发展，因此合作社应在实现自身高质量发展的同时，还要把增强与小农户的利益联结机制、扩大示范带动

作用作为主要发展目标。项目区合作社已经初步完善全产业链上"风险共担，成本分摊，利益共享"的利益联结，调研发现，扶持合作社中有分红的合作社29家，占比27.6%，基本靠土地入股保底分红，二次分红较少，小农户获得的分红金额在1 000元左右。

为此，需要构建"联得紧、带得稳、收益久"的长效机制，增强合作社带动小农户发展。一是建立权责一致、公开透明的稳定利益关系，合作社理事会成员或大股东虽然投入了资本，但需要权责一致，通过健全成员账户保障合作社股权明晰，确保理事会成员与小农户各自股权关系，同时小农户需积极参与合作社的经营管理工作，获得更多参与决策权。二是做好利益分配处理，鼓励采取订单合约方式，严格履行合同条约的同时灵活应对调整方案，为利益受损方提供其他补偿，保证权益总体不受损害，从而增强合作意愿。三是加大政策激励，保障长效利益，将合作社带动小农户与评优、评奖等挂钩，如根据合作社带动小农户数量、分红收益金额等给予政策倾斜和支持力度，加强示范引领作用。

（四）鼓励合作社产业联合，提高综合带动水平

近十年来，党中央始终高度重视合作社与农业发展、农民增收协同发展，尤其是乡村振兴战略实施以来，国家在重视农业产业化发展的同时也将注意力转移至农村全面发展中来，通过借助合作社的组织平台带动农村一二三产业融合发展。本项目有部分合作社与企业等经营主体联合，促进产业发展的同时带动小农户发展。

为此，建议进一步增强合作社带动能力，提升综合带动水平。一是在鼓励单体合作社发挥作用的同时，积极引导合作社与其他新型经营主体相互融合，遵循开放、协调、共享等新发展理念，以产业发展为桥梁和纽带，构建多元复合、功能互补的协作共享机制，探索形成具有本土特色的"企业＋联合社＋家庭农场＋基地＋小农户"的发展模式。二是积极探索合作社联合社、农业企业协会、产业化联合体等模式，使农业产业链上各主体分工协作、各要素互联互通，形成更加紧密、更加稳定的新型组织联盟——农业产业化联合体，并成为利益共同体和命运共同体，提升综合带动水平。

下篇 项目区典型案例

项目实施以来，共扶持合作社 119 家。课题组根据项目实施内容，先后多次开展跟踪调查和专项调研，收集扶持合作社生产经营、产业发展情况，凝练合作社发展带动小农户的主要做法与进展成效。结合四川、宁夏项目区产业特点，研究形成一批种植、养殖、种养结合、农业社会化服务和产业融合类合作社带动小农户的经验做法与运行模式。现精选 25 个案例作为典型，主要类型如下：

序号	产业类型	具体产业	合作社 / 基地名称
1	种植业	粮油	宣汉项目区桂刚种植专业合作社
2			原州项目区新星土地股份专业合作社
3		蔬菜	苍溪项目区高成山蔬菜专业合作社
4			红寺堡项目区周福贵黄花菜种植专业合作社
5		水果	苍溪项目区五福猕猴桃专业合作社
6			利通项目区烽火台苹果种植专业合作社
7		中药材	苍溪项目区雍河桃园天麻中药材专业合作社
8			宣汉项目区寿口岩种植专业合作社
9		茶叶	叙州项目区功益茶叶专业合作社
10			宣汉项目区佳和种植专业合作社
11		食用菌	仪陇项目区茂园种植农民专业合作社
12	养殖业	牛	原州项目区中河村益农养殖示范基地
13			彭阳项目区山牛源肉牛科技养殖专业合作社
14		羊	红寺堡项目区香园村肉羊养殖基地
15			红寺堡项目区水套村养殖基地
16		鸡	原州项目区宏科农民养殖专业合作社
17			原州项目区六盘山生态养殖专业合作社
18		猪	仪陇项目区丰泰养殖农民专业合作社
19			宣汉项目区江鑫生态养殖专业合作社
20	种养结合		叙州项目区顺盈桑蚕养殖专业合作社
21	农业社会化服务类		苍溪项目区金永丰农机服务专业合作社
22			利通项目区吴忠市海之峰种植农民专业合作社
23	产业融合类		仪陇项目区勇旗种养殖农民专业合作社
24			广安项目区初山农谷种养专业合作社
25			银川项目区月益农农艺专业合作社

1. 宣汉项目区桂刚种植专业合作社

（1）基本情况

桂刚种植专业合作社成立于 2013 年 4 月 23 日，位于四川省宣汉县君塘镇明月社区，主营优质绿色水稻种植、加工和销售等服务，出资金额 230 万元。合作社拥有成员 65 户，成员以土地、资金入股合作社，共有 359 亩土地和 122 万元资产，折股量化后理事长占股 26.1%。2021 年，合作社获得项目扶持，用于购买插秧机、运输车、抛光机、色选机、包装机等。桂刚种植专业合作社生产基地见图 1。

图 1　桂刚种植专业合作社生产基地

（2）主要做法

一是生产机械化，降低成本。合作社利用扶持资金积极引进了一系列先进的农业机械设备（图 2）。截至 2023 年底，合作社拥有拖拉机、插秧机、植保无人机等农机装备 15 台，实现粮油作物"耕、种、管、收、烘"全程机械化。这种模式不仅降低合作社的运营成本，还提高了农产品的产量与附加值。

图 2　桂刚种植专业合作社加工设备

二是提供社会化服务。2021 年，合作社仅拥有农机具 3 台，无法进行农产品加工。2023 年，合作社利用项目扶持资金采购农机设备，并提供农产品加工服务，为周边小农户提供社会化服务（图 3）。服务价格为翻耕 150 元 / 亩，收割 120 元 / 亩，目前有 40 户小农户使用代耕代收服务。

图 3　桂刚种植专业合作社农机正在收割

三是探索订单农业，稳定销售渠道。合作社与宣汉县桂花米业有限公司签订订单合同，内容包含水稻种植品种、种植规模、收购价格等。合作社按照订单要求制定下一年的种植计划，通过统一生产资料、统一农机具、统一化肥农药的方式在基地种植水稻，实现标准化生产和规模化经营。收获后，宣汉县桂花米业有限公司按照订单约定收购水稻。为规范生产，合作社还积极举办技术培训班，2023 年共培训 40 人。桂刚种植专业合作社带动模式见图 4。

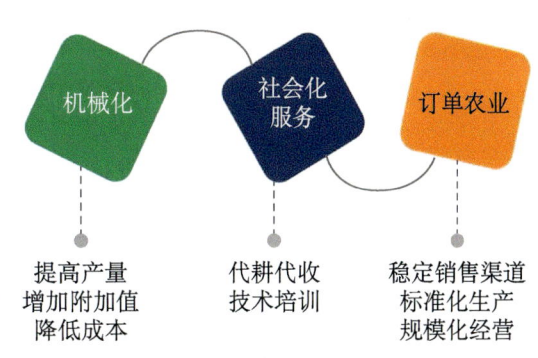

图 4　桂刚种植专业合作社带动模式

（3）取得成效

2023 年，合作社年产水稻 360 吨，销售额达 145.26 万元。合作社产品销售和社会化服务共获得盈余 66 万元，并将占盈余 69.7% 的 46 万元进行收益分红。此外，合作社为周边小农户提供更多的就业机会，带动就业 45 人，其中临时就业岗位 40 人，长期就业岗位 5 人。合作社薪酬标准为日常管理 110 元 / 天，农机师傅 300 元 / 天。通过项目扶持，合作社在自我发展的同时带动能力增强，促进当地农村经济发展。

2. 原州项目区新星土地股份专业合作社

（1）基本情况

新星土地股份专业合作社成立于2016年4月2日，位于固原市原州区彭堡镇彭堡村，该合作社主营小杂粮的种植、收购、加工和包装（图5），出资金额300万元。合作社拥有成员68户，成员以土地、资金入股合作社，折股量化后理事长占股8.9%。2022年，合作社获得项目扶持，主要用于基础设施建设、购买加工设备和加强成员培训、技术指导等。

图5 新星土地股份专业合作社产品

（2）主要做法

一是购置生产服务设备。合作社利用项目资金建设小杂粮标准化加工车间440平方米，糠皮除尘车间80平方米，加工厂场地硬化300平方米，小杂粮加工设备1套，皮带传输机1台（图6）。将合作社土地分户管理，合作社提供农资、技术、机械收割、统一代加工、订单销售的一条龙服务。收获季节收购周边小农户种植的小杂粮进行统一包装和销售，同时解决了小农户的粮食晾晒和贮藏等问题。

图 6　新星土地股份专业合作社设备

二是开展新品种试验，提升产品品质，打造自身品牌价值。合作社充分利用项目区土地肥沃、土壤富硒、昼夜温差大、日照相对较长、无工业污染等优越的自然资源条件，每年用100亩土地做新品种引进试验示范，主要试验示范晋谷、张杂谷等40多个品种，辐射带动大户种植谷子9 000余亩。合作社引进新品种后，经过反复试验、调研、种植，小杂粮的产量高、质量好、销量高，大部分销往中国山西、黑龙江、河北，甚至出口日本、韩国、俄罗斯。合作社选择绿色有机肥、富硒肥、缓释肥进行土壤保育，再用配方施肥给秧苗提供营养。通过生产环节减少农药施用量、增加有机肥或农家肥施用量，提升产品品质，顺应人们安全、健康的消费理念，打造绿色产品品牌，提高产品价值。新星土地股份专业合作社收获见图7。

图 7　新星土地股份专业合作社收获

三是开展成员及小农户种植技术培训，带动当地农民就业（图8）。合作社每年开展技术培训2期以上，培训种植及养殖150人次，也为周边小农户种植小杂粮增强信心。对于脱贫户和无法从事重体力劳动的小农户，合作社提供务工机会。新星土地股份专业合作社带动模式见图9。

图 8　新星土地股份专业合作社培训

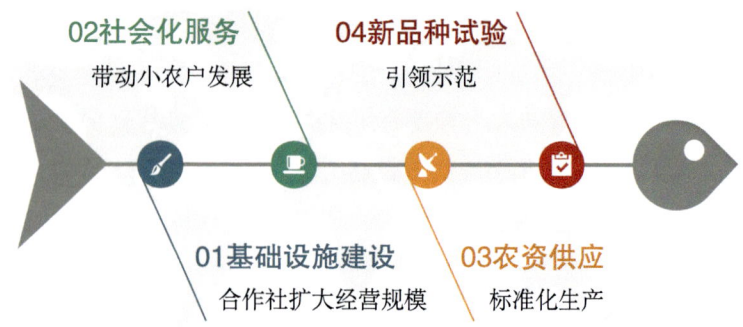

图 9　新星土地股份专业合作社带动模式

（3）取得成效

新星土地股份专业合作社已建设电商平台和网站，开展农民培训、管理软件应用和产品绿色认证等工作。新星土地股份专业合作社已经成为宁南山区小杂粮样板基地，同时也是土地股份制改革成功的先进典型。

3. 苍溪项目区高成山蔬菜专业合作社

（1）基本情况

高成山蔬菜专业合作社成立于2013年10月28日，位于苍溪县东青镇高峰村，该合作社主要从事蔬菜种植、销售等服务，出资金额320万元。合作社现有成员60户，成员以土地、资金加入合作社，共有243亩土地和22万元资金，土地、资金折股量化后理事长占股15.8%。合作社生产基地农产品已通过无公害农产品认证，认证面积3 000亩。合作社成员大多是小农户，投资能力有限，且文化水平不高，对种植、加工、营销方面知识了解不足。合作社自身发展受到没有分拣、加工、冷藏等设施设备的限制。2021年，合作社获得项目扶持，扶持资金主要用于购买蔬菜分级、冷藏保鲜等设施设备和专业知识培训及技术支持（图10）。

图10 高成山蔬菜专业合作社厂房

（2）主要做法

一是与小农户签订合同。合作社通过签订合同的方式，与小农户建立稳定的合作关系。这种模式不仅保证合作社的产品供应，也为小农户提供稳定的销售渠道和价格保障，降低市场风险。同时，合作社还根据市场需求和小农户实际情况，灵活调整合同内容和数量，促进农业生产的可持续发展。

二是统一农资供应。合作社根据所种植蔬菜品种的需要，统一组织种子、种苗、肥料等农资的供应，并以成本价与小农户结算。这大大降低小农户的生产成本，使小农户能够以更优惠的价格获取到高质量的农资产品，从而提高小农户的生产效益。

三是提供农机服务。合作社为小农户提供农机服务，包括整地、田间管理等，有效减少小农户劳动力投入，降低生产成本。农机服务的收费标准低于市场价，如整地费用为80元/亩，这使得更多小农户能够享受到现代化的农业生产服务。

四是建设现代化农业设施。通过项目的扶持，合作社安装滴灌系统、新建分拣中心和冷藏保鲜库、购买冷链物流车等现代化农业设施（图11）。这些设施的建设不仅提升合作社自身的加工、储藏能力，还通过统一的标准和服务，间接带动小农户的生产向标准化、现代化迈进。

图11　高成山蔬菜专业合作社冷藏运输车

五是专业知识培训与技术支持。在蔬菜种植和管理的关键时期，合作社组织专家进行技术培训，不仅面向合作社内部成员，还积极邀请与合作社签订订单的小农户参与，甚至欢迎其他小农户参加。这些培训活动显著提高小农户的种植技能和管理水平，为提升农产品产量和质量奠定了坚实基础。高成山蔬菜专业合作社带动模式见图12。

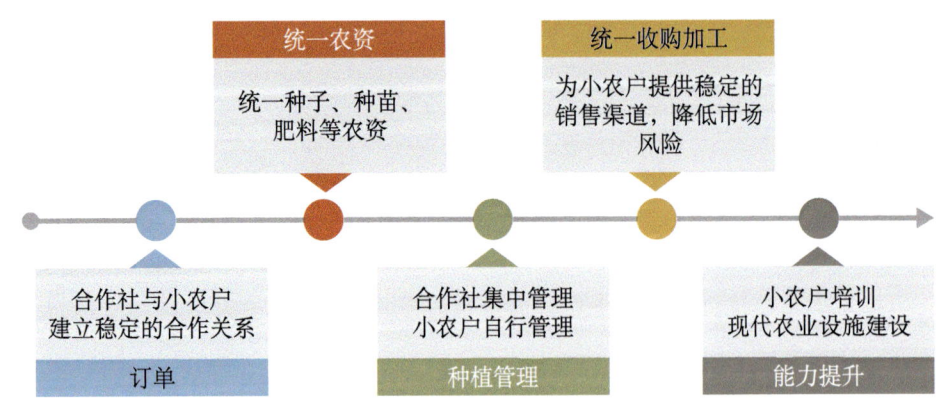

图12　高成山蔬菜专业合作社带动模式

（3）取得成效

在项目的扶持下，高成山蔬菜专业合作社取得显著的成效。合作社通过基础设施建设，解决了产品加工与储藏等瓶颈问题。合作社通过优先吸纳、照顾原贫困户等弱势群体，带动周边小农户共同发展。2023年接受合作社组织培训的小农户在1 500户以上。合作社通过统一供应生产物资、重点环节的生产技术培训等措施，将先进的生产技术和管理要求带入田间生产过程中，保证农产品的质量和产量，保障种植小农户的收益。通过提高整地水平和田间管理质量，减少小农户的劳动力投入、降低生产成本。目前合作社农机服务成员户及周边小农户1 000户以上。

4. 红寺堡项目区周福贵黄花菜种植专业合作社

（1）基本情况

周福贵黄花菜种植专业合作社成立于2016年8月10日，位于吴忠市红寺堡区太阳山镇周新村周新组，该合作社主要从事黄花菜的种植（图13）、加工与销售，出资金额150万元。合作社拥有成员60户，成员以土地入股合作社，共有1 147.8亩土地，折股量化后理事长占股30.5%。2022年，合作社获得项目扶持，将扶持的资金投资于库房、晾晒场地硬化与成员培训等。

图13 周福贵黄花菜种植专业合作社产品

（2）主要做法

一是扩建晾晒场地。在项目扶持之前，合作社的黄花菜晾晒场地不足，采摘旺季鲜菜因无法及时晾晒出现霉变、腐烂等现象，影响黄花菜干菜品质和种植经济效益。在项目扶持之后，合作社扩建库房（图14）、硬化晾晒场地，扩大了合作社的生产规模，解决了黄花菜晾晒问题，提高了成员种植黄花菜的积极性。

图14 周福贵黄花菜种植专业合作社库房

二是培训提升小农户能力，理论与实践结合。在项目扶持之前，小农户在黄花菜的种植生产中大多延续传统的经验和做法，缺乏科学的选育经验、高质量的田间管理、精准计量的施肥、合理的水肥标准、安全有效的病虫害防治技术和适宜杀青的温度及时间段的把控。项目扶持之后，合作社委托固原市原州区育才农业技能培训学校开展两期培训班，学习乡村振兴战略、农户素养与现代生活、合作社的成立、合作社规范化运行、农业生产经营管理与黄花菜高产栽培技术等理论知识（图15）。

图 15　课堂理论知识培训与田间课堂培训

在培训过程中，开展田间课堂，传授小农户黄花菜的育苗技术规程、黄花菜的制干技术规程、黄花菜的统防统治和统一施肥与黄花菜田间管理等实践操作。为巩固成员知识，合作社将培训的资料汇编成册，供成员后续学习（图16）。

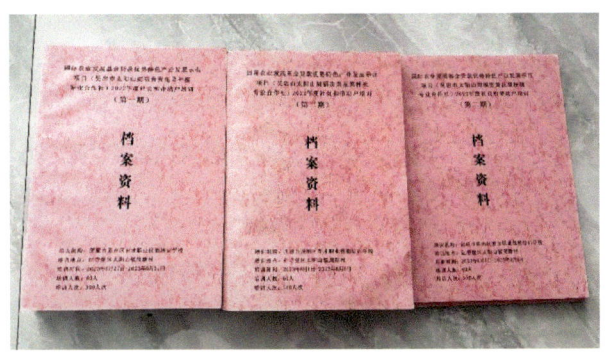

图 16　周福贵黄花菜种植专业合作社汇编的培训资料

三是提供临时就业岗位带动周边小农户。暑假期间，周边大学生参加到合作社的临时工岗位中，以赚取学费。在黄花菜采摘等环节，合作社创造临时岗位102个。目前，合作社有15个包装工人，小农户包装一箱黄花菜可获得2.2元，小农户通过包装黄花菜，一天最多可得240元（图17），周福贵黄花菜种植专业合作社带动模式见图18。

图 17　小农户正在务工

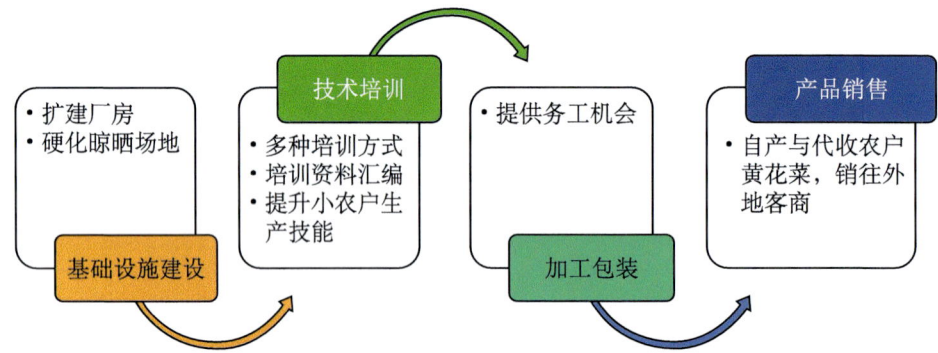

图 18　周福贵黄花菜种植专业合作社带动模式

（3）取得成效

项目扶持以来，合作社累计培训成员 120 人次，为 33 个成员提供代收代销服务。2023 年，合作社拿出近 1.7 万元进行分红，平均每户分得 320 元。2024 年，合作社自主生产 22 吨干黄花菜（图 19），收购干黄花菜 11 吨，总销售额 190 万元，其中自主生产销售 115 万元，代收代销 75 万元。

图 19　周福贵黄花菜种植专业合作社包装厂房

5. 苍溪项目区五福猕猴桃专业合作社

（1）基本情况

五福猕猴桃专业合作社成立于 2012 年 8 月 30 日，位于苍溪县亭子镇五福村，由村里的 5 户农户共同发起，出资金额 55.8 万元，主要从事猕猴桃种植、销售等服务。合作社拥有成员 50 户，成员以土地入股合作社，共有 186 亩土地，折股量化后理事长占股 18.8%。2021 年，合作社获得项目扶持，将扶持的资金投资于生产设施建设、加工储藏设备购买和成员培训等（图 20）。

图 20　五福猕猴桃专业合作社的种植基地

（2）主要做法

一是扩大生产规模。合作社建立初期，受限于规模、人数、条件以及经验的不足，合作社运营效果并不理想，收入和成本勉强相抵，利润所剩无几。随着项目扶持资金注入，合作社迎来新的发展机遇。合作社通过申请注册登记变更，提高出资金额和成员规模，成员人数从最初的 5 户增加到 50 户，其中包括 17 户原贫困户和 17 户女性成员。这一变化不仅增强合作社的实力，也为更多小农户提供参与机会和增收途径。

二是改善生产条件。合作社新建 500 平方米的分拣中心和 100 吨的冷冻室，后续计划安装喷灌设施设备 100 亩，以提高猕猴桃的灌溉效率，确保果树的健康生长。在统一经营和自主经营相结合的模式下，合作社协助周边小农户提高猕猴桃的产量和品质。同时，合作社的保鲜库延长水果的储存和供应时间，为成员创造更多的销售机会，增加成员收入。

三是分红激励机制。合作社的分红方式在保障小农户基本收益的基础上，通过激励机制提升小农户的积极性。小农户将土地流转给合作社，获得土地流转费。产品销售后合作社将利润的50%按照交易量返还成员，另外50%计入合作社账户用于合作社运营发展。五福猕猴桃专业合作社带动模式见图21。

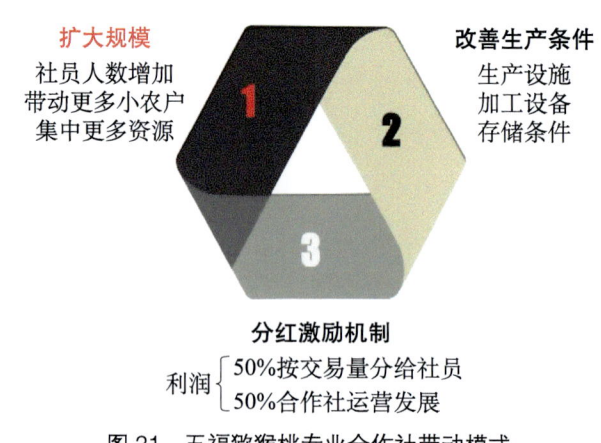

图 21 五福猕猴桃专业合作社带动模式

（3）取得成效

五福猕猴桃专业合作社采取一系列措施来促进小农户和合作社的发展。建成100亩猕猴桃园水肥一体化系统，解决了猕猴桃不同生长阶段对水肥的不同需求，把精准施肥技术与节水灌溉技术相结合，提高产量和品质、保护土壤结构、降低污染和减少病虫害。实行喷灌施肥方式后，合作社每年可减少施用肥料20吨、节约用水2.5万立方米、节约人工300人次，可节约生产成本约12万元，实现利润增长10余万元。

分拣中心建成后，合作社可将猕猴桃分类分级包装，根据不同等级差异化销售，合作社每年可实现利润增长30余万元。冷藏保鲜库（图22）建立后，合作社通过保鲜贮藏后实现错季销售，增值收入40万元。

2023年合作社培训成员50人，通过专家对合作社的技术指导和对成员的技术培训，成员提高猕猴桃的种植管理技术，获得猕猴桃绿色食品认证1个，每亩可实现增产100千克，每亩增收1 500余元。通过绿色食品认证，提高合作社产品的市场认可率和品牌效益，拓宽合作社的销售渠道，提高合作社的经济效益。

5. 苍溪项目区五福猕猴桃专业合作社

图 22　五福猕猴桃专业合作社仓库

6. 利通项目区烽火台苹果种植专业合作社

（1）基本情况

烽火台苹果种植专业合作社成立于 2015 年 4 月 16 日，位于吴忠市利通区扁担沟镇烽火墩村，主要从事苹果种植、育苗及销售，出资金额 1 575 万元。2016 年，合作社被宁夏回族自治区林业厅、吴忠市利通区林业局列为有机富硒苹果示范园项目实施单位。合作社拥有成员 50 户，9 个成员以果园的形式入股合作社，经折股量化后，理事长占股 5.7%。2021 年，合作社获得项目扶持 150 万元，将获得的扶持资金投资于库房、果树枝条粉碎机、拖拉机、机械叉车与广告宣传等。烽火台苹果种植专业合作社产品见图 23。

图 23 烽火台苹果种植专业合作社产品

（2）主要做法

一是采取"四统一"降低小农户生产成本。合作社形成统一品种、统一培训、统一管理、统一销售的"四统一"模式。在统一品种方面，合作社已种植 3 类新品种苹果，果园以维纳斯黄金苹果为主要品种，因其高甜浓香的特质被广大消费者喜爱。在统一培训方面，合作社除了接受项目、村委会组织的生产技术培训，还邀请灵武市农技人员前往果园开展田间教学课程，通过多种培训学习，大多成员已掌握嫁接、桥接等技术，小农户的生产能力不断提升。在统一管理方面，合作社统一管理成员的果园，施肥、套袋、采摘、储存（图24）与包装等环节均由合作社组织，提升小农户生产效率。在统一销售方面，成员的销售渠道由合作社打通，2023年，合作社生产280万千克苹果，收购农户5万千克苹果，销往4家超市与周边市场，拓宽了小农户的销售渠道。

图24 烽火台苹果种植专业合作社的仓库

二是多主体合作保障小农户权益。合作社与同村的合作社建立合作关系，通过微信群聊共享市场信息，且共同使用"扁担沟苹果"的品牌，利用品牌效应增加产品的经济价值，进而带动小农户增收。在农资供应方面，合作社与山西中农乐农业科技有限公司建立合作关系，合作社使用该公司的化肥与农药，该公司则定期为合作社提供果树生产技术培训指导（图25），有效预防大规模病虫害的发生，为小农户种植的苹果提供坚实的技术支撑与保障。烽火台苹果种植专业合作社带动模式见图26。

图25 烽火台苹果种植专业合作社开展田间培训活动

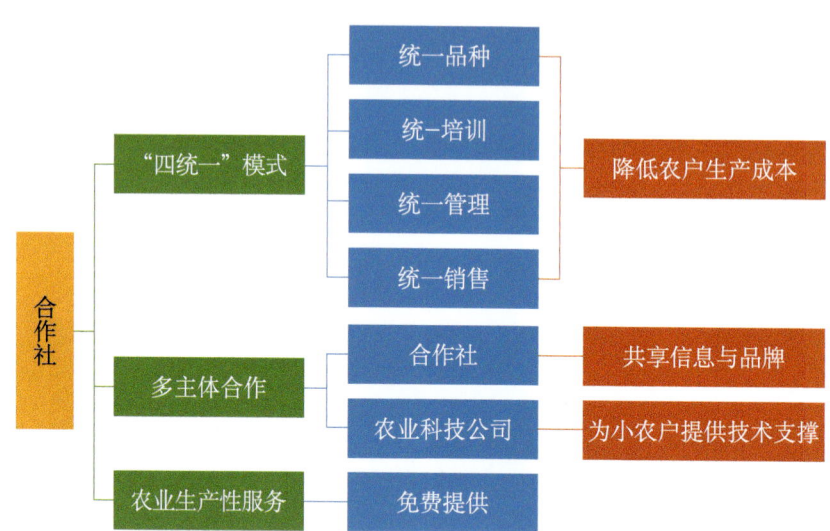

图26 烽火台苹果种植专业合作社带动模式

（3）取得成效

2023年，合作社已为41位成员免费提供农资服务、代耕代收服务、防疫防控技术培训等农业生产性服务以及包装服务、产品存储和销售服务。2023年，合作社已拥有"扁担沟苹果"品牌。合作社在建设产业链的同时，正不断扩大种植规模，果园由2021年的50亩扩大到2023年的1 400亩。规模的扩大，为周边小农户提供了更多工作岗位，合作社拥有中长期工作岗位6个，在采摘季节，合作社最多可提供120个临时岗位，临时工工资达140～150元/天。

7. 苍溪项目区雍河桃园天麻中药材专业合作社

（1）基本情况

雍河桃园天麻中药材专业合作社成立于2014年5月7日，位于苍溪县雍河乡桃园村，合作社主要从事天麻、百合、中药材的种植、加工与销售（图27），出资金额总额200万元。合作社拥有成员101户，理事长占股27.5%。2013年元月，合作社创始人杨敏返乡创业，引进云南优质乌天麻，投资入股组建天麻中药材专业合作社，在全村大力推广天麻种植技术，带领全村和周边群众共同致富。合作社注册有"苍之园""天麻姑娘"商标。2023年，合作社获得项目扶持，将扶持的资金投资于生产设施建设、加工储藏设备购买和成员培训等。

图27 雍河桃园天麻中药材专业合作社天麻种子育种基地和天麻

（2）主要做法

一是为小农户提供技术支持，包括天麻种植技术培训，受训人数近1 000人次，其中妇女达到800人次，实现了成员家家户户有个"种植能手"的目标（图28）。

二是采取"代农户垫资、定价回收产品、统一结算扣除"的方式，解

图28 雍河桃园天麻中药材专业合作社培训

决小农户从事天麻种植无资金的难题，极大地激发了群众种植天麻的热情，种植面积成倍扩大。利用"五统"标准化技术管理，品种统一、技术统训、四季统管、农资统供、品牌统创，既保证产品同步同质同效，又降低成本。

三是带动周边小农户增收。目前合作社种植天麻200余亩，有固定工人11人（其中脱贫户2人），年临时用工1 200多人次，以脱贫户为主。2023年合作社给固定工人和短期固定工人共发放工资近18万元，周边小农户实现就近务工。同时，合作社以点带面，带动全镇9个村种植中药材2 000余亩，家庭农场、企业、大户等新型经营主体10余家，以大户带动周边小农户种植，如石牛村黄精基地100亩、市场村丹参基地50亩等，形成"净作、林下套作、药药套作、猕药套作、粮药套作"种植模式，中药材以天麻、丹参、黄精、重楼、淫羊藿、茯苓等多个品种种植，推动全镇中药材产业健康发展。雍河桃园天麻中药材专业合作社带动模式见图29。

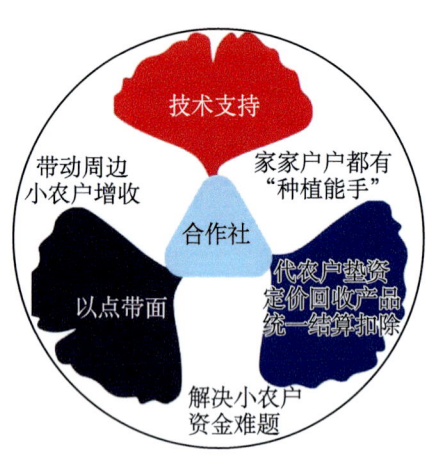

图29 雍河桃园天麻中药材专业合作社带动模式

（3）取得成效

合作社利用项目资金，生产设备不断完善，合作社生产效率显著提升，为进一步扩大规模奠定了基础。随着合作社生产规模与业务的扩张，劳动力需求也日益增长，为周边小农户提供了更多就业岗位，有力促进区域经济的发展与就业稳定。同时新设备的投入，延长产业链条，新开发多系列食用天麻产品，如天麻粉、天麻干片、天麻面条、食用鲜天麻等。合作社以"合作社+基地+小农户+服务+产品+销售"为发展思路，致力打造集天麻种植、收购、加工、经营于一体的全新中药材经营模式，实现中药材产业的规范化、集约化、品牌化发展。2023年合作社实现总收入69万元。

8. 宣汉项目区寿口岩种植专业合作社

（1）基本情况

寿口岩种植专业合作社成立于2018年1月9日，位于四川盆地东北大巴山南麓的宣汉县明月乡重石村，主要从事枳壳（图30）、花椒的种植、加工与销售，出资金额516万元。合作社拥有成员115户，共有387.8亩土地和245万元，土地、资金折股量化后理事长占股29.4%。2020年，合作社获得项目扶持，将扶持的资金投资于园区灌溉管道安装、管理培训与烘干房建设等。

图30 寿口岩种植专业合作社枳壳加工

（2）主要做法

一是产业链延伸和品牌建设。在项目的支持下，合作社投资现代化加工设备，建立烘干厂房等（图31），提高中药材的加工能力和产品质量，同时注重品牌建设和产品认证，加强产业链建设，提升品牌意识，增强市场竞争力。目前合作社已拥有商标注册证1个，农产品品牌1个。

二是扩大生产规模、提供就业岗位。2023年，合作社将黄精、石菖蒲套种于枳壳中，种植枳壳416亩、黄精100亩、石菖蒲100亩。生产规模的提升，为合作社带来更高的经济收益，也带动了周边更多小农户就业。目前合作社长期就业岗位10人，临时就业岗位30人。寿口岩种植专业合作社带动模式见图32。

图 31　寿口岩种植专业合作社烘干设备

图 32　寿口岩种植专业合作社带动模式

（3）取得成效

合作社自成立以来，一直按每亩 400 元 / 年的保底分红标准支付给成员，即便在合作社尚未产生利润的情况下，成员的收益也得到了保障。2024 年，合作社开始二次分红。合作社在发展中注重联农带农，通过培训和技术指导带动周边小农户，完善利益联结机制，促进产业增值收益留在农村，惠及农户。合作社成员中包含大量的小农户和脱贫户，为乡村振兴作出积极贡献。

9. 叙州项目区功益茶叶专业合作社

(1) 基本情况

功益茶叶专业合作社成立于2011年12月，位于叙州区蕨溪镇简湾村（天宫山），主要从事茶叶种植、加工与销售，农机具销售、农业旅游观光、农作物病虫防治服务等，出资金额515万元，合作社现已建成茶叶种植基地3 200亩。合作社拥有成员126户，其中脱贫户39人、少数民族2人、女性成员49人，成员覆盖蕨溪镇的8个村。

合作社于2020年入选项目扶持合作社，获得扶持资金360万元，并在2021年入选项目子项目农超项目，获得扶持资金150万元。功益茶叶专业合作社的新建园区见图33。

图33 功益茶叶专业合作社的新建园区

(2) 主要做法

一是与小农户签订合作协议，建立利益联结。合作社通过强化产品质量宣传、生产技术指导以及生产资料统一化、标准化等形式保证小农户订单的产品质量（图34）。若小农户产品不符合要求，合作社会依据农产品品质选择不收，或以较低价格收购作为其他农副产品；若小农户产品满足合作社需求，合作社以高于市场价1.3元/千克的价格收购小农户产品。合作社将市场需求与小农户生产直接对接，农业生产实现科学化、系统化与专业化。订单方式不仅提高了小农户的生产积极性，还解决了农产品的销售难题，保障了小农户收入。

图 34　功益茶叶专业合作社产品

二是通过生产性服务带动小农户发展。合作社免费为小农户提供农资、农机、代耕代收等社会化服务。2023 年，功益茶叶专业合作社为 18 户提供农资服务，为 124 户提供农业生产技术服务。这些服务显著提高了农作物的产量和质量，减少因技术不当或病虫害等造成的损失，降低了小农户的农业生产成本，增加了农产品的市场竞争力。同时，合作社的生产过程也需要大量的劳动力支撑，随着合作社茶园规模的扩大，茶叶采摘的高峰期，合作社招募临时工 84 人。合作社为周边小农户增加了收入来源，周边小农户为合作社缓解了用工难题。

三是提供产后加工、销售服务。合作社免费为小农户提供加工、包装、存储、运输和销售等社会化服务（图 35）。合作社为 124 户提供产品加工、包装等服务，为 82 户提供产品存储服务，为 67 户提供产品运输服务，为 124 户提供产品销售服务。2023 年，合作社收购农户鲜叶等 93 145 千克，利用自身的品牌效应和市场渠

图 35　功益茶叶专业合作社的新建车间及设备

道，实现代收代销额 178.1 万元。合作社提供产后社会化服务的同时也为小农户带来了长期就业岗位，小农户参加农产品的加工、包装、运输等工作，合作社与小农户之间形成了优势互补、互利共赢的利益联结，促进乡村产业经济的持续发展。功益茶叶专业合作社带动模式见图 36。

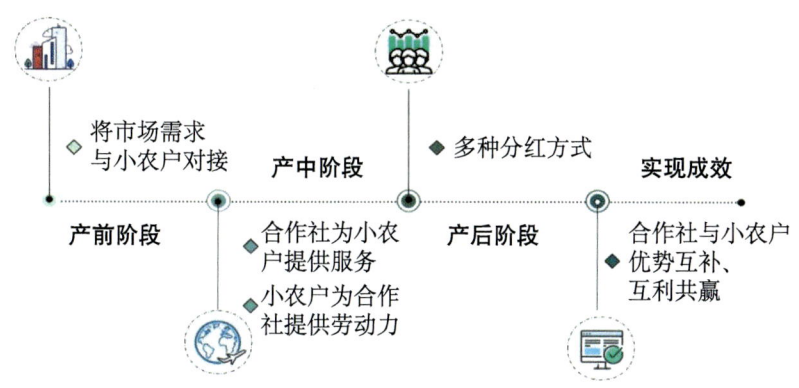

图 36　功益茶叶专业合作社带动模式

（3）取得成效

通过项目扶持，合作社引进新茶苗 500 万株，新引进品种有复选九号、131、乌牛早、黄金芽等新品种茶苗，注册了"野谷春""溪檀"等商标。2021 年被评为"国家级示范社"，2022 年通过 ISO 9001 质量认证。合作社通过合作社能力提升活动及合作社成员技能培训等，实现了合作社成员技能提高、产能增加、收入增长。合作社成员通过劳务收益、利润分红等方式直接受益，直接受益小农户达到 120 多人。2023 年，合作社营业收入达到 754 万元，本年盈余 67 万元，提取 40 万元作为分红，户均 3 000 多元；增加了合作社上下游企业的营业收入，带动山区妇女和弱势群体临时就业 2 200 多人次；实现当地茶农增产增收，带动合作社以外小农户增加收入 1 200 元 / 人。

10. 宣汉项目区佳和种植专业合作社

（1）基本情况

佳和种植专业合作社成立于2016年11月28日，位于宣汉县樊哙镇花梨村，该合作社主要从事茶叶种植、加工及销售（富硒绿茶）等服务，出资金额1 095万元（图37）。合作社拥有成员306户，共有1 000亩土地和494万元资金，土地、资金折股量化后理事长占股19.6%。合作社理事长和副理事长是兄弟俩，一个拥有建筑和农业生产的技术背景，另一个资金充裕，两人经其他项目经营管理启发，决定利用本地悠久的茶叶种植历史和丰富的生产经验，结合技术、资金和农户的意愿，整合并完善当地的茶叶种植产业，从而带动小农户增收致富。2020年，合作社获得项目扶持，将扶持资金用于购买采茶机、揉茶机、杀青机、制作微信小程序等。

图37 佳和种植专业合作社基地

（2）主要做法

一是吸引新农人。合作社的发展吸引了村里的年轻人返乡或留在家乡工作，他们拥有专业知识，为合作社注入新的活力。合作社聘请专家对小农户进行专业化和系统化的培训，提高小农户的种植技能和加工水平。佳和种植专业合作社加工车间见图38。

二是整合产业链。合作社通过农户资金入股的方式，筹集到大量资金，为合作社的发展提供了有力保障。合作社将茶叶的种植、加工和销售环节进行整合,形成一个完整的产业链。这不仅降低小农户的生产成本和风险,还提高产品的附加值和市场竞争力。

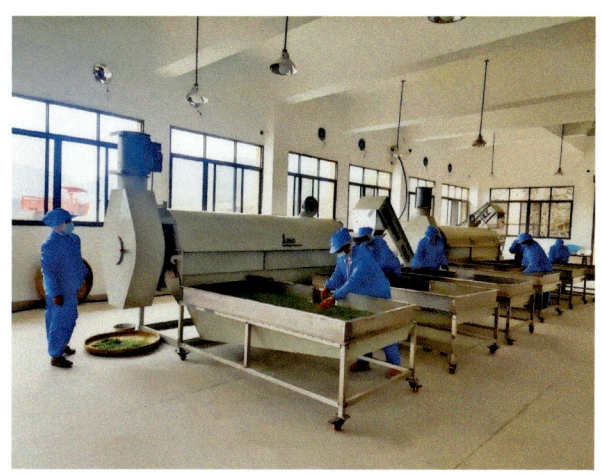

图 38　佳和种植专业合作社加工车间

三是拓展市场。合作社通过电商平台向省外消费者销售茶叶,打开新的销售渠道,提高产品的知名度和美誉度。同时,合作社还向当地的销售公司、建筑协会等供应茶叶,实现多渠道销售。佳和种植专业合作社带动模式见图39。

（3）取得成效

通过专业化和系统化的培训,小农户的种植技能和加工水平得到提高,茶叶的产量和品质也有显著

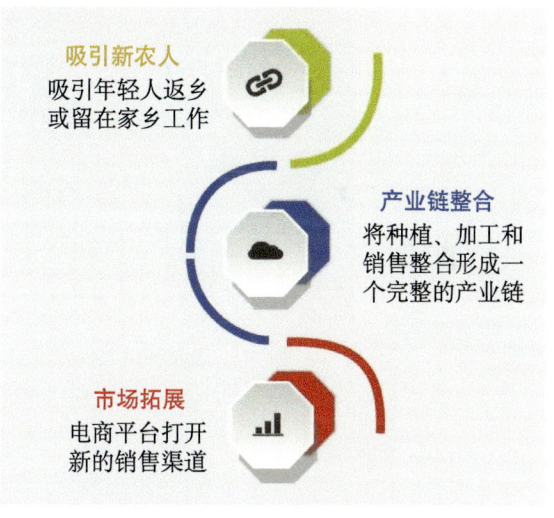

图 39　佳和种植专业合作社带动模式

提升。随着茶叶产业的发展,小农户通过套种、务工和分红等方式获得更多的收益,小农户增收效果显著,生活质量得到改善。同时,通过电商平台和多渠道销售,合作社的茶叶产品得到更多消费者的认可和喜爱,合作社的品牌影响力逐渐增强。

合作社的发展不仅带动小农户增收致富,还促进当地乡村经济的繁荣和发展。同时,合作社还吸引返乡人才的加入,为乡村振兴提供人才支持。

11. 仪陇项目区茂园种植农民专业合作社

（1）基本情况

茂园种植农民专业合作社成立于2018年1月2日，位于四川省南充市仪陇县新政镇高堂沟村，该合作社主要从事香菇、木耳（图40）等食用菌的种植、加工、运输及销售服务，出资金额550万元。合作社拥有成员130户，资金折股量化后理事长占股0.6%。2021年，合作社获得项目扶持，将扶持的资金用于搭建出菇大棚、冷冻库与烘干房等生产设施，还用于建立电商平台等宣传营销平台。

图40 茂园种植农民专业合作社生产的黑木耳

（2）主要做法

一是基础设施建设与资源整合。合作社利用项目支持，投入大量资金用于生产设施建设（图41）、加工和营销、服务培训以及产品品牌投资，现已建设出菇大棚8座，占地1 280平方米，冷链厂房250平方米，冷冻库3处，烘干厂房240平方米，烘干设备1套。采购电脑、打复印机、办公桌椅6台（套）等，为合作社的发展奠定了坚实基础。同时，整合土地资源，通过建设无公害种植基地，推广良种标准化种植技术，提高农村土地资源的产出率。

图 41　茂园种植农民专业合作社基地

二是发展循环农业，延长产业链。合作社通过走循环农业发展之路，利用桑枝做菌包种木耳（图 42），菌包堆肥施给桑树，形成资源循环利用的闭环系统，预估黑木耳市场价 60～70 元/千克。实现了资源的循环利用和产业链的延伸，延长产业链不仅增加农产品的附加值，还促进项目区域农业产业结构向高附加值方向升级。

图 42　茂园种植农民专业合作社出菇大棚

三是引进技术与创新产品。引进新品种和新技术，提高产品品质，形成品牌，扩大影响力。通过培育桑枝食用菌平菇、木耳、金耳、香菇等品种，丰富产品种类，满足市场需求。同时合作社注重技术培训，帮助小农户提高种植技能，推动香菇产业的规模化、标准化和产业化发展，为当地小农户带来更多的经济收益和发展机会。

四是拓展市场与销售渠道。通过电商平台、批发市场、商超等多元化销售渠道，扩大产品的市场覆盖面，提高产品的市场竞争力。合作社积极推广产品，吸引顾客进合作社基地采摘购买,增加产品的直接销售额。茂园种植农民专业合作社运营模式见图43。

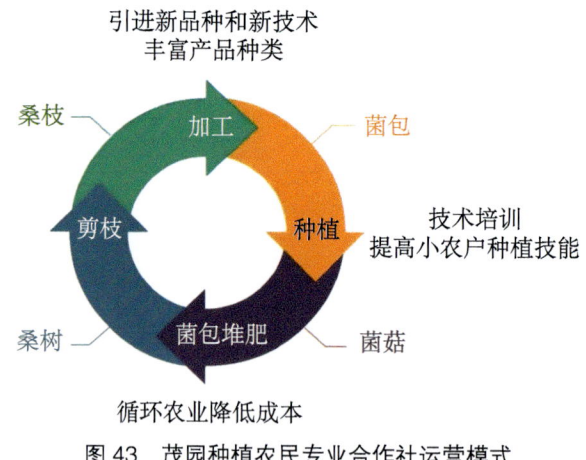

图43 茂园种植农民专业合作社运营模式

(3)取得成效

合作社通过提高生产效率、延长产业链、技术创新和市场拓展等手段,实现利益最大化。合作社将小农户纳入合作社的生产体系,鼓励小农户参与基地采摘,增加小农户的参与感和获得感,促进小农户与合作社的紧密联系。另外,通过吸纳就业、提供土地流转费用等方式,直接带动小农户增收。

12. 原州项目区中河村益农养殖示范基地

（1）基本情况

宁夏固原市原州区中河村是"人畜分离"育肥牛养殖基地示范性养殖园，通过养殖肉牛发展壮大村集体经济。在乡村振兴扶贫资金支持下，中河村益农养殖示范基地建设 3 栋养牛大棚（图 44）。项目扶持后，基地又增加 4 栋钢结构养牛大棚，配套建成青贮池、饲草房、集污池、输变电线路、园区道路、围墙等附属设施（图 45）。

图 44　中河村益农养殖示范基地

（2）主要做法

中河村集体探索走"出户入园"的路子发展肉牛养殖产业，坚持规模化标准化养殖，不断提升产品附加值。基地为小农户代养肉牛 120 多头，采取小农户筹资托养、集体购牛饲养，采用统一疫病防控防治、粪便无害处理的科学管理模式，全程标准化、机械化、科学化的养殖方式，提升了养殖效率。100 余头肉牛的投食工作仅需一个小时。小农户只需支付牛犊价格，后续培育销售均由村集体负责。中河村益农养殖示范基地带动模式见图 46。

图 45　项目扶持建设的消毒室与库房

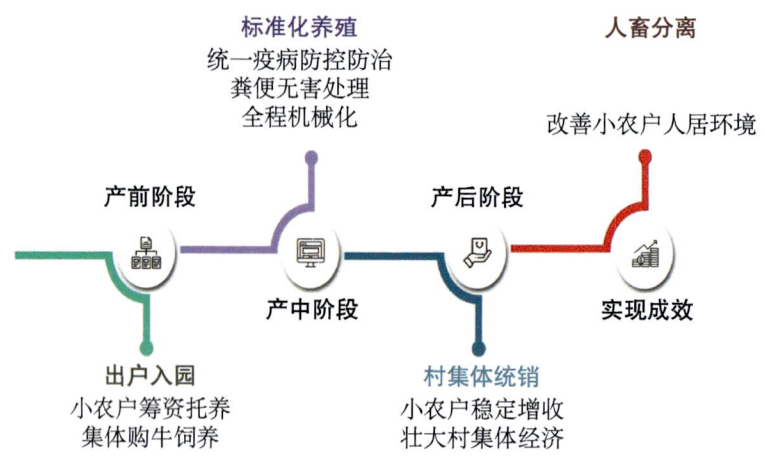

图 46　中河村益农养殖示范基地带动模式

（3）取得成效

2024 年，养殖基地长期工 4 人，共养殖 400 余头牛，预计年底出栏 300 余头牛。中河村益农养殖示范基地与周边小农户签订托养协议，为周边 40 多小农户提供代养服务，小农户一年分红 3 000 元，帮助小农户稳定增收。

13. 彭阳项目区山牛源肉牛科技养殖专业合作社

（1）基本情况

山牛源肉牛科技养殖专业合作社成立于 2012 年 11 月 1 日，位于固原市彭阳县古城镇任河村，合作社主要从事肉牛的养殖及销售（图 47），饲料加工，出资金额 100 万元。合作社拥有成员 50 户，成员以土地、资金加入合作社，土地、资金折股量化后理事长占股 11.3%。2020 年，合作社获得项目扶持，将扶持的资金投资于饲料收获机、粉草机与管理培训等。

图 47 山牛源肉牛科技养殖专业合作社的肉牛养殖

（2）主要做法

项目实施以来，合作社探索建立起"321"带动机制，3 代表"三个免费"，合作社免费为小农户进行养殖技术指导、免费为小农户提供优质客商外销渠道、免费为脱贫户赠送育肥牛；2 代表"两个支付"，合作社支付劳务工资、支付土地流转费；1 代表"一个激发"，合作社的一系列措施旨在激发小农户自力更生致富的内生动力。山牛源肉牛科技养殖专业合作社带动模式见图 48。

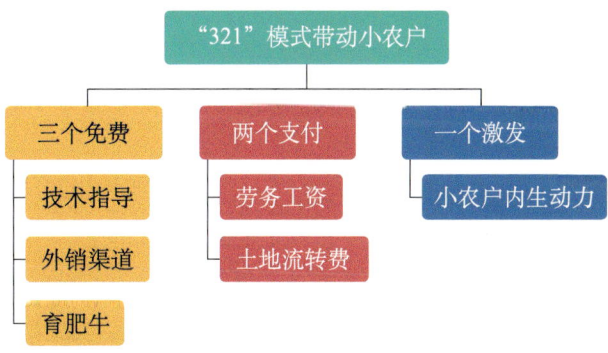

图 48 山牛源肉牛科技养殖专业合作社带动模式

（3）取得成效

山牛源肉牛科技养殖专业合作社作为宁夏大学饲料工程技术研究中心的试验示范基地，合作社在饲料配方、饲养品种上得到专业认可。2023 年，山牛源肉牛科技养殖专业合作社以每头 1.4 万元的价格出栏 80 头牛（图 49），免费为 60 户提供技术指导服务，免费为 10 户组织肉牛外销服务。

图 49　山牛源肉牛科技养殖专业合作社的牛棚

14. 红寺堡项目区香园村肉羊养殖基地

(1) 基本情况

宁夏红寺堡移民开发区来自9个乡的村民组建了香园村，小农户靠种植玉米和饲养山羊维持生计。村民一年大约能卖15只羊，10千克的小羊羔能卖700～800元，除去电费、水费等各类成本每只羊能赚40多元。项目扶持后，村里本着选择以前没有接受过财政补助并且优先扶持原贫困户的原则，确定为30户小农户提供羊棚。

(2) 主要做法

项目扶持前，养殖农户养殖的30多只大羊和小羊挤在土砌的羊圈里面，由于阳光不足，活动空间受限，养殖的绵羊品质与品相不佳。项目实施后，每家羊棚上都是用水泥建成的现代化羊棚（图50）。建成一座现代化羊棚需要花费3万多元，目前村里已建成28座。村里为养殖农户开设养殖培训班，传授养殖经验，还通过上门疫苗接种，保障全村养殖业健康发展。香园村带动模式见图51。

图50 红寺堡项目区羊圈改造

(3) 取得成效

现代化羊棚建成后，养殖农户共养殖40多只羊，种植的玉米混合麸皮和豆粕作为饲料，在小羊长到10～15千克的时候（3个月大）卖出去，每只可以卖500～600元，

图 51　香园村带动模式

养殖农户可根据自己的需求卖掉羊羔换钱，一年养殖收益达 4 万元。部分养殖农户将羊直接卖到市场上去，每只大约可以卖 2 000 元。

15. 红寺堡项目区水套村养殖基地

(1) 基本情况

滩羊养殖是水套村的特色产业，村中养殖农户农业经营以圈养滩羊为主。水套村在项目扶持下，共建设了 19 座羊棚，村集体将新建的养殖圈棚建成出租，为养殖户提供养殖场和饲料棚（图 52）。

图 52　水套村养殖基地饲料棚与羊棚

(2) 主要做法

水套村利用项目资金新建养殖场，完工交付使用后，养殖基地将养殖场和饲料棚租赁给村中养殖大户，租赁 1 个棚，一年需要支付 4 500 元。水套村在红寺堡农业农村局的指导下，多次组织养殖技术员、授课老师走村入户，现场讲解养殖技术。在多次培训下，养殖农户开阔视野，转变养殖观念，提高养殖技术。水套村养殖基地带动模式见图 53。

村集体　　　**养殖大户**　　　**农业农村局**
建设养殖场、养殖　提高养殖技术　组织技术员走村入户
圈棚、饲料棚　　　　　　　　　现场讲解养殖技术

图 53　水套村养殖基地带动模式

（3）取得成效

养殖大棚与技术培训解决了养殖农户在养殖中的诸多实际问题，小农户在培训指导下逐渐放开手脚，加大养殖规模。第二批建设的羊棚中，10户养殖农户租赁2栋羊棚，部分养殖农户租赁1栋羊棚，养殖规模多达200多只。

16. 原州项目区宏科农民养殖专业合作社

（1）基本情况

宏科农民养殖专业合作社注册成立于2009年4月21日，位于固原市原州区彭堡镇彭堡村，该合作社主要从事家禽饲养、饲料原谷物销售等服务（图54），出资金额1 518万元。合作社拥有成员54户，成员以土地、劳动力方式入股合作社，折股量化后理事长占股50.9%。2021年，合作社获得项目扶持，通过晾晒场地硬化、饲料玉米烘干厂、培训与服务等多个方面的投入，有效带动了小农户的发展。

图54　宏科农民养殖专业合作社雏鸡与鸡蛋

（2）主要做法

一是提供社会化服务，形成从产前到产后一整套服务体系。通过提供统一金融信贷、统一技术培训、统一提供鸡苗、统一饲料配送、统一疫病防治、统一鲜蛋销售、统一粪污处理"七统一"服务，构建"生产在家、服务在社"的组织模式。理事长积极争取各类培训资源，不仅自己带头参加培训，还安排合作社成员参加各类培训，一年至少开展3次培训，提高成员的养殖技术和经营管理能力。

二是建立循环农业发展链。合作社借助项目扶持资金建成饲料玉米烘干厂，并与新星土地股份专业合作社、家庭农场等经营主体合作，收购其玉米（图55）并加工成饲料，给周边养殖户配送饲料5 000吨。合作社建设的粪污发酵池服务于周边养殖户，实现了玉米种植→饲料玉米烘干→蛋鸡健康养殖→畜禽粪便无害化腐熟处理→还田利用的循环农业。循环农业减少了化学肥料过度使用及农作物对农药的依赖性。蛋鸡饲喂水分含量14%~15%的烘干玉米饲料后，鸡蛋产量增加约3%，肠道炎病害发生率下降70%左右，既减少损失又降低成本，达到农作物提质增产的目的。

图55　宏科农民养殖专业合作社晾晒场的玉米

图56　宏科农民养殖专业合作社带动模式

三是分红方式多样化。合作社建立成员账户，实现按股分红，确保成员的利益，提高养殖户的经济效益。合作社还按交易量分红，收购成员玉米返利0.03元/千克、其他农户玉米返利0.02元/千克。这些措施的实施提升了小农户的养殖信心，使合作社蛋鸡养殖规模不断扩大，带动周边小农户通过养殖蛋鸡走上致富之路。宏科农民养殖专业合作社带动模式见图56。

（3）取得成效

项目实施后，合作社取得显著的成效。2023年，合作社在宁夏首次被农业农村部推介入选"全国农民合作社典型案例名单"。合作社晾晒场解决周边种植户粮食烘干问题，直接受益者是本合作社54个养殖户，间接受益114个种植户。接受项目扶持以来，合作社为54个成员免费提供生产技术培训和金融贷款服务，近些年户均贷款达到7.5万元。

17. 原州项目区六盘山生态养殖专业合作社

（1）基本情况

六盘山生态养殖专业合作社注册成立于 2015 年 10 月 10 日，位于固原市原州区头营镇杨河村，合作社主要从事生态鸡（图 57）、灰雁、火鸡、土公鸡等家禽养殖，出资总额为 70 万元。合作社建立初衷就是以杨河村为中心，带领更多的山区老百姓走散养生态鸡的路。合作社拥有成员 58 户，成员均以资金形式加入合作社，折股量化后理事长占股 57.1%。2020 年，合作社获得项目扶持，将扶持的资金投资于养殖区建设与技术管理培训等。

图 57　六盘山生态养殖专业合作社生态鸡

（2）主要做法

一是完善基础设施，奠定产业发展基石。合作社通过项目的支持，完善养殖区的基础设施，包括道路、饮水、电力和通信，缩短了交通运输时间，保障了水质安全，确保农用机械的正常运行（图 58），为小农户提供了现代通信手段，便于接收市场信息和开展电子商务。

图 58　六盘山生态养殖专业合作社农机

合作社统一规划养殖区，设置养殖区与隔离区，配备标准化棚舍，减轻小农户的体力劳动，集中资源进行养殖，提高养殖效率和防疫能力，降低养殖风险。合作社实现饲草料种植、收割、加工和贮存的统一化管理，避免资源浪费，减轻小农户的经济负担，使小农户能够专注于养殖主业，提升养殖质量和效益。

二是加强农户培训，提升科学养殖能力。合作社与当地农业技术推广服务中心合作，构建区、乡镇、村三级技术服务网络，对小农户进行畜禽生态养殖技术、乡村振兴、乡村文明建设以及合作经营知识的培训，转变小农户的观念，提高养殖技术。采用现场教学和集中教育相结合的方式，组织小农户参观宁夏项目区内的典型示范点，直观感受现代农业技术的应用效果，增强小农户的发展信心和市场适应能力。

三是打造销售网络，拓宽市场渠道。合作社鼓励小农户团结协作，规模化养殖，提升市场占有率，与客户签订供应合同，形成品牌效应，统一销售，避免价格战，确保小农户的利益最大化。合作社开拓了常规养殖和生态养殖两条价值链，常规养殖面向宁夏、青海、内蒙古等地市场，生态养殖则通过网络销售和线下配送服务于注重品质的消费群体。同时进行品牌认证，增强消费者信任。合作社严格把控养殖绿色肉产品质量，以质量求生存，以诚信求发展，巩固和拓展消费群体，为小农户提供更广阔的市场空间，增强小农户养殖的信心和积极性。六盘山生态养殖专业合作社带动模式见图59。

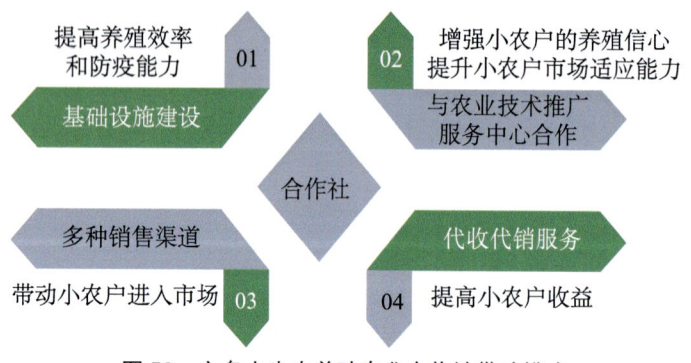

图 59　六盘山生态养殖专业合作社带动模式

（3）取得成效

合作社通过拓展市场销路，生态商品鸡销售价格显著提升，小农户自行销售价格60元/只，合作社回收时按照均价70元/只收购。合作社养殖成员是直接受益人，其中有30户原贫困户成员，受益人数112人，共增收40万元，人均增收约3 571元。同时，合作社收购本社成员及周边种植农户玉米，收购价3 000元/吨，高出市场价600元，种植农户总增收9.6万元。

18. 仪陇项目区丰泰养殖农民专业合作社

（1）基本情况

仪陇县丰泰养殖农民专业合作社成立于2023年6月13日，位于仪陇县大寅镇回龙村，出资总额为100万元。合作社主营业务为生猪的托养，目前与温氏签订生猪代养订单。合作社在回龙村建有牧草基地200亩（图60），利用自有养猪场的猪粪沼液进行施肥。同时还动员合作社成员冬播油菜300亩、小麦300亩、豆类200亩。这些成员主要涉及大寅镇回龙村、川星村、尖峰村、花山村等100多户小农户，其中脱贫户占比为32%。

图60　丰泰养殖农民专业合作社基地

（2）主要做法

一是免费提供干粪给小农户。购买肥料是农业生产中的一项重要成本支出。干粪是一种优质的有机肥料，富含氮、磷、钾等营养元素以及大量的有机质。小农户获得免费的干粪后，可以将其施用于农田、果园、菜地等，改善土壤结构，提高土壤肥力。免费获得干粪可以为小农户节省购买肥料的费用，降低农业生产成本。

二是收购秸秆进行饲料加工（图61）。在村里设置回收点，将村民出售的秸秆统一收集运输回合作社。收购秸秆可增加小农户收入，有助于提高小农户的生活质量。同时收购秸秆可以激励小农户更加注重秸秆的收集和整理，减少秸秆焚烧和随意丢弃的现象，不仅有利于环境保护，还可以提高土地的肥力和农作物的产量。

图61 丰泰养殖农民专业合作社购置的部分农机设备

三是沼液还田用于牧草种植。沼液中含有丰富的氮、磷、钾等营养元素以及多种微量元素和大量的有机质。有机质的增加可以改善土壤结构，提高土壤的保水保肥能力和通气性，有利于牧草根系的生长和发育。同时，沼液还可以减少病虫害的发生，降低农药的使用量，降低种植成本。种植的牧草可以为合作社生猪养殖提供优质的饲料来源，减少对外部饲料的依赖，进一步降低养殖成本。优质的牧草还可以改善猪肉的品质和口感，提高市场竞争力，增加养殖收益（图62）。丰泰养殖农民专业合作社模式见图63。

图62 丰泰养殖农民专业合作社牧草收割

（3）取得成效

合作社每年可有两批生猪出栏，每批约3 000头猪。温氏收购价约300元/头，统一提供猪苗、饲料、防疫药物和技术服务等价格为130元/头。为降低养殖成本，提高小农户收益，合作社将生猪粪污干湿分离，液体粪污沼气发酵处理，实现种养循环，提升资源利用效率。

18. 仪陇项目区丰泰养殖农民专业合作社

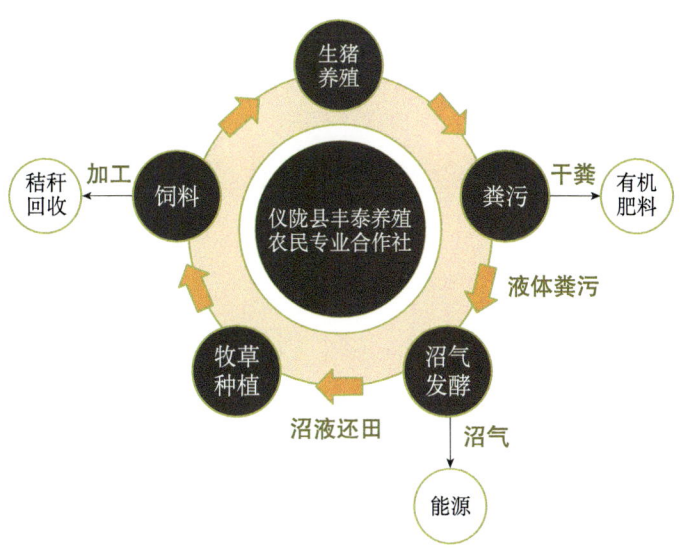

图 63　丰泰养殖农民专业合作社模式

19. 宣汉项目区江鑫生态养殖专业合作社

(1) 基本情况

宣汉县江鑫生态养殖专业合作社成立于2021年1月14日，位于宣汉县樊哙镇花梨村，该合作社主要从事家禽饲养、食用农产品初加工等服务，出资总额500万元。合作社养殖户基地平均海拔1 300米，成了天地山水之间杂交藏香猪的家。合作社共有成员100户，成员以土地、资金入股合作社，折股量化后理事长占股40.6%。合作社的发展受到客观条件的限制，种猪繁育场、加工厂、冻库等基础设施建设需要大量的资金投入，这对于起步阶段的合作社来说困难重重。2021年，宣汉县江鑫生态养殖专业合作社成为项目扶持的合作社，扶持资金主要用于种猪繁育场圈舍（图64）、冻库及烘干房修建，生产、加工设施设备采购，运营宣传等。

图64 江鑫生态养殖专业合作社黑猪养殖

(2) 主要做法

一是收购养殖户猪肉进行加工。合作社产品逐步丰富，合作社在售卖新鲜藏香猪肉的同时，还制作特色川味香肠、腊肉等产品，并销往农贸市场。合作社收购小农户的猪肉进行加工，小农户从合作社购买仔猪，合作社指导养殖和管理技术，再收购小农户的生猪，制作成成品销售，已辐射带动周边小农户20余户。

二是分红盈余确保小农户收益。合作社的经营模式是"合作社＋小农户＋基地",小农户以山林和现金入股。合作社现有种猪场 1 000 平方米,放养山林 2 万余亩。现存栏 2 500 余头,出栏 1 500 余头,已实现规模化养殖。通过合作社经营,小农户获得分红收益。合作社保底分红每股 2 180 元,二次分红每股 500 元。江鑫生态养殖专业合作社带动模式见图 65。

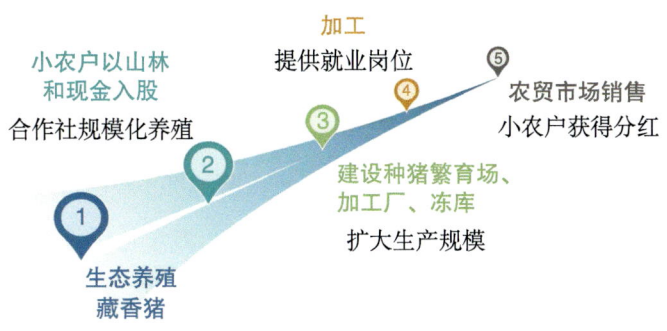

图 65　江鑫生态养殖专业合作社带动模式

(3) 取得成效

通过项目扶持,合作社发展成效明显。2023 年,合作社除部分猪肉以鲜肉形式销售外,大部分烘制成腊制品销售,实现利润 65 万元。合作社提供就业岗位 30 余个,劳务费支出 70 余万元。就业岗位全部提供给周边的小农户,其中一半是脱贫户,75% 左右提供给女性,充分照顾到农村弱势群体的利益。

20. 叙州项目区顺盈桑蚕养殖专业合作社

（1）基本情况

顺盈桑蚕养殖专业合作社成立于 2019 年 7 月 2 日，位于叙州区合什镇塘坎村爱国组，合作社主要从事蚕桑种植、桑蚕养殖（图 66）、桑枝菌种植、蚕丝被制作等，出资金额 200 万元。合作社拥有成员 102 户，折股量化后理事长占股 15%。合作社于 2022 年获批项目扶持，获得资金支持 220 万元。主要用于合作社购置生产和加工设施设备、合作社宣传推广、合作社成员技能培训等。合作社与四川省宜宾市叙州区天蚕丝绸有限责任公司、西昌蚕种场签订有购销合作协议，合作社指导生产出来的食用菌和培育的蚕种，由四川省宜宾市叙州区天蚕丝绸有限责任公司、西昌蚕种场负责收购和销售。

图 66 顺盈桑蚕养殖专业合作社蚕棚

（2）主要做法

一是加强生产设施改进。合作社借助项目资金，建设桑枝菌培育房 200 平方米（图 67），更新蚕棚喂养设备 1 000 平方米，购置农用车 1 辆，小型三轮车 1 辆，旋耕机 2 台，切桑机 8 台，喷雾器 20 台，消毒机 8 台。建设机械冷冻库 100 平方米，改建烘房30平方米。

图67　顺盈桑蚕养殖专业合作社桑枝菌生产

二是推进绿色生产。合作社通过种植桑树提高区域地面植被率，推进化肥农药减量增效，推广种养循环模式，实现农业面源污染综合防治，区域生态环境得到保护和修复（图68）。同时，通过推广秸秆覆土栽培和增施有机肥，有效改善土壤理化性状，土壤保水、保肥、保土能力得到了有效提升。

图68　顺盈桑蚕养殖专业合作社基地

三是拓展经营范围，提升盈利能力。合作社在引进新技术和培育新品种等一系列措施的支撑下，实现合作社成员增收。项目实施后，通过农民职业技能培训和专家团队技术支持有效提高妇女的生产技能和收入水平。合作社在发展过程中，不满足于处在产业链的基层，通过加工蚕茧产品、桑枝菌加工与发展旅游服务业，有效提高合作社的盈利水平，同时提供更多的就业岗位，增加成员及周边小农户的务工机会（图69）。顺盈桑蚕养殖专业合作社带动模式见图70。

图 69 顺盈桑蚕养殖专业合作社收获

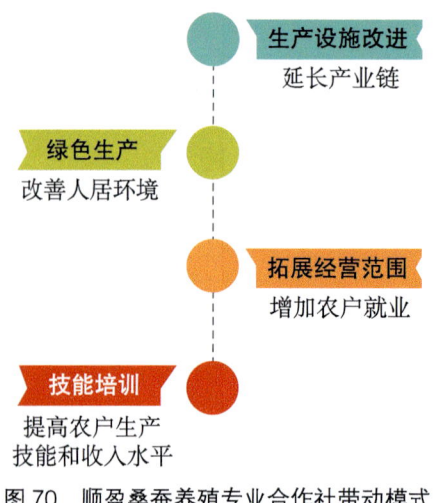

图 70 顺盈桑蚕养殖专业合作社带动模式

（3）取得成效

2023 年，合作社完成蚕茧生产 2 万千克，桑枝菌生产 2 万千克，销售收入 240 万元，实现盈余 20 万元。合作社 100 余户成员通过劳务收益、保底分红、利润分红等方式直接受益，成员务工收入 24 万元，分红 4 万元，户均 2 800 元，脱贫户获得更多分红受益。合作社通过与项目上游企业和下游企业合作增加营业收入，带动山区妇女和弱势群体临时就业 3 800 多人次，实现当地小农户增产增收，带动合作社以外小农户增加收入 800 元 / 人。

21. 苍溪项目区金永丰农机服务专业合作社

（1）基本情况

金永丰农机服务专业合作社成立于2013年11月29日，位于苍溪县永宁镇荞子村，出资金额210.8万元。合作社主要从事绿色水稻生产及农机服务，共有社员150户，社员以资金入股合作社，资金折股量化后理事长占股43.1%。合作社采取"四统一"服务模式（统一作业调度、质量标准、收费标准和维修保养）有效提升了服务效率和质量。2022年，合作社获得项目扶持，将扶持的资金投资于生产设施、加工设备等（图71）。

图71 金永丰农机服务专业合作社加工设备

（2）主要做法

一是提供农机、加工服务。合作社通过引进先进的农业机械（图72）和粮食加工、包装生产线，提升农机服务能力和农产品加工水平，为小农户提供更为高效和便捷的服务。目前，合作社建设了800亩优质水稻种植基地，并提供了1 200亩的托管耕种收机械化作业服务，同时开展了1 300亩的订单作业和跨区作业等对外农机服务。这些服务不仅提高了粮食种植的社会化服务能力，还通过配套加工设备设施对初级农产品进行加工，进一步提升了产品的附加值。

二是开展经营管理、种植技术、农机操作等方面的培训。技术培训提高合作社成员及小农户的业务技术水平，为他们的农业生产提供技术支撑。此外，合作社还

图 72　金永丰农机服务专业合作社的农机

通过推广宣传，扩大销售市场，进一步提高合作社的效益和小农户的收入。这些措施共同促进小农户的增收和脱贫户的致富。

三是从传统种植向现代化种植转变。在现代农机装备的"武装"下，逐步实现从传统种植向现代化种植的转变，每亩水稻可增产 50 千克，同时全种植周期节约人力成本 300 元，实际每亩增效 400 多元。在经营模式方面，合作社通过"合作社＋基地＋小农户"的经营模式，实现分散指导与集中经营管理的有机结合，有效降低了生产成本，提高了农产品的品质和附加值。金永丰农机服务专业合作社带动模式见图 73。

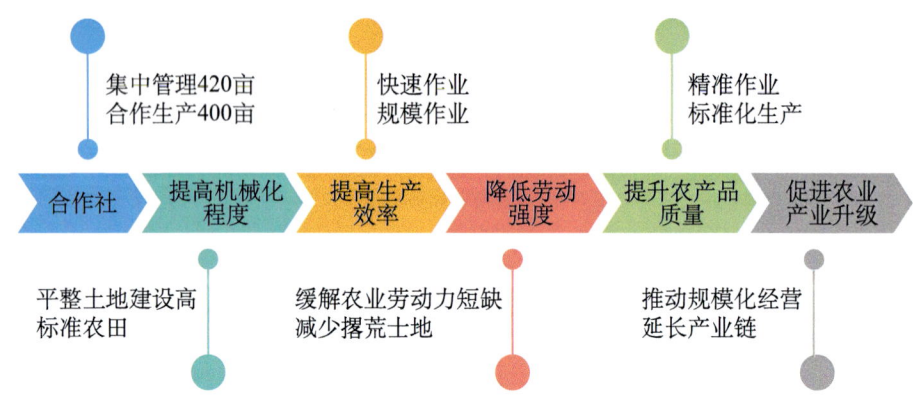

图 73　金永丰农机服务专业合作社带动模式

（3）取得成效

经过几年的发展，金永丰农机服务专业合作社的成效显著。合作社年盈利达到 27.4 万元，实现直接收入 375.5 万元，成员年户均分红达到 1 586 元，脱贫成员户均分红更是高达 1 764 元，充分体现了合作社在促进小农户增收和脱贫致富方面的积极作用。

22. 利通项目区吴忠市海之峰种植农民专业合作社

（1）基本情况

吴忠市海之峰种植农民专业合作社成立于 2023 年 7 月 31 日，位于宁夏回族自治区吴忠市利通区扁担沟镇海子井村，出资金额 10 万元。合作社在种植玉米的同时，为周边村庄提供播种施肥、托管等服务。合作社成员 51 户，成员以现金入股合作社，资金折股量化后理事长占股 1.4%，村集体以土地入股合作社并占股 30%。2023 年，合作社获得项目扶持，将扶持的资金主要用于购买拖拉机、播种机、旋耕机等机械设备（图 74）。

图 74　海之峰种植农民专业合作社农机

（2）主要做法

一是改善生产设施配套设备，奠定合作社发展基础。合作社目前已完成改造农机库 360 平方米、购置农机设备 11 台，机械化施肥使得肥料利用率提升 1 倍。合作社为满足全村 3 600 亩耕地建成高效节水灌溉项目后的统一运行管护需求，利用购置的农机设备为周边小农户提供农资、农机、托管等服务（图 75），海子井村范围内农机服务每亩优惠 10 元。

图 75 海之峰种植农民专业合作社农机服务

二是"五统一"服务模式，服务效益明显提升。随着利通区高效节水项目的开展，海子井村大部分小农户流转出土地，合作社通过村集体实现土地的规模化经营，实现统一生产、统一培训、统一灌溉、统一施肥和统一采摘销售。在生产过程中，合作社为小农户提供技术服务与培训等服务，小农户通过学习掌握种植技术，向市场提供优质的青贮玉米。产后合作社积极拓宽销售渠道，合作社既向周边小农户售卖青贮玉米，又为村集体建立的养殖场提供青贮玉米，通过生产适销对路的优质青贮玉米，逐渐形成自己的品牌效益。海之峰种植农民专业合作社带动模式见图76。

图 76 海之峰种植农民专业合作社带动模式

（3）取得成效

合作社通过完善生产设施设备，提高合作社的社会化服务能力，经合作社统一购买、收购、销售、包装和加工，亩均可降低成本150元，增加收益20%以上。合作社预计至2025年，农机作业服务面积达到3 000亩，通过农机服务实现增收15万元。

23. 仪陇项目区勇旗种养殖农民专业合作社

（1）基本情况

勇旗种养殖农民专业合作社成立于 2011 年 10 月 18 日，位于南充市仪陇县双胜镇响滩村五社，该合作社主要从事粮油种植（图 77）、加工、销售等，出资金额 630 万元。2022 年，合作社获得项目扶持，合作社将扶持的资金用于购买中型钢架大棚、新型轮式拖拉机、粮食烘干机、粮食初级筛选设备、粮食加工设备等机械设备。

图 77　勇旗种养殖农民专业合作社蔬菜产品

（2）主要做法

一是升级生产设施设备。合作社在项目扶持前虽已自建冷棚，但未达标准，在项目资助下建设了 66 个达标冷棚，并购置了一系列农业机械，包括大型拖拉机、插秧机、播种收割机械、激光平整机、植保无人机等，以及烘干设备和仓储设施，提升农业生产效率和标准化水平，降低生产成本，提高产出效益。

二是产品错峰上市，改善营销方式。合作社利用大棚交替轮作实现农产品错峰上市，通过线上线下相结合的销售模式，开拓农贸市场、学校单位等销售渠道，采用薄利多销策略，增强市场竞争力。合作社成功注册"勇旗"大米商标品牌，通过品牌效应，年销售大米 500 吨，产值达 280 万元，增强了产品市场认知度和附加值。

三是提升社会化服务。合作社采取"公司+合作社+基地+小农户"经营模式，发展优质水稻、玉米、小麦、油菜、蔬菜、水果等种植 6 280 亩，水产养殖 35 亩，实现年销售额近 2 000 万元、利润 110 万元。其中，采取代耕代种、社会化服务的方式，带动贫困户89户，户均增收3 000元以上。为5 000余户小农户提供生产资料300多吨，提供机械化服务2 300车次，为成员代运输、加工、销售产品500余吨，开展技术培训、技术交流和技术咨询2 000余人次。勇旗种养殖农民专业合作社带动模式见图78。

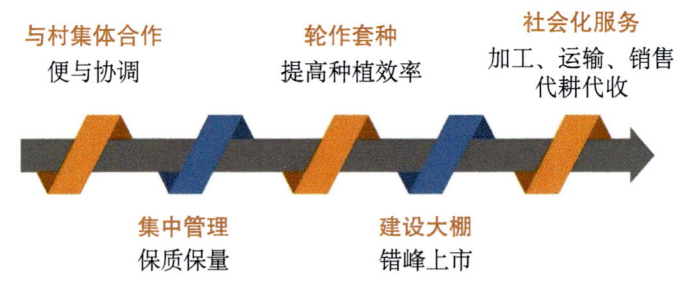

图78　勇旗种养殖农民专业合作社带动模式

（3）取得成效

一是经济效益显著。合作社年销售额近2 000万元、利润110万元，产品种植面积达6 280亩（图79），水产养殖面积35亩，展现了合作社多元化经营能力和市场适应性。

图79　勇旗种养殖农民专业合作社基地

二是受益范围扩大。合作社不仅带动89户原贫困户增收，还为5 000余户农户提供生产资料和服务，开展2 000余人次的技术培训、交流和咨询，提升小农户的生产技能和市场意识。展望未来，合作社计划进一步补齐粮油基地短板，强化营销与宣传，实现成员年均分红20万元的目标。

24. 广安项目区初山农谷种养专业合作社

(1) 基本情况

初山农谷种养专业合作社成立于 2017 年 12 月 11 日，位于广安市广安区彭家乡滑滩村，出资金额 100 万元。合作社主要通过气候智慧型农业新模式，促进当地农业和旅游业结合，实现绿色可持续发展。合作社拥有成员 55 户，成员以资金入股合作社，折股量化后理事长占股 5%。2021 年，合作社获得项目扶持，将扶持的资金投资于连栋大棚（图 80）、智能监控系统、冷链运输车和超市等。

图 80　初山农谷种养专业合作社种植大棚

(2) 主要做法

一是规范化管理。合作社强化内部管理，包括完善规章制度、用工和奖罚机制，确保小农户权益，尤其是保护原建档立卡户的利益。合作社还对成员和非成员实施统一管理和培训，合作社注重技术创新，减少化肥和农药的使用，促进农业的可持续发展。合作社与科研院校建立合作关系，引进先进技术，为小农户提供生产培训指导，提高农业科技含量，提升产品质量和生产效率，形成特色农产品品牌。合作社的规范化管理增强了农产品市场竞争力，增加了小农户的生产技能，保护了小农户的权益。

二是打造"共享农场"模式，合作社将农业与旅游结合，提供采摘、科研学习、动物互动等体验项目，顾客可以在旅游期间体验采摘、学习农业知识、与小动物亲密接触等项目。合作社期望通过"生态农场"的建设带动小农户盘活资源、参与创业，增加小农户收入。合作社将网上的"虚拟农场"变为现实中的"共享农场"，合作社雇佣小农户为不能来基地的顾客看护作物，小农户获得相应的劳动报酬。

三是建立"115城配"团购App（图81）。作为项目扶持的农超对接试点，合作社提出了定时送达、超时免单的经营理念，要求超市上午的订单11时前送达，下午的订单17时前送达。用户线上小程序下单（图82），合作社成员线下配送。合作社生产基地的新鲜蔬菜迅速配送到超市，超市再配送至餐桌，缩短流通环节，降低农产品物流成本，也创造更多服务岗位。初山农谷种养专业合作社带动模式见图83。

图81 初山农谷种养专业合作社建立的"115城配"团购超市

图82 初山农谷种养专业合作社线上购物小程序

图 83　初山农谷种养专业合作社带动模式

（3）取得成效

一是经济效益显著。合作社成员直接受益，包括大股东、小农户成员、原建档立卡贫困户、少数民族和女性成员。每个成员平均分红 2 137 元，原贫困成员平均分红更高，达到 2 653 元。合作社的建设增加了成员（尤其是原贫困成员）的收入，改善他们的生活状况。

二是促进产业发展与升级。在项目扶持之前，合作社只生产蔬菜等，扶持后，利用项目资金开启"农超板块"，增加了 B 端和 C 端客户，营业收入持续增长。通过"共享农场"项目，为城市居民提供体验农耕的机会，同时也为当地小农户提供就业机会和收入来源。合作社的示范引领作用促进了项目区其他优势特色产业的发展，推动了农业产业结构调整。

三是促进当地经济发展。合作社的建设和运营带动施工建设企业、设备设施生产企业、包装企业、运输企业等相关企业的发展。项目间接促进当地房建、餐饮、商品零售、娱乐、金融等行业的发展，为当地经济发展注入活力。

四是为乡村振兴贡献力量。合作社在成立后的五年间，吸引了 12 名优秀大学生回乡创业，推动当地农业现代化进程，成为新农人的典范。合作社的成立和运营改善了当地小农户的生活条件，提高他们的收入水平，对乡村振兴战略的顺利实施起到了积极的推动作用。通过促进当地经济的发展，合作社缓解留守儿童等社会问题，提高当地居民的幸福感和获得感。

25. 银川项目区月益农农艺专业合作社

（1）基本情况

月益农农艺专业合作社成立于 2020 年 8 月 10 日，位于银川市兴庆区月牙湖乡月牙湖村，合作社主要从事蔬菜、瓜果的种植及销售等服务（图 84），出资金额 100 万元。合作社拥有成员 70 户，成员以资金入股合作社，折股量化后理事长占股 2.8%。2021 年，合作社获得项目扶持，将扶持资金投资于大跨度温室大棚，分拣中心等。

图 84　月益农农艺专业合作社番茄种植

（2）主要做法

一是将基地温棚出租，合作社成员获取务工收入。月益农农艺专业合作社目前有温室大棚 21 栋，主要种植菌菇、果蔬等农作物，合作社与 3 个公司建立合作关系，与公司签订温室大棚租赁协议，温室大棚交由公司管理，并收取租金，成员在温室大棚中务工（图 85）。

图 85　月益农农艺专业合作社温棚与农机

二是促进农旅融合,实现基地增收。合作社位于国家AAAA级旅游景区黄沙古渡景区主入口南侧,是游客出入的必经之路,景区每年游客流量达20万人次。合作社借助这一优势将旅游和大棚采摘融合为一体,成立了宁夏热气球低空生态旅游开发有限公司(图86)让游客来景区旅游的同时进行采摘、购买,打造一个无公害、绿色的采摘园。采摘园不仅可以优化种植结构,提高综合效益,还提供更多工作岗位,帮助富余劳动力就业,带动附近的农家乐发展,增加小农户的收入。月益农农艺专业合作社带动模式见图87。

图86 宁夏热气球低空生态旅游开发有限公司

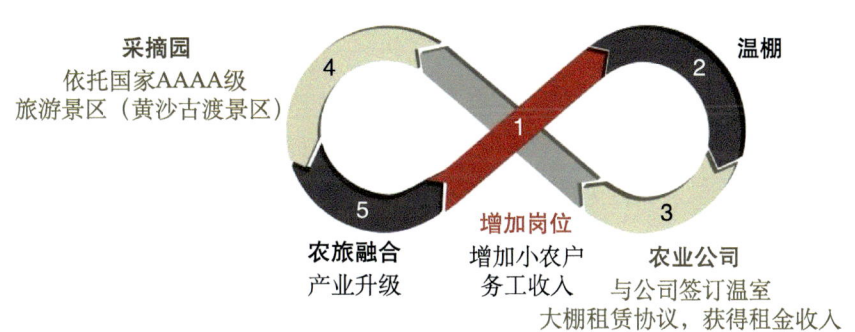

图87 月益农农艺专业合作社带动模式

(3)取得成效

2023年,合作社通过温室大棚的运营,为月牙湖村及周边小农户提供了300多个工作岗位。合作社种植小番茄5亩,销售额10万元,合作社拿出5.7万元给成员二次分红。合作社的成功运营不仅改善当地小农户的生活水平,还促进乡村旅游的发展,增强农村地区的吸引力。

致谢

中国农业科学院农业资源与农业区划研究所承担的国际农业发展基金贷款优势特色产业发展示范项目（IPRAD-SN）课题"带动小农户发展的制度安排、产业选择与价值链建设"，由尹昌斌研究员牵头，负责课题整体设计、确定研究方案、组织实施调研；课题专家团队包括中国农业科学院农业经济与发展研究所吕开宇研究员、中国农业科学院资划所易小燕研究员、任静副研究员、李福夺副研究员、杨晓梅助理研究员；郑玉雨博士后、赵玙璠助理、尹彦舒博士、杨紫洪博士、周礼君硕士等参与课题研究。

课题研究得到了指导委员会的悉心指导和帮助，感谢农业农村部农田建设管理司（国家项目办）相关领导给予的支持，感谢国际农业发展基金中国办公室主任孙印洪先生和项目监评专家史茵茵女士给予的认可和建议。

课题组人员先后到四川、宁夏各项目区开展多次调研，省（自治区）项目办及各县（市、区）项目办的唐捷、刘红兵、梁繁、张奇、韦伟、吴昊、吴焜玥、袁芳、赵涛、曾继红、兰光明、邓德全、刘海龙、马少君、雍艳霞、郝丹东、梁生藩、王芳芝等给予大力支持和帮助，在此一并表示感谢！

此外，感谢研究过程中提出宝贵建议的专家，他们是中国人民大学孔祥智教授、钟真教授，中国宏观经济研究院姜长云研究员，中国农业科学院农业信息研究所聂凤英研究员，农业农村部管理干部学院邵科副研究员，中国农业科学院农业经济与发展研究所张姝副研究员，宁夏回族自治区原农村经济经营管理站谈晓昀老师和四川省农业科学院农业信息与农村经济研究所阿木补出等专家。

需要说明的是，课题在研究过程中参考了大量的文献资料，尽可能在文中列出，但难免有疏忽或遗漏的可能，书中不足之处，敬请读者批评指正！

编著委员会

2024 年 12 月

北京

附件1：调研问卷

专业合作社调研问卷

一、合作社基本信息与经营管理情况

序号	问题	选项/单位，选择题在相应的序号上打"√"，填空题在相应的空格上填写数值	2023年
1	合作社与农业发展基金签订商业计划书时间	_____年	
2	商业计划国际农业发展基金支持资金	_____万元	
3	商业计划自筹资金	_____万元	
4	商业计划资金用途（可多选）	1=直接折算股权；2=基础设施建设；3=加工设备等产业链延伸；4=加强社员培训、技术指导等；5=加大合作社宣传、品牌推广；6=拓宽销售渠道；7=其他，请说明	
5	合作社注册名称		
6	合作社注册年份	_____年	
7	注册地址		
8	注册资金	_____万元	
9	注册类型	1=种植类；2=养殖类；3=加工类；4=销售类；5=产加销综合类；6=农机服务类；7=金融服务类；8=土地托管服务类；9=其他，请说明	
10	合作社社长/理事长姓名		
11	合作社社长/理事长年龄	_____岁	
12	合作社社长/理事长性别	1=男；2=女	
13	社长/理事长的教育程度	1=小学；2=初中；3=高中；4=大专及以上	
14	社长/理事长是否自办企业	1=是；2=否	
15	社长/理事长占股比例	_____%	
16	理事会人数	_____人	

(续表)

序号	问题	选项/单位，选择题在相应的序号上打"√"，填空题在相应的空格上填写数值	2023年
17	理事会中小农户数	_____户	
18	理事会中女性人数	_____人	
19	合作社是否有专职会计	1=是；2=否	
20	合作社总人数（包括理事会和社员）	_____人	
21	其中：社员人数	_____人	
22	青年社员（18~45）人数	_____人	
23	社员户数	_____户	
24	社员中过去是建档立卡户	_____户	
25	合作社召开社员大会的频率	_____次/年	
26	合作社召开理事会的次数	_____次/年	
27	合作社召开监事会的次数	_____次/年	
28	社员加入合作社方式（可多选）	1=土地；2=劳动力；3=资金；4=技术；5=农机具；6=其他，请说明	
29	如果是土地入社，是否折股量化？	1=是；2=否	
30	如果是资金入社，是否折股量化？	1=是；2=否	
31	合作社分红方式是什么？	1=保底分红（即土地流转费）；2=利润分红（二次分红）；3=其他，请说明	
32	二次分红的依据是什么？	1=按照交易量分红；2=按照股份分红；3=按照交易量与股份分红相结合的方式	
33	2023年利润大约有多少？	_____万元	
34	2022年利润大约有多少？	_____万元	
35	2023年是否有二次分红？	1=是；2=否	
36	如果有，二次分红总金额是多少？	_____万元	
37	二次分红金额占利润的比例是多少？	_____%	
38	平均每户社员能分多少？	_____元	
	合作社固定资产情况		
39	2022会计年度固定资产净值是多少？	_____万元	

(续表)

序号	问题	选项/单位，选择题在相应的序号上打"√"，填空题在相应的空格上填写数值	2023年
40	2023会计年度固定资产净值是多少？	_____万元	
	合作社自身能力建设情况		
41	合作社是否制定合作社管理制度？	1=是；2=否	
42	理事会成员是否参加合作社发展相关学习培训？	1=是；2=否	
43	引进新品种	_____个	
44	新品种投资	_____元	
45	引进新技术	_____项	
46	新技术费用	_____元	
47	是否为示范性合作社？	1=是；2=否	
48	如果是，示范级别为	1=国家级；2=省级；3=市级；4=县级	
49	是否经营农产品加工？	1=是；2=否	
50	是否有自己的农产品品牌？	1=是；2=否	
51	农产品"三品一标"通过几项（可多选）？	1=无公害农产品；2=绿色农产品；3=有机农产品；4=农产品地理标志	
52	是否获得商标注册证？	1=是；2=否	
53	是否与其他合作社进行联合发展？	1=是；2=否	
54	是否与其他家庭农场进行联合发展？	1=是；2=否	
55	是否与农业企业联合发展？	1=是；2=否	
56	合作社与销售合作伙伴合作方式	1=订单合同；2=口头约定；3=其他	
57	合作社提供就业岗位共有多少人？	_____人	
58	其中：原有贫困户/建档立卡户多少人？	_____人	
59	女性	_____人	
60	中青年人（18～45岁）	_____人	
61	提供岗位中长期工多少人（1年及以上）	_____人	
62	提供岗位中临时工多少人	_____人	

（续表）

序号	问题	选项/单位，选择题在相应的序号上打"√"，填空题在相应的空格上填写数值	2023年
63	合作社日常运营费用需要多少？不包括扩大投资，只是日常人员费、管理费等	_____万元/年	
64	合作社目前是否有贷款？	1=是；2=否	
65	贷款渠道？（可多选）	1=农村信用社；2=商业银行；3=其他，请说明	
66	获得金融服务（贷款）的用途？	1=购买农机具；2=建设仓储等厂房；3=购买良种；4=购买办公设备；5=招纳合作社专业技术人员；6=其他，请说明	
67	合作社应对气候变化采取的措施有哪些？（可多选）	1=节水灌溉/水肥一体化；2=有机肥替代化肥；3=绿色生物农药；4=秸秆还田；5=其他，请说明	
68	有农业生产基地的合作社购买农业（商业）保险吗？	1=是，_____元/亩；2=否	
69	近5年合作社遭遇几次自然灾害？	_____次	
70	自然灾害类型是什么？	1=洪涝；2=干旱；3=霜冻；4=其他，请说明	
71	受灾面积有多少？	_____亩	
72	产量损失比例有多大？	_____%	
73	有哪些途径帮助您恢复生产？（多选）	1=地方政府应急处理；2=保险公司赔偿；3=企业/合作社等帮扶；4=其他，请说明	
74	近5年合作社遭遇几次病虫灾害？	_____次	
75	病虫灾害类型是什么？	请具体说明_____	
76	受灾面积有多少？	_____亩	
77	产量损失比例有多大？	_____%	
78	有哪些途径帮助您恢复生产？（多选）	1=地方政府应急处理；2=保险公司赔偿；3=企业/合作社等帮扶；4=其他，请说明	
79	农发基金支持的商业计划给合作社带来什么变化？（按重要性程度从大到小排序）	A. 解决了资金问题 B. 加强了技术指导 C. 加大了合作社做大的信心 D. 加强了产业链管理、品牌意识、宣传等 E. 帮助了小农户增加收入 F. 其他，请说明	
80	对商业计划支持的满意程度	1=非常满意；2=比较满意；3=一般满意；4=比较不满意；5=非常不满意	

二、合作社生产、收购、加工、销售、服务情况

年份	产品类型 1.粮食作物； 2.油料作物； 3.设施蔬菜； 4.露地蔬菜； 5.水果；6.苗木花卉；7.药材；8.圈舍畜禽养殖；9.林下养殖或流转地散养；10.其他	产品名称 产品名称按照原料产品名称，如柑橘、牛、羊等逐一列出	自主生产规模：种植或养殖/（亩或头）	自主生产产量/千克	收购数量/千克	收购成本/（元/千克）	收购农户数/户	其中：①贫困户/户	②本合作社农户/户	合作社未加工农产品销售价格（元/千克）	合作社未加工农产品销售渠道 1=自由市场；2=企业订单；3=农超对接；4=电商；5=其他，请说明	合作社加工产品数量/千克（这里指加工前的农产品）	加工成本/（元/千克）
2023年													

（续表）

加工后产品（千克）	加工后产品销售价格/（元/千克）	加工后销售渠道 1=自由市场；2=企业订单；3=农超对接；4=电商；5=其他，请说明	如果是网络方式销售，销售量占总销量的比例是多少/%	销售总金额/万元	其中：① 自主生产销售额/万元	② 合作社成员销售额（合作社代销）/万元	销量和上年相比变化情况（1=减少；2=不变；3=增加）				
2023 年											

序号	问题及选项	农资服务（种子、化肥、农药、饲料等代销）	代耕代收（包括农机服务和托管）	农业生产技术（包括防控防疫等技术培训和指导）	产品加工、包装等（包括初加工、包装和深加工）	产品存储	产品运输	产品销售（包括代销和订单）	金融贷款
1	是否为成员提供该服务？	1=是；2=否	1=是；2=否	1=是；2=否	1=是；2=否	1=是；2=否	1=是；2=否		
2	过去12个月内，多少成员使用过项目提供的服务？								
3	农发项目实施以来一共多少成员使用过项目提供的服务？								
4	服务是否收费？	1=是；2=否	1=是；2=否	1=是；2=否	1=是；2=否	1=是；2=否	1=是；2=否		

农户调研问卷

一、农户及家庭基本情况

农户类型：1. 项目区公共基础设施与气候智慧型农业受益户；2. 项目区宁夏基地建设受益户；3. 项目区扶持合作社受益户；4. 非项目户（请选择相应的农户类型，并打√，可多选）

1. 家庭成员情况（从回答者开始，先列成人，后列小孩，与子女分家的不算作一个家庭）

代码	A1	A2	A3	A4	A5	A6	A7	A8	A9	A10
序号	姓名	性别：1=男；2=女	身份：1=户主；2=户主配偶；3=子女/儿媳/女婿；4=外孙子（女）；5=父母/岳父母/公婆；6=其他，请说明	年龄/周岁	婚姻状况：1=已婚；2=未婚；3=丧偶；4=离异	民族：1=汉族；2=少数民族	文化程度：0=没上过学；1=小学；2=初中；3=高中；4=大学及以上	健康状况：1=良好；2=轻度残疾，可劳动；3=中重度残疾，不能劳动	是否从事非农务工：1=是；2=否	如果是，主要做什么？1=外出打工；2=在公司上班；3=个体经商；4=事业单位；5=公务员；6=村干部；7=其他，请说明
1										
2										
3										
4										
5										
6										

2. 家庭经营基本情况

	指标内容	选项/单位	2023年
1	您家曾经是否为建档立卡户？	1=是；0=否	
2	您在村里担任什么职务？	1=村民委员会主任；2=村党支部书记；3=村委会其他干部；4=普通村民	
3	家里女性是否参与村级活动？（如选举投票等）	1=是；0=否	
4	您家中的家务劳动最主要承担者为（单选）：	1=父亲（丈夫）；2=母亲（妻子）；3=儿子（女婿）；4=女儿（儿媳）；5=其他	
5	母亲（妻子）对于家中买房、贷款、经营、子女上学等大事的决定权	1=90%以上；2=50%~90%；3=30%~50%；4=30%以下	
6	家中财政收入由谁掌管？	1=父亲（丈夫）；2=母亲（妻子）；3=各自管自己收入	
7	家庭可支配收入？（包括农业经营、个体工商户、工资性、财产性、转移性收入）	今年_____万元；去年_____万元	
8	其中：农业经营净收入	今年_____万元；去年_____万元	
9	工资净收入	今年_____万元；去年_____万元	
10	家庭住房建筑面积（不包括院子）	_____平方米	
11	房屋类型	1=平房；2=楼房；3=土坯房	
12	住房修建时间	_____年	
13	2020—2023年内是否有修缮	1=是；2=否；	
14	住房是否有独立卫生间？	1=是；2=否；	
15	你家厕所类型是	1=可冲水厕所；2=旱厕；3=其他	
16	家庭生活用水主要来源（单选）	1=自来水；2=井水；3=山泉水；4=河流水；5=雨水；6=其他	
17	除用电之外，家庭生活是否使用其他能源（照明、煮饭等）	1=太阳能；2=燃气；3=沼气；4=薪柴；5=煤炭；6=其他	
18	近两年是否购置农机具？	1=是，2=否；	
19	如果有，花费多少？	_____万元	
20	近两年是否购置汽车？	1=是，2=否；	
21	如果有，花费多少？	_____万元	

（续表）

	指标内容	选项/单位				2023年
22	购置汽车主要用途	1=生活便利；2=运货；3=客运车				
23	每年家庭生活支出	_____元				
24	其中：购买食物支出	_____元				
25	每年家庭人情往来支出	_____元				
26	您家有多少耕地？	_____亩				
27	家庭拥有的畜禽类型	牛/（头/只）	羊/（头/只）	猪/（头/只）	家禽/只	
28	出栏数量					
29	您家到最近市场有多远？	_____分钟（通用交通方式所需要的时间）				
30	近2年到最近市场的基础设施或交通方式是否有改建或修缮？	1=是；2=否				
31	近2年您到市场的时间是否因为基础设施改善而缩短？	1=是；2=否				
32	你是否在用加工设施加工部分产品？	1=是；0=否（如果"否"，跳过33至37）				
33	您生产的农产品加工渠道（可多选）	1=自己加工；2=附近加工厂；3=合作社				
34	该加工设施是否实用？	1.非常实用；2.有点儿实用；3.有点儿不实用；4.非常不实用				
35	到该加工设施有多远（时间）？	_____分钟（时间）				
36	近2年到该加工设施的时间是否有减少？	1=是；2=否				
37	近2年到使用加工设施的渠道是否有增加？	1=是；2=否				
38	家庭是否持有如股票、基金、国债、信托产品、外汇产品等金融产品？	1=是；2=否				
39	家庭有贷款或欠债吗？	1=有；2=没有				
40	如果有，金额多少？	_____万元				

（续表）

	指标内容	选项/单位	2023年
41	贷款或借款来源是（可多选）	1=政府贴息贷款；2=个人信誉或财产抵押贷款；3=民间私贷；4=亲戚朋友借款；5=其他，请说明	
42	家里谁决定贷款用途？	1=父亲（丈夫）；2=母亲（妻子）；3=其他	
43	家里由谁偿还贷款或借款？	1=父亲（丈夫）；2=母亲（妻子）；3=子女；4=其他	
44	现在饮食结构和营养有改善吗？	1=改善较大；2=有所改善；3=没变化；4=比以前差	
45	近5年您家遭遇几次自然灾害？	_____次	
46	自然灾害类型是什么？	1=洪涝；2=干旱；4=霜冻；4=其他，请说明	
47	受灾面积有多少？	_____亩	
48	有哪些途径帮助您恢复生产？（多选）	1=地方政府应急处理；2=保险公司赔偿；3=企业/合作社等帮扶；4=其他，请说明	
49	近5年您家遭遇几次严重的病虫害？	_____次	
50	病虫害类型是什么？	请具体说明_____	
51	受灾面积有多少？	_____亩	
52	有哪些途径帮助您恢复生产？（多选）	1=地方政府应急处理；2=保险公司赔偿；3=企业/合作社等帮扶；4=其他，请说明	
53	您与附近的合作社有何关系？	1=务工；2=向合作社出售农产品；3=使用合作社提供的服务（如农资服务、代耕代收等）；4=无任何关系	
54	您家是否加入某个合作社？	1=是；2=否	
55	您是否是合作社理事会成员？	1=是；2=否	
56	您是否参加过社员大会？	1=是，_____次，2=否	
57	加入合作社的方式是什么？（可多选）	1=土地；2=劳动力；3=资金；4=技术；5=农机具；6=其他，请说明	
58	您在合作社拥有多少股份？	_____股	
59	每年获得多少分红？	_____元	
60	参加合作社培训次数？	_____次	

二、农业生产、环境友好型技术采纳、销售情况 [如果既有种植又有养殖，表（一）和表（二）都需要填写]

（一）种植业（按照每种作物生产季零填写，如上半年玉米、下半年小麦）

年份	作物类型 [1.粮食作物；2.油料作物；3.设施蔬菜；4.露地蔬菜；5.水果；6.苗木花卉；7.药材；8.其他，请说明（品种编码且写出具体作物）]	种植面积/亩	是否采用新品种 1=是；2=否	灌溉方式 1=大水漫灌；2=水肥一体化；3=滴灌	化肥投入量（千克/亩）	化肥投入依据是什么？1=凭经验；2=看说明书；3=农资销售人员建议；4=农技推广人员建议	有机肥投入量（千克/亩）	有机肥类型 1=堆沤农家肥；2=商品有机肥	有机肥投入依据是什么？1=凭经验；2=看说明书；3=农资销售人员建议；4=农技推广人员建议	使用的有机肥是否为合作社提供的 1=是；2=否
2023年	例如：1=玉米									
	1=小麦									
	2=油菜									
	3=番茄									
	4=胡萝卜									
	5=柑橘									

附件1：调研问卷

年份	作物类型 [1.粮食作物；2.油料作物；3.设施蔬菜；4.露地蔬菜；5.水果；6.苗木花卉；7.药材；8.其他，请说明（品种编码目写出具体作物）]	作物价格是否比市场价优惠 1=是；2=否	农药使用依据 1=凭经验；2=看说明书；3=农资销售人员建议；4=农技推广人员建议	地膜使用后处理方式 1=留在地里；2=捡起来丢到专门的回收站；3=有公司来收	农作物秸秆处理方式 1=粉碎还田；2=用作饲料；3=用作燃料；4=食用菌基料；5=就地焚烧	作物产量较去年有无变化 1=增加；2=减少；3=没变化	产量增加的原因 1=风调雨顺；2=品种改良；3=生产管理技术改进	产量减少的原因 1=自然灾害；2=病虫害；3=其他	销售量较去年有无变化 1=增加；2=减少；3=没变化	销售渠道 1=合作社代销；2=商贩收购；3=自己零售
2023年 例如：1-玉米										
1-小麦										
2-油菜										
3-番茄										
4-胡萝卜										
5-柑橘										

（二）养殖业

年份	养殖类型（写明编码和具体名称）1=圈舍畜禽养殖；2=林下养殖或荒地散养	是否购买新品种 1=是；2=否	购买饲料来源：1=自由市场；2=合作社代销；3=与其他企业合作订单；4=其他，请说明	粪便是否堆沤成肥料或商品有机肥 1=是；2=否	如果否，粪便如何处理 1=直接排放；2=卖给企业；3=免费或有偿给种植户	粪便是否干湿分离 1=是；2=否	如果是，尿液处理方式 1=直接排放；2=污水池存放；3=沉淀池处理后排放；4=排入沼气池；5=氧化塘处理；6.其他，请说明	干粪处理方式（可多选）1=堆肥发酵还田；2=出售给合作社；3=出售给企业；4=其他，请说明	病死畜禽处理方式 1=卖给收购商；2=扔到河里或海里；3=深埋；4=焚烧；5=分解池分解；6=其他	销售渠道（可多选）1=自行零售；2=通过合作社销售；3=订单合同；4=电子商务；5=收购商；6=其他	出栏量较去年是否变化 1=增加；2=减少；3=不变
2023年	例如：1-牛										
	1-羊										
	2-猪										
	3-鸡										

三、农户项目参与程度及技术采纳、满意度情况（非项目区农户不作答）

代码	内容	您是否受益于下列工程建设？ 1= 是；2= 否（如否则不用打分）		对这些项目满意吗？（1～5 打分，5 分最满意）	
	1. 基础设施建设（灌排系统、水源工程、人畜安全饮水、供电系统、村庄道路、基础设施运营维护）				
1	灌排系统（包括沟渠）				
2	农业生产水源工程（山坪塘、蓄水池、拦河堰等）				
3	人畜安全饮水工程（输水管、净化设备等）				
4	电网电路				
5	村庄道路				
	2. 气候智慧型生产基地建设	是否采用该项设施或接受过相关培训：1= 是；2= 否	你认为这些做法是否有用？ 1= 是；2= 否	你是否将继续采用？ 1= 是；2= 否	对这些项目满意吗？ （1～5 打分，5 分最满意）
6	土地平整（坡改梯等）				
7	种植设施大棚 / 养殖大棚				
8	水肥一体化设施				
9	滴灌设施				
	3. 农业生产性服务	是否采用该项设施或接受过相关培训：1= 是；2= 否	你认为这些做法是否有用？ 1= 是；2= 否	你是否将继续采用？ 1= 是；2= 否	对这些项目满意吗？ （1～5 打分，5 分最满意）
10	农资采购服务（种子、化肥、农药、饲料等）				

(续表)

代码	内容	您是否受益于下列工程建设？1=是；2=否（如否则不用打分）	对这些项目满意吗？（1~5打分，5分最满意）
11	测土配方施肥		
12	病虫害绿色防控		
13	有机肥替代化肥		
14	代耕代收（包括农机服务和托管）		
15	休耕轮作、间作、套作，深翻深耕等保护性耕作		
16	秸秆还田或综合利用		
17	废弃地膜处理		
18	养殖饲料配比		
19	畜禽疫病防治		
20	畜禽粪污处理		
21	产品加工、包装等（包括初加工、包装和深加工）		
22	产品存储		
23	产品运输		
24	产品代销售（包括代销和订单）		

附件 2：调研照片

1. 2022 年 7 月 四川南充市、达州市与广安市调查合作社建设与生产情况

2. 2023 年 9 月 宁夏固原市、四川广元市、南充市调查合作社、基地建设与生产情况

3. 2023年11月 宁夏固原市受益农户入户调查

4. 2024年5月 四川宜宾市、宁夏红寺堡合作社产业发展与带动农户状况专题调研

5. 2024年10月 宁夏各项目区、四川各项目区合作社与受益农户专题调研

附件2：调研照片

121

附件2：调研照片

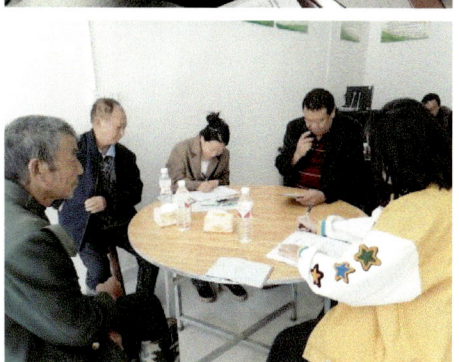

Research on Institutional Arrangement, Agro-industrial Choice and Value Chain Construction for Promoting Smallholders' Development

—The IFAD Program for Specialized Agribusiness Development in Sichuan and Ningxia

Yin Changbin et al.

Research on Institutional Arrangement, Agro-industrial Choice and Value Chain Construction for promoting Smallholders' Development
—The IFAD Program for Specialized Agribusiness Development in Sichuan and Ningxia

Steering Committee

Director: Guo Yongtian

Deputy Director: Su Wei   Sun Yinhong

Members: Zheng Miao   Shi Yinyin

Editorial Committee

Editor-in-chief：Yin Changbin Wu Hongwei

Associate Editor：Su Wei Yi Xiaoyan

Editor Members：

Zheng Miao	Ren Jing	Yang Xiaomei
Li Fuduo	Wei Wei	Tang Jie
Liu Hongbing	Wu Hao	Zhang Qi
Yuan Fang	Wu Kunyue	Liang Fan
Zhao Tao	Zeng Jihong	Lan Guangming
Deng Dequan	Liu Hailong	Ma Shaojun
Yong Yanxia	Hao Dandong	Liang Shengfan
Wang Fangzhi	Li Linglu	Ni Zixuan
Yang Zihong	Zhang Zewei	Zhou Lijun
Xu Keyi	Zhao Yufan	Yin Yanshu

Preface

The report of the 20th National Congress of the Communist Party of China (CPC) outlined significant strategies and arrangements for developing agriculture and rural in the new era. Rural industry is the foundation of rural revitalization, and upgrading the capacity of agricultural business entities is the support for industrial revitalization. Smallholders are the basic form of Chinese agricultural operations and the majority of the rural population. Promoting smallholders' development is crucial to achieve modernization of agriculture and rural areas, which is an essential component of the Agricultural Powerhouse in China.

The CPC Central Committee and the State Council have consistently prioritized the role of smallholders in agricultural development. Chinese President Xi Jinping has repeatedly emphasized that Smallholders in the Large Country is a basic characteristic in China. It is essential to resolve the challenges faced by smallholders and integrate them into the framework of modern agricultural development. In 2019, the General Office of the CPC Central Committee and the General Office of the State Council issued the Opinions on Promoting the Integration of Smallholders with Modern Agriculture. It put forward guiding opinions on supporting smallholders, enhancing their capacity and advancing modern agriculture. The No.1 central document for 2022 emphasized the significance of consolidating and enhancing the distinctive agro-industry in poverty alleviated regions. It also underlined the importance of improving the mechanisms for connecting and benefiting smallholders and increasing the household operational income. The No.1 central document for 2024 stated the necessity to accelerate the creation of a high-quality production and management team for smallholders, such as new types of agribusinesses and socialized agricultural services. The document also stressed enhancing the operational capacity of family farms and agricultural cooperatives in order to strengthen the ability to serve and promote smallholders.

It is a long-term process for supporting the development of smallholders that requires financial support and technical guidance and resolution of many problems faced in their operations. To draw on the concepts and experiences of international organizations in modern agricultural development, which will help the development of agricultural and rural modernization in China. Chinese government applied for an $80 million loan and grant from the International Fund for Agricultural Development (IFAD) in October 2018. The fund supports the Project for Specialized Agribusiness Development in Sichuan and Ningxia (IPRAD-SN, hereinafter referred to as "the Project"). The project aims to build and improve agricultural infrastructure, enhance the capacity of smallholders and cooperatives, and establish inclusive, equitable and sustainable value chain. The goal of the project is to promote the development of advantageous agro-industry, consolidate poverty alleviation outcomes and contribute to rural revitalization in the targeted regions. The project spans six years across ten counties(districts)in two provinces. The regions include Cangxi, Yilong, Xuzhou, Guang'an and Xuanhan in Sichuan Province, and Xingqing, Litong, Hongsibu, Yuanzhou and Pengyang in Ningxia Hui Autonomous Region. There will be 43 townships, 121 villages and 199,000 rural population benefited from the project. The project comprises three parts, they are infrastructure construction, the establishment of climate-smart production bases along with agro-industry value chain, and the enhancement of management and coordination capabilities.

On May 16, 2022, the National Project Office (NPO, located in the Department of Farmland Construction and Management, Ministry of Agriculture and Rural Affairs, MARA) signed a research contract with the Institute of Agricultural Resources and Regional Planning of the Chinese Academy of Agricultural Sciences (IARRP, CAAS). The aim of the research is threefold. First, it is to promote the construction of institution for the development of smallholders driven by farmers' cooperatives. Second, it focuses on enhancing the selection and growth of local advantageous and specialized agro-industries. Third, it endeavors to improve value chain, facilitating the shift from traditional to modern agriculture. The research title is Institutional Arrangement, Agro-industry Choice and Value Chain Construction for Promoting Smallholders' Development(GB-21005). The research team sorted out the national strategic arrangements and policy measures throughout the project implementation. Then the team assessed the fundamental strengths of the region's advantageous and characteristic industries. The team designed a set of questionnaires on cooperative driven smallholder development for the project implementation. Using stratified random sampling, the team had one-by-one, face-to-face exchanged with cooperatives and smallholders to gather data. The team has carried out four surveys, obtained first-hand data and imformation, dissected typical cases, and wrote four survey reports, on the basis of which this book was prepared.

The book is one of the outcomes of the research and is divided into two parts. The first part is a comprehensive report. It sorts out China's current strategic arrangements, institutional frameworks, and policy measures for promoting smallholder development. Then it analyzes the development status of advantageous and characteristic industries in the project areas and the selection of key agro-industries. The research focuses on the cooperatives supported by the project. It summarizes their growth and the ways they engage smallholders. It also clarifies the practices and effectiveness of these cooperatives. These aspects cover agro-industry progress, value chain construction and smallholder promotion. Finally, it distills the principal modes through which project-supported cooperatives promote smallholder development. The second part is typical cases in the project areas. Based on these, 25 typical cases have been selected. These cases are about the development of advantageous and characteristic industries such as grain, oil, vegetables, fruits, tea, cattle and sheep farming. The English version provides a corresponding translation of the Chinese content.

The IPRAD-SN Project of IFAD on the Institutional Arrangement, Agro-industry Choice and Value Chain Construction for Promoting Smallholders' Development (GB-21005) provided funding for this book.

Editorial Committee
December 2024, Beijing

Part I Comprehensive Report

Chapter 1   Project Background and Research Overview

1. Background and Progress of IPRAD-SN Project

To implement the strategic goals set by the Central Committee of the Communist Party of China (CPC) and the State Council for rural revitalization and accelerate the modernization of agriculture and rural areas. And drawing on the concepts and experience of modern agricultural development of international financial organizations, the Chinese government signed a loan agreement with the International Fund for Agricultural Development (IFAD) on October 30, 2018, for the Demonstration Project for Advantageous and Characteristic Agribusiness Development in Sichuan and NingXia (IPRAD-SN, hereinafter referred to as "the Project"). The total loan and grant amount for the Project was 80 million US dollars.

The project is organized and implemented by the Department of Farmland Construction Management under the Ministry of Agriculture and Rural Affairs (National Project Office). It is conducted across 10 counties(districts) in Sichuan (County District of Cangxi, Xuanhan, Guang'an, Xuzhou and Yilong) and Ningxia (County District of Yuanzhou, Pengyang, Hongsibu, Litong and Xingqing). The project cover 43 townships and 121 administrative villages, benefiting a rural population of 199,000, including 93 impoverished villages and 39,000 people living in poverty.

The Project has a six-year implementation period, with a total approved investment of CNY (Chinese Yuan) 1.04 billion. Of this amount, the International Fund for Agricultural Development (IFAD) invested 80 million US dollars, which was equivalent to 520 million yuan[①], accounting for 49.8% of the total investment. The loan was borrowed and repaid

---

[①] according to the exchange rate between the US dollar and the Chinese yuan of 1 : 6.5 in the year when the Loan Agreement was signed.

by the Central Finance in a unified manner. The loan includes CNY 279.5 million (USD 43 million) allocated to Sichuan and CNY 233.9 million (USD 36 million) allocated to Ningxia. Local government funding amounts to CNY 524.7 million, making up 50.2% of the total investment, with CNY 274.5 million contributed by Sichuan and CNY 250.2 million by Ningxia.

The Project aims to build and improve infrastructure, develop agricultural product processing and sales, and strengthen the exploitation of the agricultural value chain. These efforts focus on extending, improving, and upgrading the agricultural value chain to improve the production, management, trading, and service capabilities of smallholders and cooperatives, thereby boosting their market competitiveness. Ultimately, the project endeavors to construct a stable income growth value chain for smallholders, which features inclusiveness, equality and sustainability, contributes to regional development. At the same time, the project explores, innovates and forms a replicable, scalable mode for industry development. The specific construction contents of the project mainly include three aspects:

(1) Optimizing Infrastructure to Expand Market Access for Smallholders

Improve, develop, rehabilitate and maintain the infrastructure within the project area. Specific construction efforts include irrigation and drainage systems, water source projects, safe drinking water systems for humans and livestock, power supply networks, roads in villages and fields and other construction contents. As of the end of 2024, total investment in public infrastructure exceeded CNY 280 million, among which the funds from the IFAD amount to 9.22 million yuan, accounting for 3.29%. The infrastructure development improves the production and living conditions of smallholders and provides a fundamental guarantee for the development of specialized agricultural industries.

(2) Establishing Climate-Smart Production Bases to Enhance Smallholders' Climate Resilience

The project has also focused on the construction of climate-smart production bases, which enable the scalable use of farmland through land levelling and other engineering measures. By the end of 2024, the total investment in climate-smart production bases reached

CNY 79.09 million. The funds from the IFAD amount to 61.44 million yuan, accounting for 77.68%. These bases incorporate advanced technologies, such as water-saving irrigation, integrated water and fertilizer systems, and remote monitoring of pests and diseases. These technologies enhance smallholders' resilience to risks such as droughts, floods, and pest outbreaks. They also help smallholders master green agricultural production technologies, improve agricultural productivity, and enhance the quality of agricultural products. By leveraging these improvements, spur smallholders to break free from the shackles of single agricultural production and expand industrial chain into industry and service industries, increasing smallholders' income through multiple channels.

(3) Supporting the Development of Cooperatives and Driving the Capacity Improvement of Smallholders

The project is dedicated to bolstering the development of cooperatives, aiming to promote smallholders and industry growth. Specifically, business plans were signed with cooperatives in need, thereby rendering their development goals more targeted and their planning more scientific and rational. By the end of 2024, the project had supported 119 cooperatives (89 in Sichuan and 30 in Ningxia). These cooperatives provide technical training and employment opportunities to their members, in order to strengthen members' market competitiveness and bargaining power. Cooperatives utilize Apps and digital platforms to showcase their on-field production processes to the public. Through innovative marketing modes such as field adoption and cooperative-managed trusteeship, the sales of high-quality agricultural products have been successfully realized. Furthermore, the industrial chain has been extended and its quality has been enhanced through strategies like agricultural-supermarket linkage, online sales platforms, and the integration of agriculture and tourism.

2. Research Purpose and Significance

The target group of the project implementation is smallholders, so that more smallholders can obtain direct or indirect benefits through the project's infrastructure construction and value chain construction, participate in project activities, acquire more skills and achieve capacity enhancement. Smallholders are the main force of rural revitalization, and their development directly impacts the prosperity of rural economies and social stability. "A large country with a large number of smallholders" is the basic national condition of China. The data of the Third National Agricultural Census shows that the number of smallholders in the country accounts for more than 98% of the agricultural business entities. The cultivated area managed by smallholders constitutes approximately 70%[1] of the overall cultivated land area. However, smallholders face numerous challenges, including limited production scale, severe land fragmentation, low mechanisation rates, and insufficient market participation. These factors hold back their effective integration into modern agricultural and market economy systems, inhibiting improvements in agricultural productivity.

With the organizational advantages of new agricultural entities becoming increasingly apparent and their service capacities continuously improving, enhancing the scale and specialisation of smallholders is an essential pathway to connecting them with larger markets and improving overall agricultural efficiency. Cooperatives, as mutual aid organisations with both economic and social characteristics. It's an organizational approach for sustainable development in modern agriculture. The No. 1 Central Document has repeatedly redefined the social status, organizational structure and legal status of cooperatives. To ensure cooperative's operation, Farmers' Cooperative Law of the People's Republic of China has been amended. The number of cooperatives in China has shown a trend of vigorous development. According to the Ministry of Agriculture and Rural Affairs, by the end of 2023, over 1.09 million organizations provide agricultural socialized services in the whole country. The service area has exceeded 2.14 billion mu times and benefited over 94 million[2] smallholder households. Cooperatives form interest-linked entities with smallholders. They drive smallholders to participate more deeply in the construction of agricultural industrial chains and value chains. This is of great significance for stimulating the internal motivation of smallholders.

---

[1] Promoting the Organic Integration of Smallholders and Modern Agricultural Development (Economic Daily, Page 10, August 27, 2024), http://www.moa.gov.cn/ztzl/ymksn/jjrbbd/202408/t20240827_6461328.htm.

[2] Giving Play to the Driving Effect of New Agricultural Business Entities (Economic Daily, Page 8, April 25, 2024), http://www.moa.gov.cn/ztzl/ymksn/jjrbbd/202404/t20240425_6454364.htm.

Chapter 1 Project Background and Research Overview

To keep abreast of cooperative development dynamics in project areas in a timely manner and summarise the practices and outcomes of cooperatives in supporting smallholders, the research team of the Institute of Agricultural Resources and Regional Planning of the Chinese Academy of Agricultural Sciences(IARRP, CAAS) has carried out multiple field investigations. These involved one-by-one and face-to-face interviews with cooperative representatives and beneficiary smallholders (see Attachment 1 and 2 for survey questionnaires and photos), a large amount of First-hand information was collected.

3. Survey Methodology and Data Collection

(1) Survey Scope and Sample Selection

The survey covered 10 project areas across Sichuan and Ningxia, targeting beneficiary smallholders and supported cooperatives. Beneficiary smallholders were selected through stratified random sampling, with 3 project villages chosen from each project area (except Xingqing District) and 10 to 15 households randomly selected per village, (except that of Xingqing District) resulting in a total of 426 households (Table 1-1). We also considered the potential impact of establishment timing on the project. Therefore, supported cooperatives were selected based on those established and operational by the end of June 2023, and 105 were selected.

Table 1-1 Survey scope

Province	County (District)	Village	Sample	
Sichuan	Cangxi	Daying Village, Qingyan Village, Quanjia Village	45	225
	Guang'an	Gannian Village, Qiaoliang Village, Tongxin Village	45	
	Xuzhou	Ganxi Village, Sankuaishi Village, Xuanhua Community	45	
	Xuanhan	Niubei Village, Gaolun Village, Longdong Village	45	
	Yilong	Gaotanggou Village, Guoshan Village, Qixingqiao Village	45	

(continue)

Province	County (District)	Village	Sample	
Ningxia	Xingqing	Haitaonan Village, Yueyahu Village	10	201
	Litong	Baisitan Village, Fenghuodun Village, Haizijing Village	40	
	Hongsibu	Chaoyang Village, Liushutai Village, Shuitao Village	49	
	Yuanzhou	Biezhuang Village, Caojing Village, Jiangkou Village	55	
	Pengyang	Chengyang Village, Ciwan Village, Gaozhuang Village	47	
Total				426

(2) Survey Methodology and Main Contents

The research team interviews the cooperatives one-by-one and face-to-face, and conducted a field study on their products, services, and economic performance (Figure 1-1). The research team also made a visit to Ningxia's Facility Agriculture Bases to evaluate the outcomes of production base construction (Figure 1-2).

Figure 1-1 Products and services of cooperatives business

Chapter 1　Project Background and Research Overview

Figure 1-2　Construction of Ningxia' production bases

The questionnaire utilized two types, smallholders and cooperative. The smallholders' questionnaire covers basic information of rural households, agricultural operations, cooperative participation, and approaches to interest alignment. The cooperative questionnaire includes members composition, equity structures, business management, and value chain construction (Attachment 1). Additionally, research team combined the project's mid-term research data (2020, 907 farm households and 43 cooperatives) to compare and analyze the practices and effectiveness of cooperatives in the project area in driving smallholder development.

Chapter 2　Institutional Arrangement for Promoting Smallholders' Development

1. National Strategic Deployment

The report of the 19th National Congress of the CPC put forward the rural revitalization strategy. It pointed out that issues concerning agriculture, rural areas, and rural people are fundamental to the national economy and people's livelihood, and that resolving the "Three Rural Issues" must always be the top priority of the whole Party's work. The No. 1 Central Document of 2018 provided a top-level framework design for the rural revitalization strategy. Centering around this long-term and historic task, as well as the overarching guideline for the work related to agriculture, rural areas and farmers in the new era, each year's No. 1 Central Document, except for those during the decisive stage of poverty alleviation which focused on phased tasks and shored up the weakest links, has centered on rural revitalization in its theme. In February 2018, the CCCPC and the State Council issued the National Rural Revitalization Strategy Plan (2018–2022), making an overall deployment for implementing the Rural Revitalization Strategy.

To implement and fulfill the rural revitalization strategy and enhance smallholders' capacity to engage in modern agriculture, General Office, CCCPC and the General Office of the State Council issued the Opinions on Promoting the Integration of Smallholders with Modern Agriculture in 2019. It was put forward to adhere to the coordination between taking smallholders' family-based operations as the foundation and taking various forms of appropriately scaled operations as the leading factor. Coordinate it with appropriate scaled operations led by various modern agricultural modes, enhancing smallholders, and enriching smallholders, accelerate the construction of a policy system for supporting the development of smallholders. Facilitate traditional smallholders' transition into modern farmers so as to accomplish the effective integration of theirs into the development of

Chapter 2　Institutional Arrangement for Promoting Smallholders' Development

modern agriculture.

In 2020, with the complete victory in China's battle against poverty, the nation achieved the historic milestone of lifting 98.99 million rural poor people under the current standards out of poverty. All 832 impoverished counties were officially removed from the poverty list, and 128,000 impoverished villages were no longer classified as poor, effectively eradicating regional poverty and accomplishing the formidable task of eliminating absolute poverty[①]. Following this achievement, the CCCPC and the State Council issued the Opinions on Effectively Linking Poverty Alleviation Results with Rural Revitalization, proposing a five-year transition period. The document pointed out that it should shift resources from poverty alleviation towards consolidating the achievements and comprehensively promoting rural revitalization. The document also put forward suggestions on supporting the development and expansion of rural characteristic industries and on continuously improving infrastructure in formerly impoverished regions, in order to strengthen efficient connection between poverty alleviation and rural revitalization.

In 2022, Chinese President Xi Jinping, in the report delivered at the 20th National Congress of CPC, pointed out "accelerate the building of a strong agricultural nation and solidly advance the revitalization of rural industries, talent, culture, ecology, and organizations." The report emphasized the principle of prioritizing agricultural and rural development, consolidating and expanding the results of poverty alleviation, and accelerating the construction of a strong agricultural nation. It called for taking solid steps to promote the revitalization of rural industries, talent, culture, ecology and organizations, and to strengthen the foundation of food security. The No. 1 Central Document of 2024 further stated "anchored to the goal of building a strong agricultural nation, taking the ensuring national food security and preventing large-scale return to poverty as the bottom line. Furthermore, focusing on elevating agro-industry rural industries, improving the level of rural construction and enhancing rural governance, strengthening the dual driving forces of science and technology and reform, intensifying measures to boost farmers' incomes, thereby accelerating the modernization of agriculture and rural areas to better promote Chinese-style modernization."

---

① Xi Jinping's Speech at the National Conference on Poverty Alleviation and Award Ceremony in February 2021.

2. Institutional Arrangement

In recent years, the country has deepened reforms in key fields of rural areas, promoted the modernization of agriculture and rural areas, and spurred historic changes in work related to agriculture, rural areas, and rural people. During the project implementation, continuous reforms and innovations have been made in aspects such as the rural land system and the agricultural operation and management system, providing support and guarantee for the smooth progress of the project.

(1) Rural Land "Three Rights Separation" Provides Institutional Support for Smallholders' Development

In 2016, General Office, CCCPC and the General Office of the State Council issued the Opinions on Improving the Separation of Ownership, Contractual Rights and Operational Rights of Rural Land. This policy divided the right to contractual management of rural land into contractual rights and operational rights, establishing a parallel system of ownership, contractual rights, and operational rights. Under this framework, "holders of operational rights have the legal right to possess, cultivate, and derive income from transferred land for a specified period." This reform represents a significant institutional innovation following the household responsibility system. With the "three rights separation" in place, farmers who migrate to cities for work retain stable contractual rights, allowing them to confidently transfer their land's operational rights. Meanwhile, farmers seek to expand their operations can acquire additional operational rights through various channels, thereby increasing their scale of production. This arrangement enables the collective, contracted farmers, and new agricultural business entities to share land rights. Landowners, contract holders, and operators all benefit without losing their respective rights. Collective land becomes a fluid production factor, farmers transferring operational rights gain property income, and new agricultural business entities achieve economies of scale and higher returns.

(2) New Agricultural Entities Support Policies Provide Pathways for Smallholders' Development

On 31 May 2017, the General Office of the CPC Central Committee and the General

Chapter 2 Institutional Arrangement for Promoting Smallholders' Development

Office of the State Council issued the Opinions on Accelerating the Construction of Policy System for Cultivating New Agricultural Business Entities. This policy made key deployments in aspects such as fiscal and tax incentives, infrastructure development, financial credit, insurance, marketing, and talent cultivation and recruitment. It emphasized the need for comprehensive policy support to foster new agricultural business entities, leveraging their economies of scale to drive ordinary farmers, making them both participants and beneficiaries of modern agricultural development. In January 2018, the important document Opinions of the Central Committee of the Communist Party of China and the State Council on Implementing the Rural Revitalization Strategy put forward that "We should make overall plans to cultivate new agricultural business entities and support smallholders, and adopt targeted measures to introduce smallholder production into the track of modern agricultural development." In September of the same year, the Rural Revitalization Strategy Plan (2018–2022) pointed out that "We should strengthen new agricultural business entities, implement the cultivation project for new agricultural business entities, and encourage the conduct of moderately scaled operations through multiple forms." In February 2019, General Office, CCCPC and the General Office of the State Council issued the Opinions on Promoting the Organic Integration of Smallholders and Modern Agriculture, creating policy guarantees for supporting and enhancing the ability of smallholders to develop modern agriculture, and helping to better play the principal role of smallholders in rural revitalization. To further improve the quality of new agricultural business entities, the Ministry of Agriculture and Rural Affairs released the High-Quality Development Plan for New Agricultural Business Entities and Service Providers (2020–2022) on 3 March 2020. This plan outlined specific development requirements for different types of agricultural business entities, providing clear guidance for policy implementation. And it includes driving smallholders as part of the cultivation content, further deepening the connection between them.

(3) The Improvement of the Agricultural Support and Protection System Provides Support for Strengthening, Benefiting and Enriching Agriculture

On 26 November 2019, the 11th Meeting of the Central Committee for Comprehensive Deepening Reform (19th CCCPC) reviewed and approved the Opinions on Improving the Agricultural Support and Protection System and the Opinions on Strengthening the Construction of the Socialized Service System for Agricultural Science Technology. The meeting put forward that in establishing and improving the agricultural support and protection system, it is necessary to adhere to giving priority to the development of agriculture and rural areas and take the implementation of the Rural Revitalization Strategy as the overall starting point. It called for in-depth reforms in areas such as agricultural supply-side structural reform, sustainable agricultural development, agricultural investment guarantees, agricultural subsidies and compensation, management of agricultural support funds. The goal is to gradually build an agricultural support and protection system that is tailored to national conditions, comprehensive in scope, clear in direction, targeted in focus, complementary and coordinated in the measures, and easy to operate. This system aims to continuously enhance the precision, stability, and effectiveness of policies for strengthening, benefiting, and enriching farmers(Table 2-1). Meanwhile, the meeting pointed out that in strengthening the construction of the agricultural science and technology socialized service system, efforts should be focused on increasing the effective supply of agricultural science and technology services and strengthening the connection between supply and demand, with the goal of improving the efficiency of agricultural science and technology services. These measures aim to promote the service innovation of agricultural technology extension institutions, strengthen the service functions of universities and research institutes, expand the strength of market-oriented and socialized services, and accelerate the construction of an open, competitive, diversified, complementary and highly efficient agricultural science and technology socialized service system.

Table 2-1 Institutional reforms for smallholders' development

Vintages	Policy Documents	Policy Content
2015	Ministry of Finance issues Guidance on Comprehensive Agricultural Development to Support Agricultural Advantageous Characteristic Industries and Promote the Development of Agricultural Industrialization	Focusing on optimizing layout, highlighting advantages, providing targeted support, and improving benefits, the strategy aims to promote the integration of primary, secondary and tertiary industries in rural areas, driving continuous income growth for farmers, with the creation of agricultural advantage and specialty industry clusters as the focus.

Chapter 2　Institutional Arrangement for Promoting Smallholders' Development

(continue)

Vintages	Policy Documents	Policy Content
2016	General Office, CCCPC and the General Office of the State Council issued the Opinions on Improving the Separation of Ownership, Contractual Rights and Operational Rights of Rural Land	The rural land contract management rights are divided into contract rights and management rights, with ownership, contract rights, and management rights operating concurrently. Land management rights holders are entitled by law to occupy, cultivate, and obtain returns from transferred land within a specified period.
2016	The Central Committee of the Communist Party of China and the State Council issued the Opinions on Steadily Advancing the Reform of the Rural Collective Property Rights System	To clarify property ownership and safeguard members' rights, efforts are focused on advancing reforms of collectively owned operational assets, exploring new forms of realization and operating mechanisms for the collective economy.
2017	General Office, CCCPC and the General Office of the State Council issued the Opinions on Accelerating the Construction of Policy System for Cultivating New Agricultural Business Entities	Accelerating the cultivation of new agricultural business entities, establishing a complete policy support system, and give play to the leading role of new agricultural business entities in promoting agricultural modernisation.
2019	General Office, CCCPC and the General Office of the State Council issued the Opinions on Promoting the Organic Integration of Smallholders and Modern Agriculture	Through measures such as policy support, service improvement, and mechanism innovation, promoting the organic integration between smallholders and modern agricultural systems.
2019	Opinions on Improving the Agricultural Support and Protection System and the Opinions on Strengthening the Construction of the Socialised Service System for Agricultural Science and Technology considered and adopted at the Eleventh Meeting of the Nineteenth Central Committee for Comprehensively Deepening Reforms	It called for in-depth reforms in areas such as agricultural supply-side structural reform, sustainable agricultural development, agricultural investment guarantees, agricultural subsidies and compensation, management of agricultural support funds. The goal is to gradually build an agricultural support and protection system that is tailored to national conditions, comprehensive in scope, clear in direction, targeted in focus, complementary and coordinated in the measures, and easy to operate. Meanwhile, the meeting pointed out that efforts should be focused on increasing the effective supply of agricultural science and technology services and strengthening

(continue)

Vintages	Policy Documents	Policy Content
2019		the connection between supply and demand, with the goal of improving the efficiency of agricultural science and technology services. These measures aim to promote the service innovation of agricultural technology extension institutions, strengthen the service functions of universities and research institutes, expand the strength of market-oriented and socialized services.
2021	Law of the People's Republic of China on Promotion of Rural Revitalization	It comprehensively outlines the overall requirements, guiding principles, key tasks, and support measures for rural revitalization, providing a legal foundation to ensure the successful implementation of rural revitalization initiatives.

3. Local Policy Measures

During the Project implementation, Sichuan and Ningxia actively formulated and implemented policies tailored to local agricultural development(Table 2-2). These policies emphasized agricultural transformation and upgrading, agro-industry integration, and brand building, and the organic integration of smallholders with modern agriculture. In doing so, they aimed to ensure food security, enhance agricultural benefits, and increase farmers' incomes, all while working towards the long-term goal of agricultural and rural modernization.

Sichuan, according to "Sichuan Rural Poverty Alleviation and Development Outline (2011–2020)", proposed initiatives tailored to local conditions. These included promoting agro-industry restructuring, supporting the growth of farmers' cooperatives and other new agricultural business entities, and driving agricultural industrialization and farmers' income growth. Efforts focused on developing specialty industries and agricultural cooperative organisations by leveraging the natural resources of poverty-stricken areas. Comprehensive industry development plans were formulated and refined, with increased support to advance specialty agriculture. Mechanisms linking the interests of farmers were improved, and organizational modes such as "cooperatives+ smallholders" and "leading

Chapter 2 Institutional Arrangement for Promoting Smallholders' Development

enterprises + cooperatives+ smallholders" were promoted. Additionally, the province emphasized strengthening the connection with the market, expanding agricultural value chains, increasing the value-added of agricultural products, and building brands for competitive and characteristic agricultural products.

In 2021, the CPC Sichuan Provincial Committee and the Sichuan Provincial People's Government issued the Opinions on Comprehensively Implementing the Rural Revitalization Strategy and Embarking on a New Journey of Agricultural and Rural Modernization Construction, proposing that "a hierarchical development system for modern agricultural parks that conforms to the actual situation in Sichuan should be constructed to drive smallholders into the track of modern agricultural development and form a new trend of integrated development of the primary, secondary and tertiary industries in rural areas." Further, in May 2021, the CPC Sichuan Provincial Committee and Sichuan Provincial Government issued the Implementation Opinions on Achieving Seamless Connection Between Poverty Alleviation and Rural Revitalization. The document put forward establishing a sound long-term mechanism for consolidating poverty alleviation outcomes, improving rural water supply security, and continuously increasing support for counties (cities and districts) that are in the former deeply impoverished areas and the hinterland of the Qinba Mountains and that have poor economic development conditions and heavy tasks in consolidating and expanding the achievements of poverty alleviation. It also emphasized the development and expansion of rural industries with local characteristics in these regions. In July 2021, the Sichuan Provincial Government released the Sichuan Provincial 14th Five-Year Plan for Advancing Agricultural and Rural Modernization, put forward initiating the comprehensive promotion of a new stage in agricultural and rural modernization. Resolutely safeguard the bottom line of food security and enhance the supply guarantee level of important agricultural and sideline products. Accelerate the development of high-quality and high-efficient modern characteristic agriculture and improve the modernization level of agro-industry and supply chains. Speed up filling the supportive shortcomings of the "10+3" agro-industry system and construct a hierarchical development system for modern agricultural parks.

In 2018, the Ningxia Hui Autonomous Region released the Three-Year Action Implementation Plan to Win the Battle Against Poverty which put forward focusing on building the self-development capacity of the population in impoverished regions and strengthening and optimizing advantageous and characteristic industries. The region's Rural Revitalization Strategy Plan and Implementation Opinions on Promoting the Organic Integration of Smallholders with Modern Agricultural Development and other documents highlighted the importance of fostering new agricultural business entities, promoting industry integration, and enhancing the market competitiveness of agricultural products.

The14th Five-Year Plan and the Implementation Opinions on Advancing Rural Revitalization and Accelerating Agricultural and Rural Modernization of Ningxia focused on green development of agriculture, key industry growth, food security, and promoting agro-industry quality and efficiency, and planned the building of modern agricultural systems. In 2021, the Autonomous Region's Party Committee and Government issued the Opinions on Supporting Key Counties for Rural Revitalization, identifying Yuanzhou District and Hongsibu District as key counties for national rural revitalization, while Pengyang County was designated a key county for regional rural revitalization. These areas, with relatively weak foundations for poverty alleviation are the key areas for preventing the recurrence of poverty and the return to poverty as well as consolidating and expanding the achievements of poverty alleviation during the 14th Five-Year Plan period.

Table 2-2 Local policy advancement for smallholders' development

Year	Local policy document	Related content
Sichuan		
2018	Opinions of the Sichuan Provincial Committee of the Communist Party of China and the People's Government of Sichuan Province on the Implementation of the Rural Revitalization Strategy and Creating a New Era of Comprehensive Development for Agriculture, Rural Areas, and Farmers	The strategy for rural revitalization outlines the overall requirements, key tasks, and support measures for implementation, with a focus on promoting appropriately scaled agricultural operations and fostering the growth of new agricultural business entities.
2019	Evaluation and Incentive Programme for the Construction of Modern Agricultural Parks in Sichuan Province	By establishing modern agricultural parks, the province aims to enhance agricultural efficiency and competitiveness, drive agricultural transformation and upgrading, increase farmers' incomes, and strengthen effective linkages with the market.

Chapter 2　Institutional Arrangement for Promoting Smallholders' Development

(continue)

Year	Local policy document	Related content
2021	Sichuan Province's "14th Five-Year Plan" for Promoting Modernisation of Agriculture and Rural Areas	The strategy integrates agricultural and rural modernisation, advancing both simultaneously with a unified design. It takes into account regional differences and development foundations, tailoring timeframes, task lists, and roadmaps to local conditions for advancing agricultural and rural modernisation.
2023	Action Programme for the Integrated Development of Rural Two-Three Industries in Sichuan Province	Key initiatives include deep processing of agricultural products, expanding markets for "Sichuan" agricultural brands, enhancing product branding, integrating agriculture with culture and tourism, and strengthening and expanding business entities with technological empowerment to promote the integrated development of primary, Secondary, and tertiary rural industries.
2024	Opinions of the Sichuan Provincial Committee of the Communist Party of China and the Sichuan Provincial People's Government on Learning and Applying the Experience of the "Thousand Villages Demonstration, Ten Thousand Villages Improvement" Project to Promote Rural Revitalization in a Comprehensive Manner	The strategy also accelerates progress by building a modern agricultural management system, developing new forms of rural collective economies, and exploring urban-rural integration reforms at the county level.
Ningxia		
2017	Opinions on Accelerating the Brand Building of Ningxia's Characteristic and High Quality Agricultural Products	Strengthening the standardised production of branded agriculture, enhance brand development through technological innovation, cultivate key players in brand agriculture, and reinforce regional public brands for Ningxia's specialty agricultural products. Establish a brand directory system for Ningxia agricultural products, expand market sales channels for branded products, and enhance quality and safety monitoring and regulation, with the overall goal of improving modern agricultural efficiency and ensuring sustained income growth for farmers.

(continue)

Year	Local policy document	Related content
2019	Strategic Plan for Rural Revitalization in the Ningxia (2018–2022)	The rural revitalization plan outlines specific measures, including the development of cooperatives and family farms as new agricultural business entities, promoting the integration of agricultural industries, and increasing the market competitiveness of agricultural products.
2020	Implementing Opinions of the Ningxia Hui Autonomous Region on Promoting the Organic Connection between Small Farmers and Modern Agricultural Development	Through policy guidance and support, smallholders are encouraged to improve their production capacity and to establish stable benefit-sharing mechanisms with modern agricultural enterprises through cooperatives and federations.
2021	"Fourteenth Five-Year Plan" for the Modernisation and Development of Agriculture and Rural Areas of the Ningxia Hui Autonomous Region	The creation of a National Agricultural Green Development Pilot Zone serve as a platform to focus on the region's "Nine Key Industries" and "Four Key Enhancement Actions," accelerating the development of modern agro-industry, production, and management systems.
2021	Implementing Opinions of the People's Government of the Autonomous Region on Comprehensively Promoting Rural Revitalization and Accelerating Modernisation of Agriculture and Rural Areas	Efforts to advance agricultural modernization focus on eight key areas: ensuring the security of grain and essential agricultural products, safeguarding arable land, improving the quality of crop and livestock farming, and accelerating the growth of modern rural industries.

Chapter 3　Advantageous Agro-industry in Project Areas

The project areas have distinct characteristics in their advantageous and specialized agro-industries. Grain, oil, vegetable, and fruit industries have a solid foundation in Sichuan, and cool-climate vegetables as well as cattle and sheep farming provide a strong foundation in Ningxia. There is a good foundation for agro-industry development in the two project areas.

1. Sichuan Project Area

Sichuan Province, located in southwestern China and situated upstream of the Yangtze River, is known as the "Land of Abundance", covering a total area of 486 thousand square kilometers, accounting for 5.1% of the country's total land area. The province spans several major geographic regions, including the Qinghai-Tibet Plateau, the Hengduan Mountains, the Yunnan-Guizhou Plateau, the Qinba Mountains, and the Sichuan Basin, with its terrain sloping from the highlands in the northwest to the lowlands in the southeast. The landforms are diverse, including four types of landforms: plains, terraces, hills, and mountains, which can be divided into the mountainous areas of southwestern Sichuan, the plateau regions of northwest Sichuan, and the basin lowlands of central Sichuan.

As a major agricultural province, Sichuan serves as a strategic base for ensuring the national supply of primary agricultural products and plays a critical role in China's agricultural development. Sichuan's advantageous and characteristic agricultural industries include grains and oils, pigs, fruits, tea, silkworms, and Chinese medicinal herbs, etc. In the first three quarters of 2024, Sichuan's pig slaughter reached 45.129 million head, with pigs production totalling 3.568 million tons, ranking firstly in the country. The pig industry, characterized by large-scale farming, and boasts several well-known local brands, such as "Sichuan-Tibetan Black Pig". Additionally, the planting area and output of late-maturing citrus also rank among the top in the country, and occupy an important position in the national citrus market by virtue of its unique advantage of dislocation of time to market. Sichuan also ranks secondly nationwide in tea cultivation, while fruits such as lemons, pomegranates, and loquats hold a prominent place in the national market. Additionally, Sichuan's vegetable, pickled vegetable, and fruit processing industries are highly competitive, with strong market performance.

The selected project areas in Sichuan include Cangxi County in Guangyuan City, Xuanhan County in Dazhou City, Guang'an District in Guang'an City, Xuzhou District in Yibin City, and Yilong County in Nanchong City, all of which have established agro-industry foundations in fruits, tea, mushrooms, peppercorns, silkworms and pigs.

2. Ningxia Project Area

Ningxia is located in the mid-upper reaches of the Yellow River in northwestern China. It is economically underdeveloped, with a relatively high concentration of formerly impoverished populations. The region features a long, narrow north-south terrain, with elevations decreasing from south to north. The western areas have significant elevation differences, while the eastern areas are relatively gently rolling. The plains are located in the central part of the region, characterized by flat and open terrain with fertile soil, forming the well-known "Jiangnan of the Frontier" through irrigation with Yellow River water. The main agricultural types here are irrigated agriculture and the cultivation of specialty melons and vegetables. The Liupan Mountains in the south have elevations mostly above 2,000 meters, with forestry and mountainous dryland farming as the primary agricultural activities. The northern part belongs to the Ningxia-Mongolian Plateau, with elevations between 1,000 and 1,500 meters, mainly consisting of grasslands and deserts. The climate is relatively arid with scarce precipitation, and the main agricultural types are grassland animal husbandry, dryland and oasis agriculture.

The key advantage and specialty agro-industries in Ningxia include cool-climate vegetables, goji berries, wine, Tan sheep, and beef cattle. Cool-climate vegetables are renowned for their quality and safety, The planting area for cool-climate vegetables remains above 3 million mu[①] (approximately 200 thousand hectares), with production stable at over 7.3 million tons. Among these, the planting area for Ningxia Caisim greens exceeds 270 thousand mu (18 thousand hectares) and annual sales exceed CNY 3.6 billion. "Ningxia Caisim" has been recognized as a national geographical indication product and is supplied to the Guangdong-Hong Kong-Macao Greater Bay Area through cold-chain logistics. Ningxia's Tan sheep is a well-known meat product both domestically and internationally, particularly in high-end dining markets. Additionally, Ningxia has registered the "Guyuan Yellow Cattle" and "Jingyuan Yellow Beef " as national geographical indication brands and established the regional public brand "Xihai Gu," alongside several enterprise brands such as "Mu He Chun" and "Zhen Hui Wei".

The selected project areas in Ningxia include Yuanzhou District and Pengyang County in Guyuan City, Hongsibu District and Litong District in Wuzhong City, and Xingqing District in Yinchuan City. The counties and districts involved in the projects are primarily agriculture-based. However, they face relatively weak foundational conditions for agricultural production, with some areas experiencing severe water shortages.

Based on the resource conditions and agro-industry strengths of Sichuan and Ningxia, the IFAD project identified representative industries for development, focusing on crops such as grains, oilseeds, vegetables, fruits, and Chinese medicinal herbs, as well as livestock farming for pigs, cattle, sheep, and poultry (the selected agro-industry for each project area are listed in Table 3-1). Through project support, on one hand, we will strengthen the infrastructure construction of agro-industry development, improve transportation conditions, and lay the foundation for more market opportunities; On the other hand, we will promote the development of science and technology to empower the development of the industry, use modern agricultural facilities and equipment and technical modes, such as automated water-saving irrigation, drone seeding, green prevention and control of pests and diseases, etc., strengthen the technical training of business entities, master production skills, and improve the agro-industry value chain.

---

① 1 hm² = 15 mu.

Table 3-1 Agro-industry selection in project area

Province	County area	Agro-industry
Sichuan	Cangxi	Red kiwi fruit, Cangxi pear, vegetables, agricultural machinery services, grains and oils, peppercorns, lemons, citrus, Chinese medicinal materials
	Yilong	Fruits, edible mushrooms, beef cattle, vegetables, grains and oils, pigs, aquatic products
	Xuanhan	Leisure agriculture, tea, peppercorns, grains and oils, Chinese medicinal materials, fruits, pigs, vegetables, beef cattle
	Guang'an	Fruits, peppercorns, Leisure agriculture, grains and oils
	Xuzhou	Silkworms, tea, vegetables, pigs, Chinese medicinal materials, flowers
Ningxia	Hongsibu	Grains and oils, fruits, cauliflower, Chinese medicinal materials, Tan sheep
	Yuanzhou	Broilers, laying hens, grains and oils, beef cattle
	Litong	Grains and oils, forage, beef cattle
	Pengyang	Chinese medicinal materials, beef cattle, laying hens, pasture, fruits, bees
	Xingqing	Fruits, vegetable, beef cattle

Chapter 4 Practices and Effectiveness of Cooperatives in Promoting Smallholders' Development

Taking cooperatives to promote the development of smallholders is an important element of project implementation. Based on data collected from 105 project-supported cooperatives, we analyzed the production and operation status as well as the agro-industry development of these cooperatives, and summarized the practices and effectiveness of cooperatives in promoting the smallholders' development. We also analyzed the status of smallholders' income and satisfaction through survey data.

1. Improvement of Infrastructures and Diversification of Business Types

With the support of project funds, cooperatives surveyed have significantly improved their office environments and upgraded their infrastructure and equipment. Office space increased by 14,279 square metres, while processing facilities and storage capacity expanded by 78,791 square metres and 40,980 square metres, respectively. The processing equipment of cooperatives increased by 933 sets, the storage equipment increased by 141 sets, and the logistics equipment increased by 52 sets(Table 4-1).

Table 4-1 Increase in cooperative infrastructure equipment

Project area	Infrastructure Area/(square meter)			Equipment/set		
	Office space	Processing facilities	Storage capacity	Processing equipment	Storage equipment	Logistics equipment
Sichuan	12,435	68,350	28,620	715	122	43
Ningxia	1,844	10,441	12,360	218	19	9
Total	14,279	78,791	40,980	933	141	52

Cooperatives have diversified their business operations into five categories: planting, livestock farming, integrated planting-livestock farming, agricultural machinery services, and agricultural tourism (Figure 4−1). Among them, planting is the most common, with 52 cooperatives, accounting for 49.5% of the total. There are 9 livestock farming cooperatives, accounting for 8.6%. There are 31 cooperative societies that combine planting and breeding, accounting for 29.5%. There are 9 agricultural tourism cooperatives, accounting for 8.6%. There are 4 agricultural machinery service cooperatives, accounting for 3.8%.

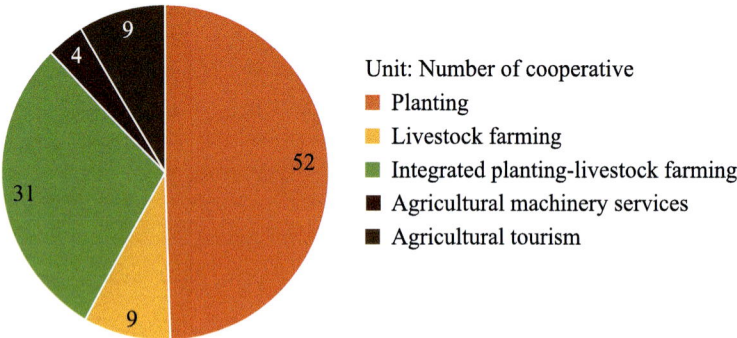

Figure 4−1　Number of different types of cooperatives

2. Strengthening the Value Chain and Enhancing Agro-industry Efficiency

(1) Improving Internal Management System and Promoting Standardized Operation

With project support, all 105 cooperatives have developed internal management systems, holding two general meetings and three board meetings annually. 68 cooperatives have hired full-time accountants, while those without in-house accountants manage their finances through external professionals or accounting firms. Additionally, 63 cooperatives are capable of independently drafting business plans (Table 4−2).

Table 4−2　Internal management of cooperatives

Unit: number of cooperative

Project area	Development of management system	With full-time accountants	Independent business plan writing
Sichuan	89	55	55

Chapter 4 Practices and Effectiveness of Cooperatives in Promoting Smallholders' Development

(continue)

Project area	Development of management system	With full-time accountants	Independent business plan writing
Ningxia	16	13	8
Total	105	68	63

(2) Enhancing the Value Chain and Extending the Agro-industry Chain

1) Introduction of new varieties and technologies

With improved production infrastructure, the cooperatives have focused on adopting new varieties and technologies. By the end of 2023, 379 new varieties had been introduced, with a total investment of 13.883 million yuan, while 111 new technologies were adopted, involving an investment of 2.653 million yuan(Table 4-3).

Table 4-3 Number and amount of new varieties and technologies introduced

Project area	New varieties/ number	Investment in new varieties/(million yuan)	New technologies/ item	Investment in new technologies/(million yuan)
Sichuan	364	13.782	105	2.628
Ningxia	15	0.101	6	0.025
Total	379	13.883	111	2.653

2) Development of specialized industries

The cooperatives operate in a range of local specialty industries, including grains and oils, fruits, vegetables, tea, and livestock such as cattle and sheep. According to survey data, the total sales[①] revenue from specialized industries in 2023 reached CNY 132.862 million. 64.334 million came from sales on behalf of collections representing 48.4% of total sales. Livestock farming generated CNY 22.921 million in sales, with CNY 3.52 million on sales, accounting for 15.4% of total sales. Livestock farming generated CNY 109.94 million in sales, with CNY 60.814 million from on behalf of collections' sales, making up 55.3% of total sales (Table 4-4).

---

① The total sales of cooperatives consist of sales from self production and sales on behalf of others.

Table 4-4 Cooperative's sales and proportion   Unit: million yuan

Industry type	Total sales	Self-production sales	Proportion/%	Sales on behalf of collections	Proportion/%
Plantation	109.94	49.127	44.7	60.814	55.3
Livestock farming	22.921	19.401	84.6	3.52	15.4
Total	132.862	68.528	51.6	64.334	48.4

3) Extending the agro-industry chain

As the project progressed, cooperatives expanded their operations from traditional agriculture into sectors such as agricultural product processing, catering, and hospitality, thereby extending the agro-industry chain. The proportion of cooperatives involved in agricultural product processing increased from 39.5% in 2020 to 43.8% in 2023. Similarly, the percentage of cooperatives engaged in catering and hospitality rose from 4.6% in 2020 to 10.5% in 2023(Table 4-5).

Table 4-5 Number and proportion of cooperatives with extended agro-industry chain

Business type	2020		2023	
	Number/count	Proportion/%	Number/count	Proportion/%
Agricultural product processing	17	39.5	46	43.8
Catering, hospitality, and related services	2	4.6	11	10.5

4) Emphasis on branding

Brand development has become an important strategy for cooperatives to enhance market competitiveness. Among the 105 cooperatives, 69 have been designated as mode cooperatives, accounting for 65.7%. Among them, there are 10 national-level mode cooperatives, 16 provincial-level mode cooperatives, 20 city-level mode cooperatives, and 23 county-level mode cooperatives. Furthermore, 47 cooperatives have established agricultural product brands, 68 cooperatives have obtained certifications for "Three Products and One Standard" (pollution-free, organic, green products, and geographical indications), and 49 cooperatives hold trademark registration certificate.

Chapter 4　Practices and Effectiveness of Cooperatives in Promoting Smallholders' Development

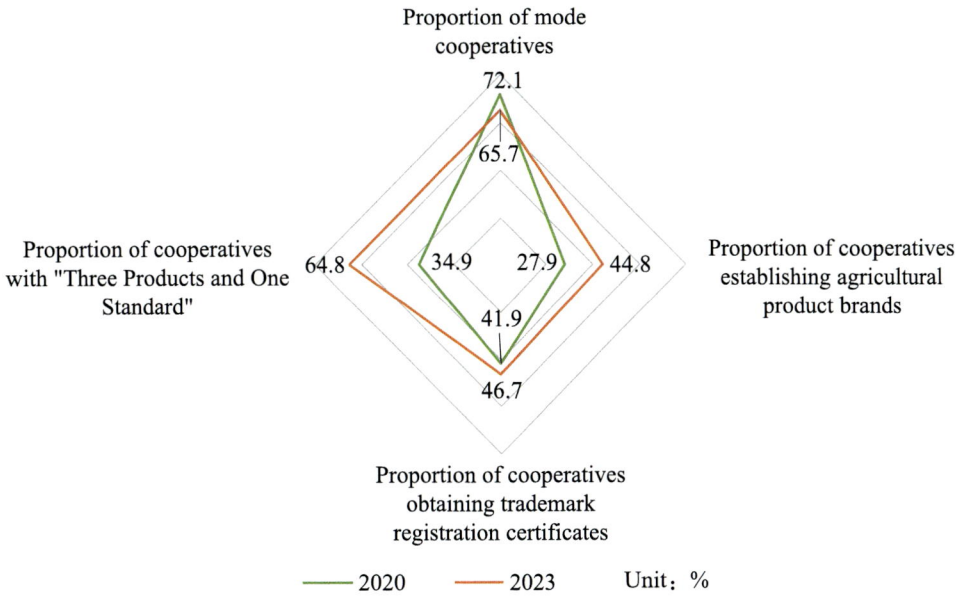

Figure 4-2　Changes in cooperative brand development

With project support, cooperatives have not only improved their operational and management capabilities but also made significant progress in brand development. Compared to the mid-term assessment, the proportion of cooperatives with agricultural product brands increased from 27.9% to 44.8%, a rise of 16.9 percentage points. Meanwhile, the proportion of cooperatives with "Three Products and One Standard" registration certificates grew from 34.9% to 64.8%, an increase of 29.9 percentage points (Figure 4-2).

5) Operational efficiency and profitability

With the continuous development of specialized industries, the operational efficiency of cooperatives has gradually improved, in 2023, 59 cooperatives (accounting for 56.2% of those surveyed) reported profits. In Sichuan, 50 cooperatives reported profits, with the profitability rate increasing from 51.8% in the mid-term to 56.2%. In Ningxia, 9 cooperatives were profitable, with the profitability rate declined slightly, likely due to market price fluctuations in 2023, which led to a general drop in cattle and sheep prices, affecting cooperative revenues(Table 4-6).

Table 4-6　Comparison of profitable cooperatives

Project area	2020		2023	
	Number/count	Proportion/%	Number/count	Proportion/%
Sichuan	14	51.8	50	56.2

	2020		2023	
Project area	Number/count	Proportion/%	Number/count	Proportion/%
Ningxia	11	68.7	9	56.3
Total	25	58.1	59	56.2

(continue)

Note: In 2020, a total of 43 cooperatives were surveyed, including 27 in Sichuan and 16 in Ningxia. In 2023, a total of 105 cooperatives were surveyed, including 89 in Sichuan and 16 in Ningxia.

3. Providing Diversified Services and Supporting Smallholders Through Multiple Channels

(1) Clear Division of Roles and Benefit-sharing

The first step in promoting the development of smallholders is to encourage them to join cooperatives. Smallholders form the majority of cooperative members, with the 105 surveyed cooperatives supporting a total of 8,708 smallholder households, representing 97.4% of all members in 2023. In the Sichuan project area, smallholders account for 7,951 small farmers in the cooperatives surveyed and researched, accounting for 97.9%, while in the Ningxia project area, smallholders total 757 households, making up 92.5% of members.

Smallholders also play a significant role in cooperative management, a holding 82.9% of board positions. In the Sichuan project area, smallholders hold 362 board positions, representing 81.7%, while in the Ningxia project area, they hold 70 board positions, accounting for 89.7%.

To strengthen the benefit-sharing mechanism with smallholders, cooperatives convert the value of land and capital contributed by smallholder members into equity shares. For members who contribute land, the cooperatives calculate the equity based on the local land transfer price, and profits are distributed according to the equity shares, allowing members to receive dividends.

(2) Providing Employment and Strengthening Collaborative Interaction

The 105 surveyed cooperatives have created 5,638 employment opportunities for farmers. The number of jobs provided depends on factors such as the number of supported

Chapter 4 Practices and Effectiveness of Cooperatives in Promoting Smallholders' Development

cooperatives, industry type, and production scale. Among these positions, approximately 20% are long-term roles, while 80% are temporary jobs (Table 4-7).

Table 4-7 Types of employment provided by cooperatives

Project area	Employment Positions/unit	Proportion of long-term positions/%	Proportion of temporary positions /%
Sichuan	4,933	21.6	78.4
Ningxia	705	8.6	91.4
Total	5,638	20.0	80.0

(3) Conducting Training to Improve Production Skills

Cooperatives play an important role in providing technical training. The 105 cooperatives surveyed organized a total of 402 training sessions, primarily targeting smallholders, with 8,299 receiving training. In Sichuan, 89 cooperatives trained 7,309 smallholders, while 16 cooperatives in Ningxia trained 990 smallholders(Table 4-8).

Table 4-8 Number of training sessions and persons in cooperatives

Project area	Number/time	Number of persons/person
Sichuan	362	7,309
Ningxia	40	990
Total	402	8,299

Cooperatives have become key players in promoting and adopting green agricultural practices. Among the surveyed cooperatives, 81 cooperatives have integrated green production technologies into their production process. 75 cooperatives have adopted organic fertilizers as a substitute for chemical fertilizers. 66 cooperatives have implemented water-saving irrigation or integrated water and fertilizer management systems. 66 cooperatives have employed green biological pesticide technologies(Table 4-9).

Table 4-9 Number of cooperatives applying green production technologies

Unit: count

Project area	Organic fertilizer as a substitute for chemical fertilizers	Water-saving irrigation/ water-fertilizer integration	Green biopesticides	Return straw to the fields
Sichuan	50	44	45	26
Ningxia	25	22	21	15
Total	75	66	66	41

(4) Providing Services to Ensure Product Quality

Cooperatives provide a range of agricultural services to farmers in the surrounding areas, covering pre-production, mid-production, and post-production stages. These services help integrate various aspects of farming, livestock rearing, and processing, enabling farmers to reduce costs and increase income. Among the surveyed cooperatives, 80 cooperatives (76.2%) provide agricultural production technology services, such as pest control. 60 cooperatives provide agricultural input services, including seeds, fertilizers, pesticides and animal feed. 57 cooperatives provide services for agricultural product sales. 39 cooperatives offer machinery services, such as custom farming and harvesting. 34 cooperatives provide product processing and packaging services. Compared to 2020, cooperatives have expanded their range of services, now including product storage and transportation, 36 cooperatives provide product storage services and 32 cooperatives provide product transportation services(Figure 4-3).

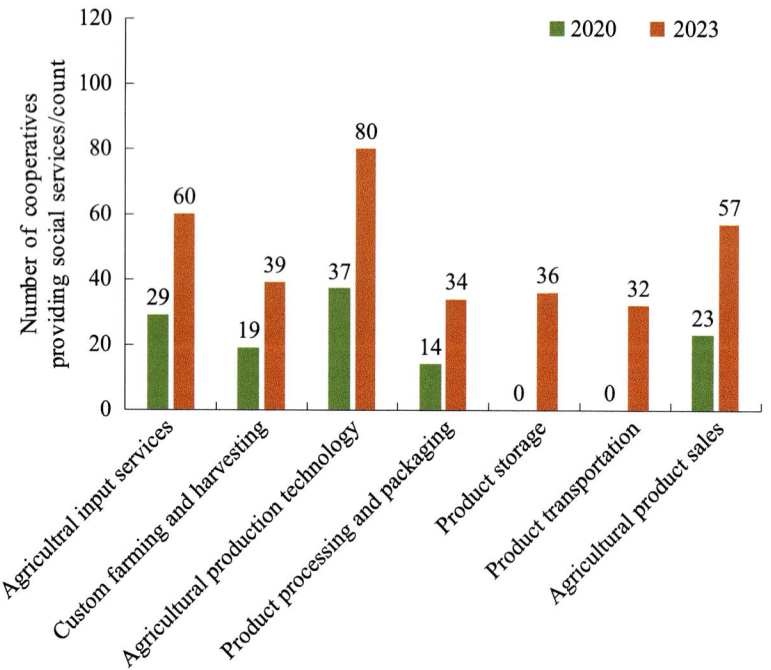

Figure 4-3　Comparison of the provision of socialized services by cooperatives

In the Sichuan project area, cooperatives primarily focus on pre-production and mid-production services, with 61.8% providing agricultural inputs, 37.1% offering custom farming and harvesting services and 82% delivering agricultural production technology support. In contrast, cooperatives in the Ningxia project area emphasize post-production services, with 25% provide product processing and packaging, 32.6 % provide storage services, 31.3% provide transportation services and 56.3% focus on product sales (Figure 4-4).

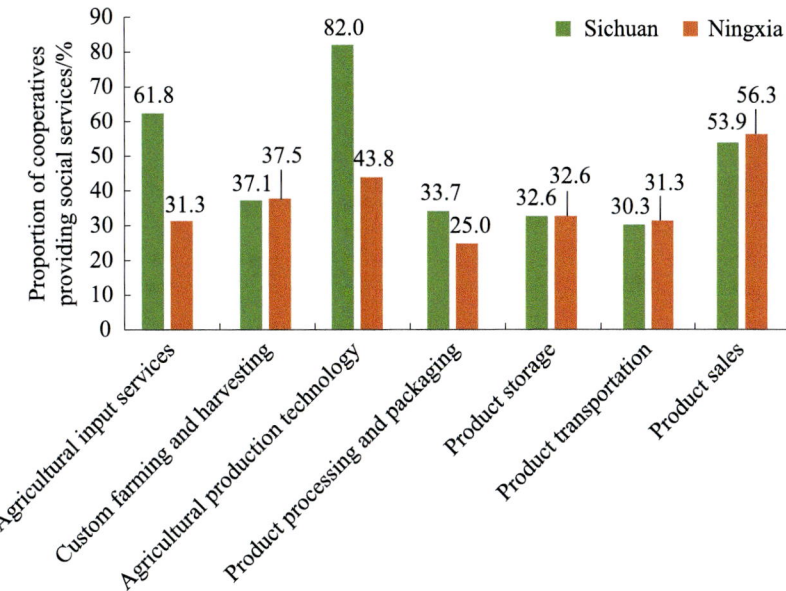

Figure 4-4   Socialisation services provided by cooperatives in different project areas

4. Effectiveness of Smallholders' Participation in Cooperatives

(1) Participation Through Land and Other Assets

Among the 426 households surveyed, 239 households (over 50%) had joined cooperatives supported by the project. Of these, 221 households (over 90%) held cooperative shares, with 63.8% contributing land as equity (Table 4-10).

Table 4-10   Farmers' membership in cooperatives   Unit: household

Project area	Land equity	Buy-in	Equity in land and capital
Sichuan	76	39	3
Ningxia	60	36	2
Total	136	75	5

(2) Participation in Training to Learn and Apply Production Techniques

Farmers actively participate in the training sessions organized by cooperatives and generally report high satisfaction with the training outcomes. Of the farmers surveyed, 231 participator had attended cooperative-led training sessions, including 223 cooperatives members. On average, farmers attend approximately three training sessions per year and perceive the training as highly beneficial(Table 4-11).

Table 4-11 Number of participants in training

Project area	Number of persons trained/person	Number of members/person	Number of training sessions/time	Effectiveness of training/point
Sichuan	123	115	4	1.6
Ningxia	108	108	2	1.2
Total	231	223	3	1.4

Note: Training effectiveness scoring of score represents: 1=very good; 2=good; 3=general; 4=poor; 5=very poor.

After attending technical training sessions, farmers actively apply green production techniques. Among the surveyed farmers, 229 households adopted green production technologies such as integrated water and fertilizer management and the use of organic fertilizers instead of chemical fertilizers. Among them, in the Sichuan project area, 187 households adopted green production technologies. In the Ningxia project area, 42 households adopted green production technologies (Table 4-12).

Table 4-12 Number and proportion of farmers adopting green production technologies

Project area	Number/household	Proportion/%
Sichuan	187	83.1
Ningxia	42	20.9
Total	229	53.7

In terms of specific technologies, 154 households adopted straw incorporation or comprehensive utilization technology, 139 households adopted organic fertilizer as a substitute for chemical fertilizers, 129 households adopted green prevention and control of pests and diseases, and 121 households adopted conservation tillage, including fallowing, crop rotation, and intercropping(Figure 4-5).

Chapter 4 Practices and Effectiveness of Cooperatives in Promoting Smallholders' Development

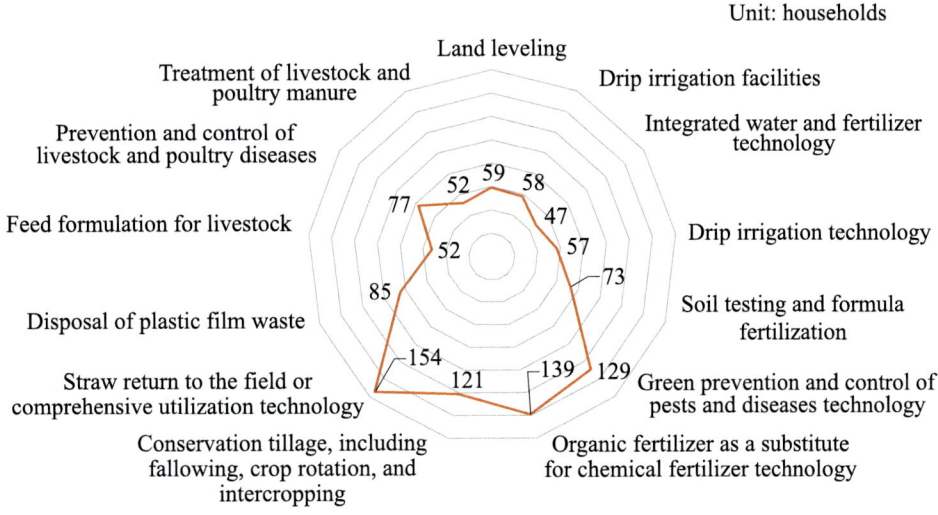

Figure 4-5 Adoption of green production technologies by farmers

(3) Adopting Cooperative Services to Promote Quality and Efficiency on Agriculture

The adoption of agricultural socialized services provided by cooperatives has effectively reduced farmers' production costs and provided strong support for the extension of the speciality industry chain and supported the extension of value chains and the expansion of industry functions for specialized agricultural products. Among the surveyed farmers, the use of cooperative-provided socialized services is widespread, with 218 households utilizing these services—98 in Sichuan and 120 in Ningxia(Table 4-13).

Table 4-13 Number and proportion of farmers adopting cooperative socialization services

Project area	Number/household	Proportion/%
Sichuan	98	43.6
Ningxia	120	59.7
Total	218	51.2

In terms of service types, the socialized services used by farmers are mainly concentrated in pre-production and mid-production services. 143 households utilized agricultural machinery services, 98 households accessed agricultural input procurement services. Post-production services are also gradually gaining traction: 64 households used storage and processing services, 26 households utilized transportation services, 23 households accessed product sales services(Figure 4-6).

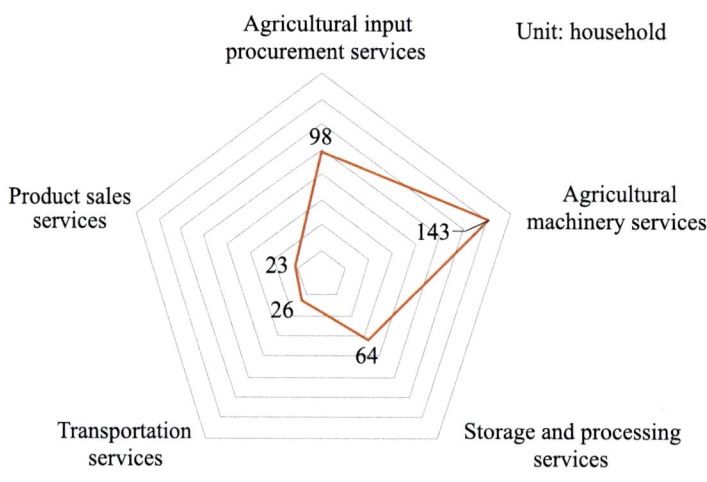

Figure 4-6 Use of cooperative social services by farmers

(4) Income Increase and Satisfaction Feedback from Smallholders

The household income of smallholders among cooperative members has shown a notable increase. According to the survey, the average annual household income for cooperative members is 59.3 thousand yuan [1], consisting of 35.5 thousand yuan from wage income, 17.5 thousand yuan from agricultural operating income, 0.3 thousand yuan from property income, and 6 thousand yuan from other income (Table 4-14, Figure 4-7). Compared to non-members, cooperative members' household income is 13.5% higher. Specifically, their wage income is 0.8% higher, while agricultural operating income is 41.2% higher. The results show that farmers can increase their income through multiple channels after joining cooperatives.

Table 4-14 Income composition of cooperative members in the project area

Unit: thousand yuan

Project area	Wage income	Agricultural operating income	Property income	Other income	Total income
Sichuan	45	13	0.3	10	68.3
Ningxia	26	22	0.3	2	50.3
Average	35.5	17.5	0.3	6	59.3

[1] Income refers to gross income. The operational income of smallholder farmers in the project area is primarily derived from agriculture. Here, only agricultural operational income is accounted for, while other income includes transfer income, income from individual businesses, and financial support from children or relatives.

Chapter 4 Practices and Effectiveness of Cooperatives in Promoting Smallholders' Development

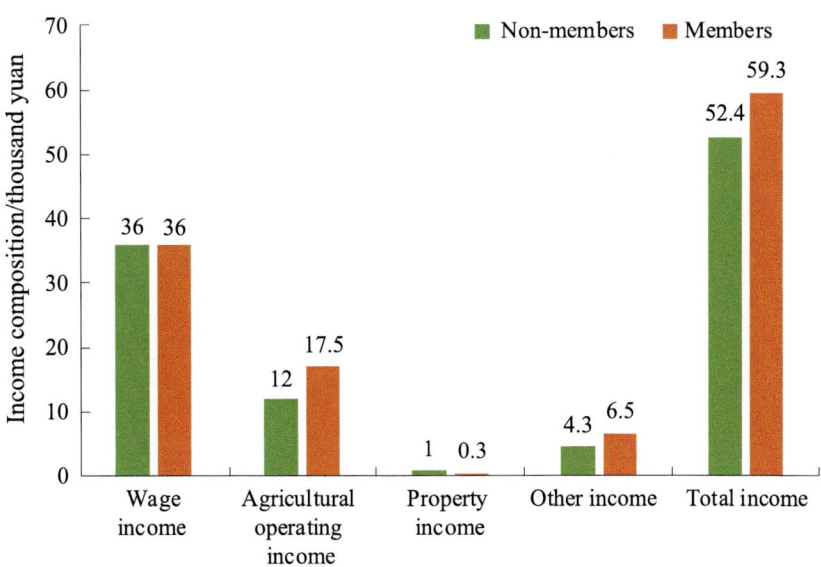

Figure 4-7   The income comparison of members and non-members of the cooperative

The income structure of cooperative members differs between the Sichuan and Ningxia project areas. In Sichuan, wage income accounts for 66.0 % of household income, while agricultural operating income contributes 18.6%. In Ningxia, wage income makes up 51.8% of household income, with agricultural operating income accounting for 43%. Within agricultural operating income, 62.9% comes from fruit planting in Sichuan, and 41% is derived from grain planting in Ningxia, and 32.1% from animal husbandry in Ningxia(Figure 4-8, Figure 4-9).

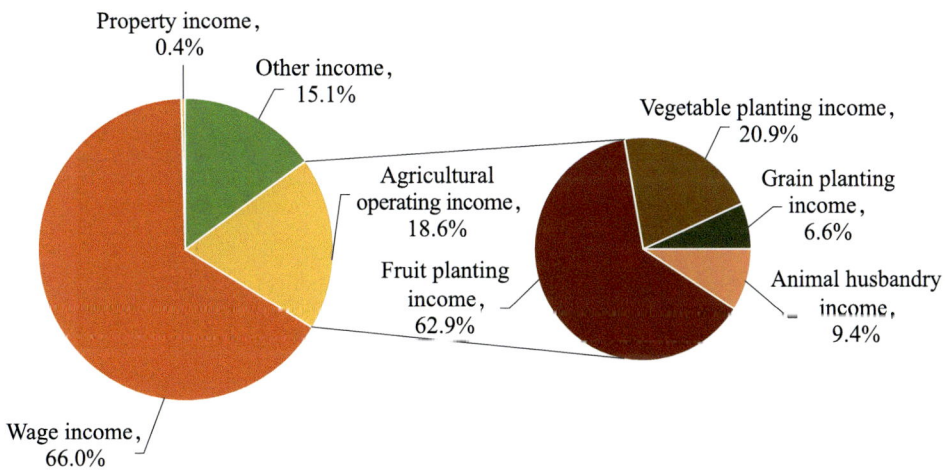

Figure 4-8   Income structure of cooperative members in the Sichuan project area, 2023

Dividend payments have become a significant source of income growth for smallholders. In 2023, five of the nine profitable cooperatives in Ningxia distributed

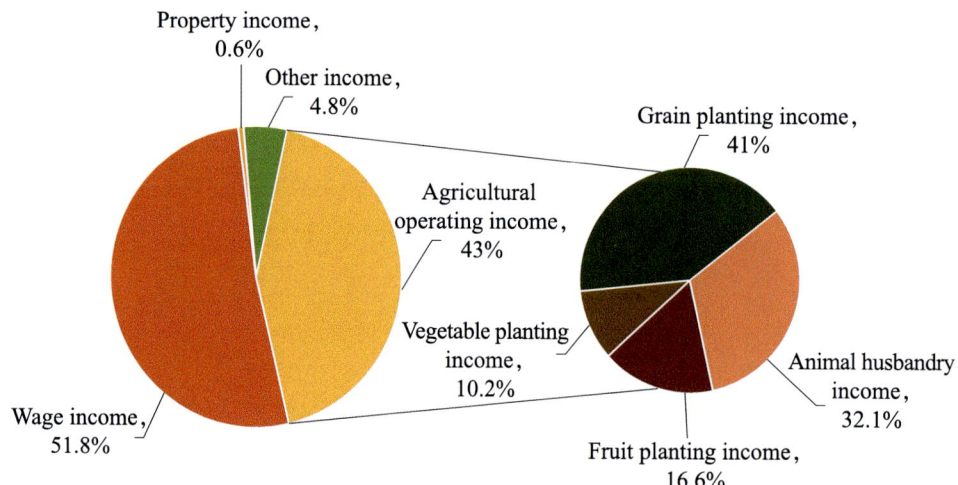

Figure 4-9 Income structure of cooperative members in the Ningxia project area, 2023

dividends to 264 households, with an average payout of CNY 446 per household, while in Sichuan, 25 out of 50 profitable cooperatives distributed dividends to 2,218 households, averaging CNY 1,556 per household.

Feedback from cooperative members underscores the diverse benefits of participation, Of the 239 member questionnaires, with 155 households identifying dividend income as the greatest advantage. Additionally, 34 households valued the employment opportunities and increased wage income provided by the cooperatives, while 32 households appreciated the chance to acquire new production techniques and gain experience in management and operations(Figure 4-10).

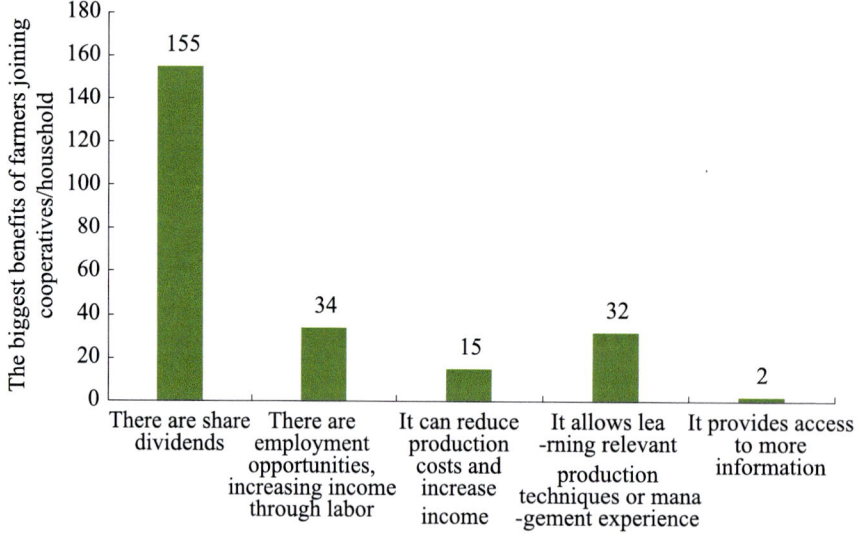

Figure 4-10 Analysis of the feedback on the benefits of cooperative members

Chapter 4 Practices and Effectiveness of Cooperatives in Promoting Smallholders' Development

Satisfaction was measured on a five-point scale, where 5 indicated "very satisfied", 4 "quite satisfied", 3 "neutral satisfied", 2 "slightly dissatisfied" and 1 "very dissatisfied". Members rated their satisfaction with skills related to prevention and control of livestock and poultry diseases, feed formulation for livestock, straw return to the field or comprehensive utilization. Conservation tillage practices, such as fallowing, crop rotation, and intercropping, are at 4.9 or higher. Satisfaction with organic fertilizer as a substitute for chemical fertilizer and drip irrigation technology above 4.5(Figure 4-11).

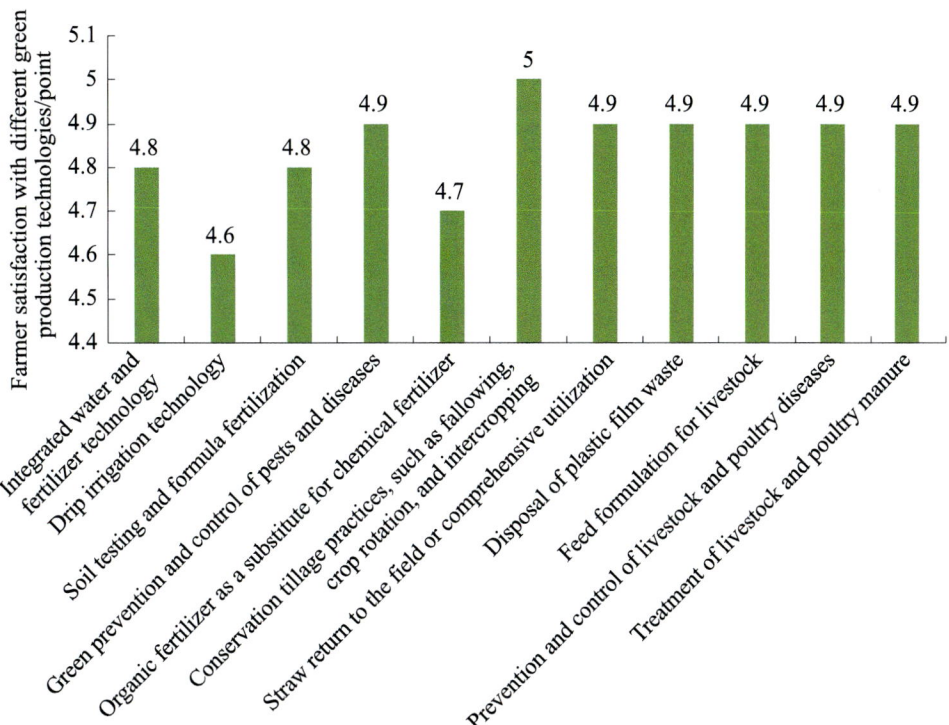

Figure 4-11 Satisfaction of cooperative members with green production techniques
Note: Satisfaction level ranges from 1 to 5, with 5 being the most satisfied, the same below.

Members were also highly satisfied with the agricultural services provided by the cooperatives. Among them, satisfaction with agricultural machinery services and agricultural input services is 4.9 points, while satisfaction with product transportation, storage and processing, and product sales services is 4.8 points(Figure 4-12).

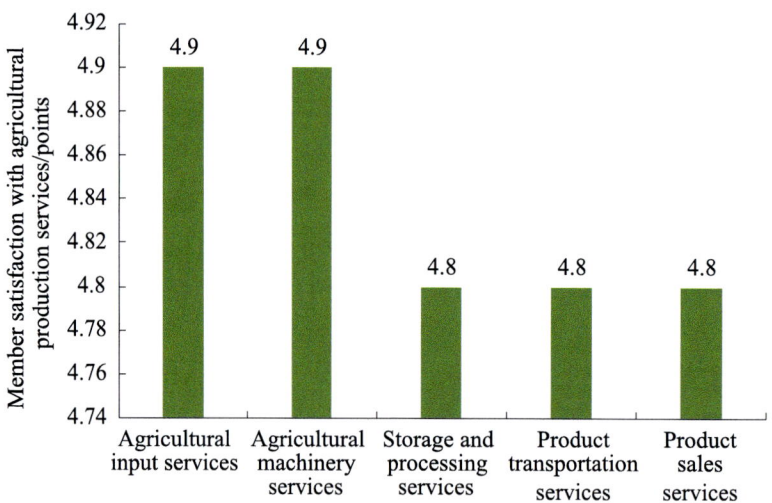

Figure 4-12 Satisfaction of cooperative members with productive agricultural services

Chapter 5 Typical Modes and Suggestions for Cooperatives Promoting Smallholders' Development

Since the project implementation, project areas have explored and developed a variety of modes to support the development of smallholders. The research team has summarized and formed five typical modes for driving the development of smallholders based on the preliminary research materials, including "Cooperatives + Smallholders", "Cooperatives + Agricultural Enterprises + Smallholders", "Village Collective + Production Base + Smallholders", "Village Collectives + Cooperatives + Production Bases + Smallholders" and "New Farmers + Smallholders". To continuously exert the influence and benefits of the project and further enhance the development capacity of smallholders, we put forward some suggestions for popularizing the operation mode of cooperatives promoting the development of smallholders.

1. Typical Modes for Promoting the Development of Smallholders

(1) The "Cooperatives + Smallholders" Mode

"Cooperatives + Smallholders" is the most direct mode for cooperatives to drive the development of smallholders. Among the 105 cooperatives surveyed, 36 cooperatives adopted this mode, accounting for 34.3%. Under this mode, the cooperatives use the funds to support their own operations, build infrastructure, and construct climate-smart production bases. In addition, they offer a range of social services to smallholders, such as processing, packaging, storage, transportation and sales. By providing these services, cooperatives also create employment opportunities for smallholders, fostering a mutually beneficial relationship that links cooperative and smallholder interests(Figure 5-1).

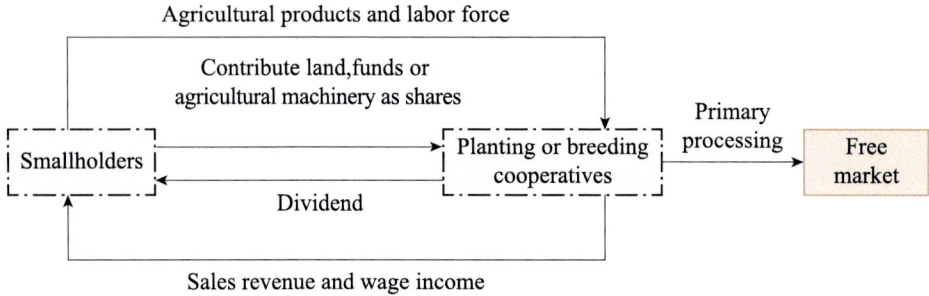

Figure 5-1 The "Cooperatives + Smallholders" mode

Under this mode, smallholders benefit mainly in two ways. Firstly, they can obtain income from the sales of agricultural products and from working for others, smallholders sell their agricultural products and provide labour to cooperatives, earning revenue from the sale and employment wages. The cooperatives assume all production and market risks. Secondly is the dividend income, smallholders can invest in the cooperative by contributing land, capital, or agricultural machinery as equity. In return, and the cooperatives follow a "sharing benefits, sharing risks" principle, distributing dividends from annual profits according to each member's share. This allows smallholders to earn additional income through their residual claim rights.

(2) The "Cooperatives + Agricultural Enterprises + Smallholders" Mode

"Cooperatives + Agricultural Enterprises + Smallholders" is a typical mode in which the cooperatives in the project drive the development of smallholders. Among the 105 cooperatives surveyed, a total of 68 cooperatives have joined forces with agricultural enterprises for development, accounting for 64.8%. Under this mode, the cooperatives sign cooperative operation contracts with enterprises and provide all-round socialized services for members before, during, and after production. This helps avoid the situation where smallholders have to "go it alone" in agricultural production and market sales, and forms an interest linkage mechanism with smallholders that features "risk, cost, and benefit sharing"(Figure 5-2).

At the production stage, the cooperatives purchase fertilizers and biopesticides from agricultural technology enterprises, which also provide regular technology guidance and training to smallholders. This support helps prevent large-scale pest outbreaks, offering a solid technical foundation for cooperative production. The training also enhances the individual skills of smallholders.

Chapter 5 Typical Modes and Suggestions for Cooperatives Promoting Smallholders' Development

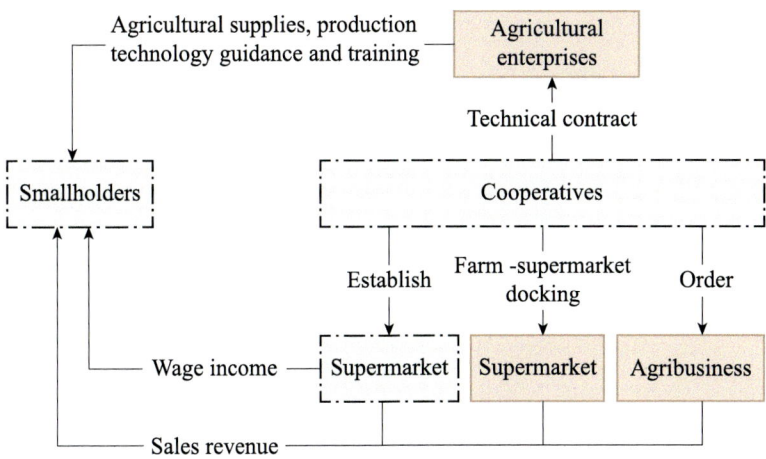

Figure 5-2 The "Cooperatives + Agricultural Enterprises + Smallholders" mode

At the sales stage, agricultural sales enterprises act as key downstream partners. Before production begins, the cooperatives sign contract farming agreements with these enterprises. The cooperatives oversee crop management and coordinates their members, while smallholders grow crops according to cooperative guidelines. The sales enterprise handles product processing, packaging, and marketing. This contract-based partnership stabilizes the cooperative's sales channels, mitigates financial losses from market fluctuations, and alleviates smallholders concerns about "unsold produce", providing them with more secure income.

A similar approach is the "Cooperatives + Supermarkets + Smallholders" mode. If the cooperative's agricultural products meet supermarket standards, such as pesticide residue testing, they can directly supply supermarkets. Supermarkets delegate production to cooperatives, share their product standards, and cooperatives produce goods that are standardized, high-quality, and safe. Supermarkets purchase qualified products directly from the cooperatives, reducing intermediary steps between the farm and the retail shelf, thus ensuring a seamless connection between the "farm" and the "consumer's basket." Given the seasonal nature products like vegetables, cooperatives and supermarkets maintain close communication to monitor production conditions and align with market demands. This direct connection eliminates middlemen, increases smallholders' earnings, and contributes to balanced urban-rural development.

Some cooperatives have also used project funds to establish their own supermarkets, equipped with sorting systems and diversified sales channels, such as online platforms, community direct sales, and express delivery services. Consumers can purchase products in-store or place online orders for home delivery. This mode ensures comprehensive coverage from production bases to retail outlets and home delivery, benefiting local consumers and providing additional employment opportunities for smallholders.

(3) The "Village Collective + Production Base + Smallholders" Mode

This mode refers to the village collective using project support funds to develop production bases for special industries. Successful implementation relies on village leaders with strong management skills to coordinate various stakeholders, organize and mobilize smallholders, and leverage local resources to develop special industries. Some planting and breeding experts in the village collective are restricted by the limited land area, making it difficult for them to expand their production scale. The construction of the production base provides them with the conditions to expand production. Large-scale planters can lease the land of the production base to expand their production and operation scale and boost their enthusiasm for production. For skilled farmers who face limitations due to insufficient land, the establishment of a production base offers greater production opportunities. Large-scale farmers can lease land from the production base to expand their operations, further motivating them to scale up their activities(Figure 5-3).

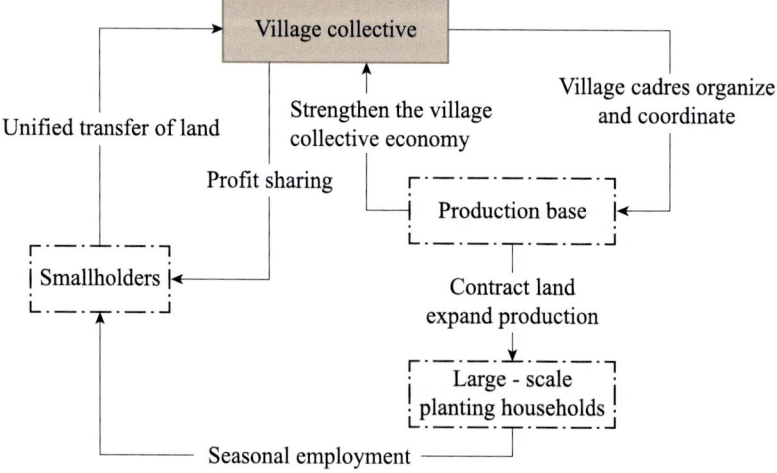

Figure 5-3 The "Village Collective + Production Base + Smallholders" mode

Smallholders collectively transfer their land to the village collective in a unified manner and work at the production base. The development of the production base creates more collective economic benefits for the village collective. The village collective and smallholders become an interest-related entity. Smallholders provide labor to ensure the normal operation of the production base, and the profit dividends from the production base and the wages from working there increase the income of smallholders.

(4) The "Village Collectives + Cooperatives + Production Bases + Smallholders" Mode

This mode is typically driven by skilled individuals or village leaders. The village collective, often through a land service cooperative, consolidates fragmented land parcels from smallholders by leasing their contracted land and integrating it into a unified production area, and then establishing specialized planting or breeding cooperatives to further develop characteristic industries(Figure 5-4).

After receiving project support, the village collective cooperatives expanded the existing production bases with the support funds. Smallholders can join these cooperatives by contributing land, capital, or skills, ensuring their active participation in production. The cooperative oversees and manages every stage of production and collaborates with agricultural enterprises to provide marketing and sales services. This reduces transaction costs and market risks for smallholders, ensuring stable income and fostering local development.

Cooperatives led by village collectives should focus more on leveraging the collective's strengths in resource integration and organizational coordination, and the whole village makes use of the production bases to develop characteristic industries, mainly focusing on the development of large-scale operations. In rural China, social relationships heavily influence whether smallholders join cooperatives, and village leaders play a crucial role in encouraging participation. The role of village collectives has evolved from merely acting as a bridge between smallholder and the government to guiding smallholder in agricultural production and business activities, while still maintaining their autonomy in managing their own operations.

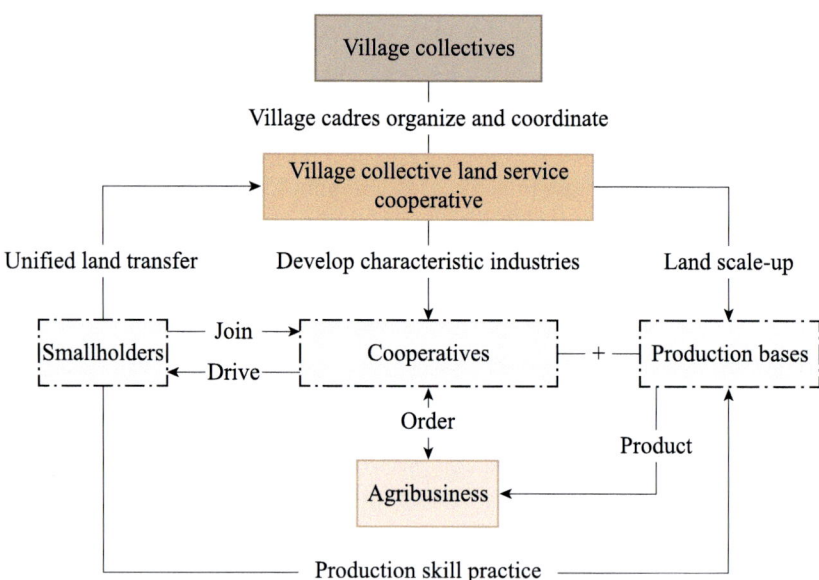

Figure 5-4　The "Village Collective + Cooperatives + Production Base + Smallholders" mode

(5) The "New Farmers + Smallholders" Mode

The "New Farmers + Smallholders" mode is a new driving mode explored and formed during the project implementation. Among the 105 cooperatives surveyed, 43 cooperatives adopted this mode, accounting for 40.9%. Under this mode, the members of the cooperative council are young people who returned to their hometowns to start businesses and are also the initiators and leaders of the cooperatives. They possess higher education levels, strong organizational and management skills, extensive social networks, and industry resources. This mode makes the management of cooperatives relatively standardized, through the implementation of robust internal governance systems—such as *cooperative charters* and *member representative assembly regulations*, cooperatives clearly define member equity, establish profit distribution plans, and ensure all members benefit directly through dividend payouts and labour income. Some cooperatives even offer special dividends to formerly registered impoverished members(Figure 5-5).

In the project area, new farmers use cooperatives to develop regional speciality industries and integrate smallholders into the value chain of these industries. For example, one group of new farmers, with abundant human and financial capital, excels at combining agriculture with other industries, creating diverse and open cooperative business modes.

They may establish partnerships with supermarkets, provide supply services to institutional canteens, or develop agritourism to attract visitors for leisure and consumption. By diversifying operations, these new farmers have improved the comprehensive benefits of the cooperatives while creating additional employment opportunities for local smallholders.

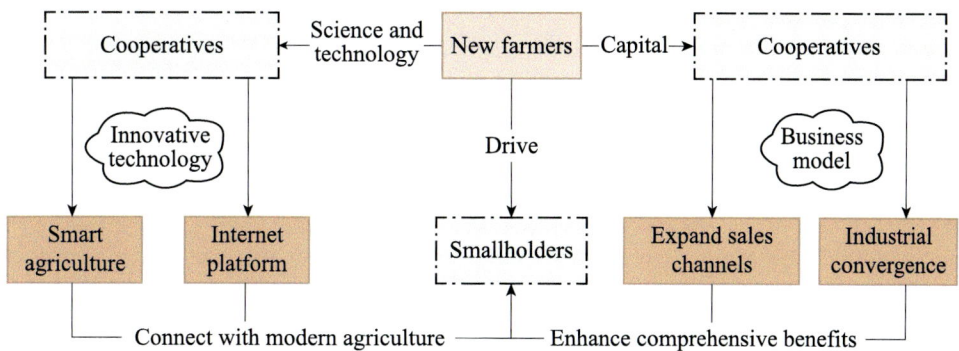

Figure 5-5 The "New Farmers + Smallholders" mode

Another group of new farmers focuses on agricultural technology. By integrating digital technologies such as the internet, artificial intelligence, and cloud computing, new farmers enhance the productivity and efficiency of cooperatives. Examples include establishing smart agricultural parks powered by 5G communication technology, incorporating automation into agricultural production, and using e-commerce platforms or social media channels like WeChat to market agricultural products and boost brand visibility. These tech-driven new farmers promote high-quality, sustainable agricultural development, enhance smallholders' capacity to adopt modern technologies, and facilitate the integration of smallholders into modern agricultural practices.

2. Suggestions for Modes of Application and Promoting Smallholders' Development

The above-mentioned modes have established relatively close mechanisms for connecting the interests of smallholders, achieving significant results, promoting employment and increasing income for smallholders, and playing an important role in smallholder development. At the same time, the research also revealed that cooperatives still have room for improvement in areas such as management standardization, brand building, and profitability, and there are opportunities to optimize the linkage of smallholder interests and benefit distribution.

(1) Strengthen the Standardized Management of Cooperatives to Promote High-Quality Development

Improving the standardization level of farmer cooperatives is crucial to achieving high-quality development. In 2019, the Central Agricultural Office, together with 11 other departments, issued the Several Opinions on Promoting the Standardization and Improvement of Farmer Cooperatives ([2019] No. 18), proposing to improve the cooperatives' standardization from aspects such as organizational structure and financial management. The cooperatives supported by this project were selected through a business plan bidding process, and their management is relatively standardized. However, survey data shows that 35.2% of cooperatives do not have full-time accountants, and most business plans are entrusted to third-party entities; only 60% of cooperatives can independently complete their business plans.

Standardized cooperatives can ensure operational stability and sustainability, reduce operational risks, and improve operational efficiency. Therefore, it is recommended that cooperatives should further standardize their management:

Establish and improve internal management systems, including financial management, production management, and marketing management, ensuring the execution and supervision of these systems.

Improve organizational structure, clarify the responsibilities and authorities of each department, and establish a scientific and reasonable decision-making mechanism to ensure the scientific and democratic nature of decisions.

Improve the protection of cooperative member accounts. The primary interest of ordinary members lies in the distribution of surplus profits, and it is necessary to accurately record members' actual contributions and transaction volumes. Any financial subsidies that the cooperative can receive from public fiscal projects must be quantified into each member's account. Establishing a complete member account system is key to ensuring legal and regulated distribution of surplus profits.

Strengthen talent training and introduction to improve the professional quality and management abilities of employees, thus ensuring the talent supply for the cooperative's

Chapter 5 Typical Modes and Suggestions for Cooperatives Promoting Smallholders' Development

standardized development.

(2) Increase Policy Support and Enhance the Service Capability of Cooperatives

The provision of agricultural socialized services is an important means for cooperatives to drive the development of smallholders. The research found that the agricultural production services provided by project-supported cooperatives were mostly concentrated in the pre-production phase. Only 34 cooperatives offered post-production services such as processing and packaging, while 36 cooperatives offered product storage services, and 32 cooperatives provided product transportation services.

Therefore, it is recommended to enhance the service capabilities of cooperatives through policy guidance, financial support, and other measures:

The government should formulate scientific and reasonable policies to create a favorable external environment for the development of cooperatives. For example, offering tax incentives, financial subsidies, and other policy supports, increasing financial support for cooperatives, establishing a public service system for cooperative development, and strengthening publicity and promotion for cooperatives to effectively stimulate their innovative vitality, improve their independent development capabilities, and promote high-quality development.

The government should establish a sound regulatory mechanism to ensure the implementation and supervision of policies, and take strict measures against cooperatives that violate laws, regulations, and policies, thus maintaining a fair and competitive market environment. Through government guidance, support, and regulation, the government can promote the high-quality development of farmer cooperatives, facilitate the transformation and upgrading of agricultural industries, and ensure continued income growth for farmers.

(3) Improve the Interest-Linked Mechanism to Stimulate the Endogenous Motivation of Cooperatives in Driving Smallholders

The original intention of establishing cooperatives is to achieve win-win cooperation and joint development with local smallholders. Therefore, cooperatives should not only aim to achieve their own high-quality development but also prioritize strengthening the interest-linked mechanism with smallholders and expanding their demonstration role. The cooperatives in the project areas have already made initial improvements in establishing a "shared risk, cost, and benefit" interest link across the entire industry chain. The survey found that 29 of the supported cooperatives (27.6%) provided dividends, primarily based on land shareholding with a guaranteed minimum dividend. Secondary dividends are rare, and smallholders receive dividends of around 1,000 yuan.

Thus, a long-term mechanism of "tight connection, steady lead, and lasting benefits" needs to be constructed to strengthen cooperatives' ability to drive smallholder development:

Establish stable, transparent, and consistent interest relationships with aligned rights and responsibilities. Although cooperative council members or major shareholders have invested capital, their rights and responsibilities must align. Through the improvement of member accounts, the ownership structure of the cooperative should be clarified, ensuring that the relationships between council members and smallholders are clear. At the same time, smallholders need to actively participate in the cooperative's management to gain more decision-making rights.

Properly manage benefit distribution. Encourage the use of order contracts, ensure the strict fulfillment of contract terms, and flexibly adjust plans as needed. Provide compensation to the party suffering from a loss to ensure that overall rights and interests are not harmed, thus enhancing willingness to cooperation.

Increase policy incentives to ensure long-term benefits, linking the cooperative's success in driving smallholders with evaluations, awards, etc. Policies should offer preferential support based on the number of smallholders driven by the cooperative and the amount of dividend income, enhancing the demonstrative and leading role.

(4) Encourage the Agro-industry Integration of Cooperatives to Improve the Comprehensive Driving Capability

In the past decade, the Party Central Committee has attached great importance to the collaborative development of cooperatives, agriculture, and farmers' income, especially since the implementation of the rural revitalization strategy. The country has shifted the focus from agricultural industrialization development to the comprehensive development of rural areas, using cooperatives as an organizational platform to promote the integration of primary, secondary, and tertiary industries in rural areas. Some cooperatives in this project have already joined forces with enterprises and other business entities to drive the development of smallholders while promoting agro-industry development.

Therefore, it is recommended to further enhance the driving ability of cooperatives and improve the overall driving level:

While encouraging individual cooperatives to play their role, actively guide cooperatives to integrate with other new business entities. Following the new development concepts of openness, integration, and sharing, cooperatives should use agro-industry development as a bridge to build a diverse, complementary, and collaborative sharing mechanism. Explore and establish a development mode featuring "Enterprise + Cooperative + Family Farm + Base + Smallholder" with local characteristics.

Actively explore modes such as cooperative federations, agricultural enterprise associations, and agro-industry joint ventures, allowing different actors along the agro-industry chain to cooperate, share, and interconnect. This will form a more tightly-knit and stable new organizational alliance — an agricultural industrialization joint body that will serve as both a community of interests and a community of shared destiny, thus enhancing the comprehensive driving capability.

Part Ⅱ　Case Study

Since the implementation of the project, a total of 119 cooperatives have been supported. According to the implementation content of the project, the research group has carried out follow-up investigations and special investigations for many times, has collected the production and operation of the cooperatives and the agro-industry development of the cooperatives, and summarized the main practices and progress of the development of the cooperatives to drive smallholders. Combined with the agro-industry characteristics of the project areas in Sichuan and Ningxia, the experience, practice and operation mode of a number of planting, breeding, the combination of planting and breeding, agricultural socialization service and agro-industry integration cooperatives which drive smallholders were studied and formed. Now, 25 cases are selected as typical cases, and the main types are listed as follows:

No.	Agro-industry type	Specific industry	Cooperative / base name
1	Planting	Grains and oils	Guigang Planting Professional Cooperative in Xuanhan
2			Xinxing Land Stock Professional Cooperative in Yuanzhou
3		Vegetables	Gaochengshan Vegetable Professional Cooperative in Cangxi
4			Zhou Fugui Day Lily Planting Professional Cooperative in Hongsibu
5		Fruits	Wufu Kiwi Fruit Professional Cooperative in Cangxi
6			Fenghuotai Apple Planting Cooperative in Litong
7		Chinese medicinal materials	Yonghe Taoyuan Gastrodia Elata Chinese Medicinal Materials Professional Cooperative in Cangxi
8			Shoukouyan Planting Professional Cooperative in Xuanhan
9		Tea	Gongyi Tea Professional Cooperative in Xuzhou
10			Jiahe Planting Professional Cooperative in Xuanhan
11		Edible mushrooms	Maoyuan Planting Farmers' Professional Cooperative in Yilong
12	Breeding	Cattle	Yinong Breeding Demonstration Base in Zhonghe Village in Yuanzhou
13			Shanniuyuan Beef Cattle Science and Technology Breeding Professional Cooperative in Pengyang

(continue)

No.	Agro-industry type	Specific industry	Cooperative / base name
14	Breeding	Sheep	Xiangyuan Village Mutton Sheep Breeding Base in Hongsibu
15			Shuitao Village Breeding Base in Hongsibu
16		Chickens	Hongke Farmers' Breeding Professional Cooperative in Yuanzhou
17			Liupanshan Ecological Breeding Professional Cooperative in Yuanzhou
18		Pigs	Fengtai Breeding Farmers' Professional Cooperative in Yilong
19			Jiangxin Ecological Breeding Professional Cooperative in Xuanhan
20	The combination of planting and breeding		Shunying Silkworm Breeding Professional Cooperative in Xuzhou
21	Agricultural socialization service		Jinyongfeng Agricultural Machinery Service Professional Cooperative in Cangxi
22			Wuzhong Haizhifeng Planting Farmers' Professional Cooperative in Litong
23	Agro-industry integration		Yongqi Planting and Breeding Farmers' Professional Cooperative in Yilong
24			Chushannonggu Planting and Breeding Professional Cooperative in Guangan
25			Yueyinong Agronomic Professional Cooperative in Yinchuan

1. Guigang Planting Professional Cooperative in Xuanhan

(1) Basic Information

Guigang Planting Professional Cooperative was established on 23 April 2013, located in Mingyue Community, Juntang Town, Xuanhan County, Sichuan Province. It is mainly engaged in high-quality green rice planting, processing and sales services, with registered capital of CNY 2.3 million. The cooperative has 65 member households, who contribute land and funds as equity shares. The cooperative collectively manages 359 mu of land and assets valued at CNY 1.22 million, with the chairman holding a 26.1% equity stake following share quantification. In 2021, the cooperative received project support, enabling the purchase of equipment such as rice transplanters, transport vehicles, polishing machines, color sorting machines, and packaging machines. Guigang planting professional cooperative production base is shown in Figure 1.

Figure 1   Guigang Planting Professional Cooperative production base

(2) Main Practices

Firstly is mechanised production to reduce costs. The cooperative uses the support funds to actively introduce a series of advanced agricultural machinery and equipment(Figure 2).

By the end of 2023, the cooperative had 15 pieces of agricultural machinery equipment such as tractors, rice transplanters and plant protection drones, realizing the full mechanization of "tillage, planting, management, harvesting and drying" of grain and oil crops. This mode not only reduces the operational costs but also increases the yield and adds value of agricultural products.

Figure 2　Processing equipment of Guigang Planting Professional Cooperative

Secondly is to provide social services. In 2021, the cooperative had only three agricultural machinery tools, unable to process agricultural products. By 2023, using project support funds, it procured additional equipment to offer agricultural processing services(Figure 3). These services are extended to surrounding smalloloders at rates of CNY 150 per mu for ploughing and CNY 120 per mu for harvesting. Currently, 40 farming smallholders utilize these outsourced ploughing and harvesting services.

Figure 3　Guigang Planting Professional Cooperative agricultural machinery is harvesting

Thirdly is to explore the order of agriculture, stable sales channels. The cooperative signed an order contract with Xuanhan County Osmanthus Rice Industry Co., Ltd., including rice planting varieties, planting scale, purchase price, etc. The cooperative formulates the planting plan for the next year according to the order requirements, and grows rice in the base by unifying production means, agricultural machinery and tools, and chemical fertilizers and pesticides to realize standardized production and large-scale operation. After the harvest, Xuanhan County Osmanthus Rice Co., Ltd. according to the order agreed to purchase rice. In order to standardize production, the cooperative also actively holds technical training courses, training a total of 40 individuals in 2023. Driving mode of Guigang Planting Professional Cooperative is shown in Figure 4.

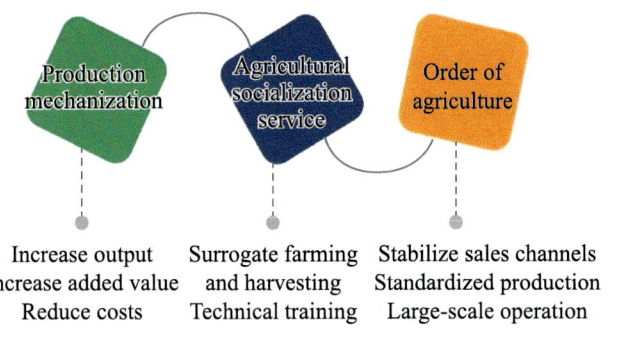

Figure 4   Driving mode of Guigang Planting Professional Cooperative

(3) Effectiveness

In 2023, the cooperative has an annual output of 360 tons of rice, with a sales volume of CNY 1.4526 million. The cooperative product sales and socialized services obtained a total surplus of more than CNY 660 thousand, and CNY 460 thousand, accounting for 69.7% of the surplus, for income dividends. In addition, the cooperative provides more employment opportunities for the surrounding smallholders, promoting employment for 45 people, including 40 temporary jobs and 5 long-term jobs. The salary standard of the cooperative is 110 CNY / day for daily management and 300 CNY / day for the agricultural machinery master. Through project support, the cooperative can enhance its self-development and promote the development of local rural economy.

2. Xinxing Land Stock Professional Cooperative in Yuanzhou

(1) Basic Information

Xinxing Land Stock Professional Cooperative was established on 2 April 2016, located in Pengbao Village, Pengbao Town, Yuanzhou District, Guyuan City. The cooperative is mainly engaged in planting, acquisition, processing and packaging of small grains(Figure 5), with a capital amount of 3 million yuan. The cooperative has 68 members, and the members invest in the cooperative with land and funds. After the share quantification, the chairman holds 8.9% of the shares. In 2022, the cooperative received project support, mainly for infrastructure construction, purchase of processing equipment, strengthening member training and technical guidance.

Figure 5　Products of Xinxing Land Stock Professional Cooperative

(2) Main Practices

Firstly, purchasing production and service equipment. The cooperative has utilized project funds to build 440 square meters of small coarse grain standardized processing workshop, 80 square meters of bran dust removal workshop, and a 300 square meters hardened processing yard. Additionally, it has purchased one set of minor grain processing equipment and a belt conveyor(Figure 6). The cooperative land is managed by household, offering an integrated service chain that includes agricultural inputs, technical support, mechanical harvesting, centralized processing, and contract sales. During the harvest season, the small grains planted by surrounding smallholders were purchased for unified packaging and sales. At the same time, it has solved problems such as grain drying and storage for smallholders.

Figure 6   Equipment of Xinxing Land Stock Professional Cooperative

Secondly, to conduct new varieties test, improve product quality, to build their own brand value. The cooperative makes full use of the superior natural resource conditions such as fertile land, selenium-rich soil, large temperature difference between day and night, relatively long sunshine, and no agro-industry pollution. Every year, it uses 100 mu of land to introduce experiments and demonstration of new varieties, mainly testing and demonstrating more than 40 varieties such as Jingu and Zhangzagu, and radiating large households to plant more than 9,000 mu of millet. After introducing new varieties, the cooperative conducted repeated experiments, research and planting, the yield of small grains was high, good quality and high sales, most of them were sold to Shanxi, Heilongjiang, Hebei of China, and even exported to Japan, the Republic of Korea and Russia. The cooperative chose green organic fertilizer, selenium-rich fertilizer and slow-release fertilizer for soil conservation, and then used formula fertilization to provide nutrition to the seedlings. Through reducing the amount of pesticide application, increase the amount of organic fertilizer or farm fertilizer in the production link, improve the quality of products, conform to peoples's safe and healthy consumption concept, create green product brand, improve product value. Harvest of Xinxing land stock professional cooperative is shown in Figure 7.

Figure 7   Harvest of Xinxing Land Stock Professional Cooperative

Thirdly, to conduct planting technology training for members and smallholders to promote the employment of local smallholders(Figure 8). The cooperative carries out more than two technical training sessions every year, training 150 people in planting and breeding, and also enhances the confidence of surrounding smallholders in planting small grains. For households that have shaken off poverty and smallholders who are unable to engage in heavy physical labor, the cooperative provides job opportunities. Driving mode of Xinxing Land Stock Professional Cooperative is shown in Figure 9.

Figure 8   Training of Xinxing Land Stock Professional Cooperative

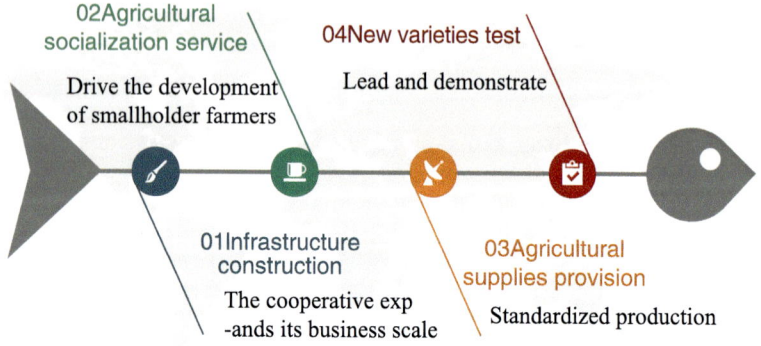

Figure 9   Driving mode of Xinxing Land Stock Professional Cooperative

(3) Effectiveness

The cooperative has built e-commerce platforms and websites to carry out farmer training, management software and green certification of products. Xinxing Land Stock Professional Cooperative has become a mode base of small grain in mountainous area of southern Ningxia, but also an advanced mode of successful land shareholding reform.

3. Gaochengshan Vegetable Professional Cooperative in Cangxi

(1) Basic Information

Gaochengshan Vegetable Professional Cooperative was established on 28 October 2013, located in Gaofeng Village, Dongqing Town, Cangxi County. The cooperative is mainly engaged in vegetable planting, sales and other services, with a capital amount of CNY 3.2 million. The cooperative has 60 members, members of whom join the cooperative with land and funds, with a total of 243 mu of land and CNY 220,000 in capital contributions. After the quantification of land and funds, the chairman holds 15.8% of the shares. Cooperative production base agricultural products have passed the pollution-free agricultural products certification, certification area of 3,000 mu. Most of the members of the cooperative are smallholders, with limited investment ability, and the education level is not high, and the knowledge of planting, processing and marketing is insufficient. The development of cooperatives themselves is limited by the lack of sorting, processing, refrigeration and other facilities and equipment. In 2021, the cooperative received project support, and the support funds were mainly used to purchase vegetable grading, refrigeration and preservation facilities, as well as professional knowledge training and technical support(Figure 10).

Figure 10　The factory building of Gaochengshan Vegetable Professional Cooperative

(2) Main Practices

Firstly, to sign contracts with smallholders. The cooperative establishes a stable cooperative relationship with smallholders by signing contracts. This mode not only guarantees the supply of the products of the cooperatives, but also provides the stable sales channels and price guarantee for the smallholders, and reduces the market risks. At the same time, cooperatives also flexibly adjust the content and quantity of contracts according to the market demand and the actual situation of smallholders to promote the sustainable development of agricultural production.

Secondly, to unify the supply of agricultural supplies. The cooperative shall organize the supply of seeds, seedlings, fertilizers and other agricultural materials uniformly according to the needs of the planted vegetable varieties, and settle the accounts with smallholders at the cost price. This greatly reduces the production cost of smallholders, so that smallholders can obtain high-quality agricultural products at more favorable prices, so as to improve the production efficiency of smallholders.

Thirdly, to provide agricultural machinery services. The cooperative provides agricultural machinery services for smallholders, including land preparation, field management, etc., effectively reducing smallholder labor input and reducing production costs. The charging standards of agricultural machinery services is lower than the market price, and the cost of land preparation is 80 CNY / mu, which enables more smallholders to enjoy modern agricultural production services.

Fourth, to build modern agricultural facilities. With the support of the project, the cooperative installed drip irrigation system, built a new sorting center and refrigerated storage, purchased cold chain logistics vehicles and other modern agricultural facilities (Figure 11). The construction of these facilities not only improves the processing and storage capacity of the cooperatives themselves, but also indirectly drives

Figure 11　The refrigerated transport vehicle of Gaochengshan Vegetable Professional Cooperative

the production of smallholders to the standardization and modernization through unified standards and services.

Fifth, professional knowledge training and technical support. In the critical period of vegetable planting and management, the cooperative organizes experts to conduct technical training, not only for the internal members of the cooperative, but also actively invites smallholders who sign orders with the cooperative to participate, and even welcomes surrounding smallholders to participate. These training activities have significantly improved smallholder planting skills and management level, laying a solid foundation for improving the yield and quality of agricultural products. Driving mode of Gaochenshan vegetable professional cooperative is shown in Figure 12.

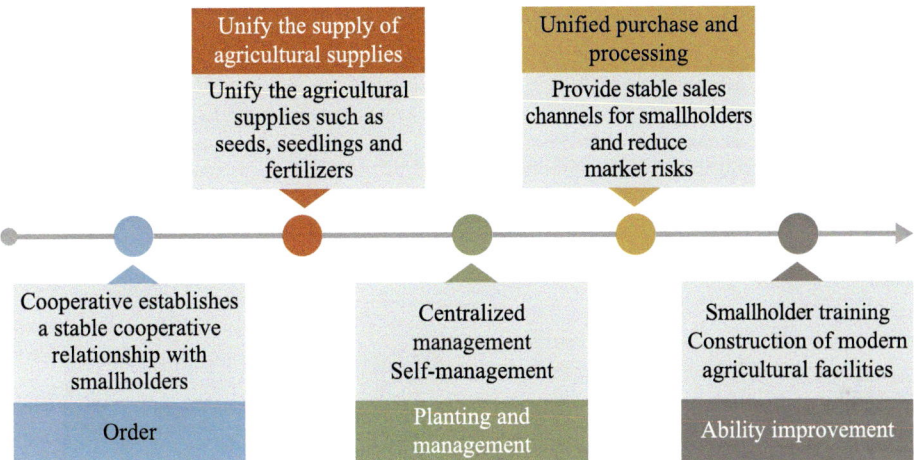

Figure 12　Driving mode of Gaochengshan Vegetable Professional Cooperative

(3) Effectiveness

With the support of the project, Gaochengshan vegetable professional cooperative has achieved remarkable results. Through infrastructure construction, the cooperative has solved bottlenecks such as product processing and storage. By giving priority to absorbing and taking care of the original poor households and other vulnerable groups, the cooperative can promote the common development of the surrounding smallholders. In 2023, more than 1,500 households received training organized by cooperatives. Through the unified supply of production materials and production technology training in key links, the cooperative brought advanced production technology and management requirements into the field production process, so as to ensure the quality and output of agricultural products and ensure the income of smallholders. By improving the level of land preparation and field management quality, smallholders labor input and production costs can be reduced. At present, the cooperative agricultural machinery service members and surrounding smallholders are more than 1,000.

4. Zhou Fugui Day Lily Planting Professional Cooperative in Hongsibu

(1) Basic Information

Zhou Fugui Day Lily Planting Professional Cooperative was established on 10 August 2016, located in Zhoucun Group, Zhoucun Village, Taiyangshan Town, Hongsibu District, Wuzhong City. The cooperative is mainly engaged in the planting(Figure 13), processing and sales of day lily, with a capital amount of CNY 1.5 million. The cooperative has 60 members, members of whom join the cooperative with land, with a total of 1,147.8 mu of land. After the share quantification, the chairman holds 30.5% of the shares. In 2022, the cooperative received project support, and invested the supported funds in warehouse, the hardening of the drying space and member training.

Figure 13 Products of Zhou Fugui Day Lily Planting Professional Cooperative

(2) Main Practices

Firstly, the cooperative expanded the air-drying site. Before the project support, the day lilies drying space of the cooperative was insufficient, and the fresh vegetables in the peak season would be mildew and rot without drying in time, which affected the quality of dried day lilies and the economic benefits of planting. After the support of the project, the cooperative expanded the warehouse(Figure 14) and hardened the drying site, expanded the production scale of the cooperative, solved the problem of day lily drying, and improved the enthusiasm of members to plant day lily.

Figure 14　Warehouse of Zhou Fugui Day Lily Planting Professional Cooperative

Secondly, training to improve the ability of smallholders, combining theory with practice. Before the project support, most of smallholders continued the traditional experience and practices in the planting and production of day lily, lack of scientific breeding experience, high-quality field management, accurate measurement of fertilization, reasonable water and fertilizer standards, safe and effective pest control technology and appropriate temperature and time control. After the project support, the cooperative entrusted the Yucai Agricultural Skills Training School of Yuanzhou District of Guyuan City to conduct two training courses to learn the theoretical knowledge of rural revitalization strategy, smallholders literacy and modern life, the establishment of cooperatives, standardized operation of cooperatives, agricultural production and management and high-yield cultivation techniques of day lily(Figure 15).

Figure 15　Classroom theoretical knowledge training and field classroom training

4. Zhou Fugui Day Lily Planting Professional Cooperative in Hongsibu

In the training process, field classes were carried out to teach smallholders the technical procedures of day lily, drying procedures of day lily, unified control and control of day lily, unified fertilization and field management of day lily. In order to consolidate the knowledge of the members, the cooperative compiled the training materials into a book for their follow-up study(Figure 16).

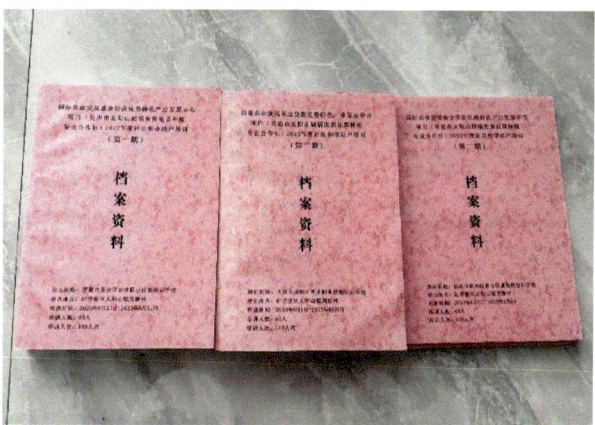

Figure 16 Training materials compiled by Zhou Fugui Day Lily Planting Professional Cooperative

Thirdly, to provide temporary jobs to promote the surrounding smallholders. During the summer vacation, nearby college students participated in temporary jobs in the cooperative to earn tuition fees. In the day lily picking and other links, the cooperative created 102 temporary positions. At present, there are 15 packaging workers in the cooperative. Smallholders can get CNY 2.2 for a box of day lilies, and smallholders can get up to CNY 240 a day(Figure 17), Driving mode of Zhou Fugui Day Lily Planting Professional Cooperative is shown in Figure 18.

Figure 17 Smallholders are working

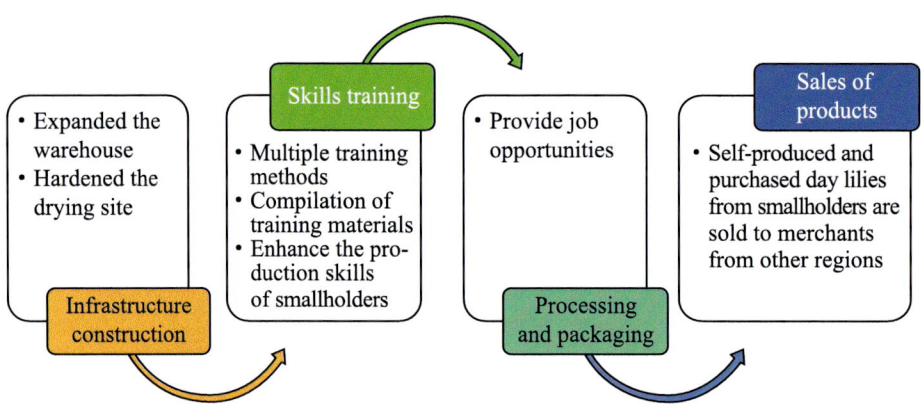

Figure 18　Driving mode of Zhou Fugui Day Lily Planting Professional Cooperatives

(3) Effectiveness

Since the support of the project, the cooperative has trained a total of 120 members and provided collection and sales services for 33 members. In 2023, it distributed nearly CNY 17,000 in dividends, with an average of CNY 320 per household. In 2024, the cooperative independently produced 22 tons of dried day lily and acquired 11 tons of dried day lily, with a total sale of CNY 1.9 million, of which CNY 1.15 million was produced and sold independently and CNY 750 thousand on commission. Packaging workshop of Zhou Fugui Day Lily Planting Professional Cooperative is shown in Figure 19.

Figure 19　Packaging workshop of Zhou Fugui Day Lily Planting Professional Cooperative

5. Wufu Kiwi Fruit Professional Cooperative in Cangxi

(1) Basic Information

Wufu Kiwi Fruit Professional Cooperative was established on 30 August 2012 in Wufu Village, Tingzi Town, Cangxi County. It was initiated by five local farming households with registered capital of CNY 558,000, mainly engaged in kiwi planting, sales and other services. The cooperative has 50 members, pooling 186 mu of land. The chairman holds 18.8% of the shares. In 2021, the cooperative was supported by the agricultural development fund, which was invested in production infrastructure, processing, storage equipment, and members training(Figure 20).

Figure 20　Planting base of Wufu Kiwi Fruit Professional Cooperative

(2) Main Practices

Firstly, to expand the scale of production. In its early days, the cooperative struggled due to limitations in scale, member numbers, conditions, and experience, barely breaking even. With the injection of project funds, it entered a new phase of development. By registering for changes in its funding and membership structure, the cooperative grew from five households to 50 households including 17 formerly impoverished households and 17 female members. This expansion not only strengthened the cooperative but also created more opportunities for local smallholders to participate and increase their income.

Secondly, to improve production conditions. The cooperative built a 500-square-meter sorting center and a 100-ton freezer, and plans to install 100 mu of sprinkler irrigation facilities to improve the irrigation efficiency of kiwi fruit and ensure the healthy growth of fruit trees. Under the mode of combining unified management and independent management, the cooperative helps the surrounding smallholders to improve the yield and quality of kiwi fruit. At the same time, the cooperative storage extends the storage and supply of fruits, creating more sales opportunities for members and increasing their income.

Thirdly, the dividend incentive mechanism. On the basis of guaranteeing the basic income of smallholders, the dividend method of the cooperative enhances the enthusiasm of smallholders through the incentive mechanism. Smallholders transfer their land to cooperative to obtain land transfer fees. After the products are sold, the cooperative will return 50% of the profits to the members according to the transaction volume, and the other 50% will be recorded into the cooperative account for the operation and development of the cooperative. Wufu Kiwi Fruit Professional Cooperative driving mode is shown in Figure 21.

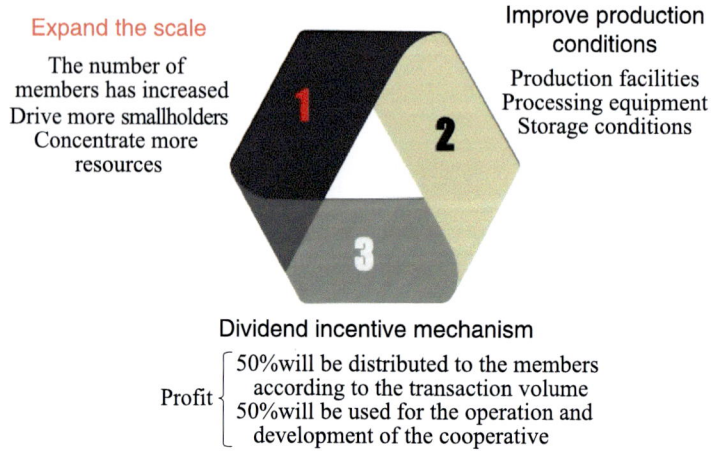

Figure 21 Wufu Kiwi Fruit Professional Cooperative Driving Mode

(3) Effectiveness

Wufu Kiwi Fruit Professional Cooperative took a series of measures to promote the development of smallholders and cooperatives. The integrated water and fertilizer system of 100-mu kiwi fruit garden has been built, which solves the different needs of water and fertilizer in different growth stages of kiwi fruit. The cooperative combined precision fertilization technology with water-saving irrigation to improve yield and quality, protect soil structure, reduce pollution and diseases and insect pests. After the implementation of sprinkler irrigation and fertilization, the cooperative could reduce the application of fertilizer by 20 tons, save 25 thousand cubic meters of water, save 300 artificial person-times, save the production cost of about CNY 120 thousand, and achieve a profit increase of more than CNY 100 thousand.

After the completion of the sorting center, the cooperative can classify and package the monkey peach, and sell them differently according to different grades. The cooperative can achieve a profit increase of more than CNY 300 thousand per year. After the establishment of the refrigerated storage(Figure 22), the cooperative realized the off-season sales through the preservation and storage, and the value-added income was CNY 400 thousand.

Figure 22 Wufu Kiwi Fruit Professional Cooperative warehouse

In 2023, the cooperative trained 50 members. Through the technical guidance of experts to the cooperative and the technical training of members, the members improved the planting management skills of kiwi fruit, and obtained the kiwi green food certification, which increased the yield of 100 kg per mu and increase the income of more than CNY 1,500 per mu. Through the green food certification, improve the market recognition rate and brand benefits of cooperative products were improued, the sales channels of cooperatives were broadened, and the economic benefits of cooperatives were enhanced.

6. Fenghuotai Apple Planting Professional Cooperative in Litong

(1) Basic Information

The Fenghuotai Apple Planting Professional Cooperative was established on 16 April 2015, located in Fenghuodun Village, Biandangou Town, Litong District, Wuzhong City. It primarily engages in apple planting, seedling cultivation, and sales, with an initial investment of CNY 15.75 million. In 2016, the cooperative was designated as an implementation unit for the Organic Selenium-rich Apple Demonstration Orchard Project by the Forestry department of Ningxia Hui Autonomous Region and the Forestry bureau of Litong district, Wuzhong City.

The cooperative consists of 50 members, with 9 members contributing orchard assets as shares. After quantification, the chairman holds a 5.7% share. In 2021, the cooperative received project support of CNY 1.5 million, which the cooperative invested in warehouses, fruit tree branch crushers, tractors, mechanical forklifts and advertising. Products of Fenghuotai Apple Planting Professional Cooperative are shown in Figure 23.

Figure 23　Products of Fenghuotai Apple Planting Professional Cooperative

(2) Main Practices

Firstly, implementing "Four Uniforms" to reduce smallholders' production costs. The cooperative has established a "Four Unified" mode: unified varieties, unified training, unified management, and unified sales. Unified varieties: the cooperative has introduced and planted three new apple varieties, with Venus Golden Apple as the primary crop. This variety is highly favoured by consumers for its sweet and fragrant qualities. Unified training: in addition to participating in production technology training organized by the project and village committee, the cooperative invites agricultural technicians from Lingwu City to deliver on-site field training. Through various learning opportunities, most members have acquired skills such as grafting and bridge grafting, significantly enhancing their production capabilities. Unified management: the cooperative oversees the management of members' orchards, organizing key activities such as fertilization, bagging, harvesting, storage(Figure 24) and packaging, thereby improving smallholders' production efficiency. Unified sales: the cooperative manages sales channels for its members. In 2023, it produced 2.8 million kilograms of apples and purchased an additional 50 thousand kilograms from smallholders. These were sold to four supermarkets and local markets, successfully expanding sales channels for smallholders.

Figure 24 Storage facility of Fenghuotai Apple Planting Professional Cooperative

Secondly, multi-stakeholder cooperation to protect smallholders' rights. The cooperative establishes collaborative relationships with other cooperatives in the same village. Through shared WeChat groups, they exchange market information and collectively use the "Biandangou Apple" brand. This branding strategy leverages the brand's market influence to enhance product value and increase smallholders' income. In terms of agricultural supply, the cooperative partners with Shanxi Zhongnongle Agricultural Technology Co., Ltd. The cooperative uses fertilizers and pesticides provided by the company, which, in turn, offers regular technical training and guidance on fruit tree production(Figure 25). This partnership effectively prevents large-scale pest infestations and provides solid technical support and guarantees for the apples grown by smallholders. Development mode of Fenghuotai Apple Planting Professional Cooperative is shown in Figure 26.

Figure 25   Field training activities by Fenghuotai Apple Planting Professional Cooperative

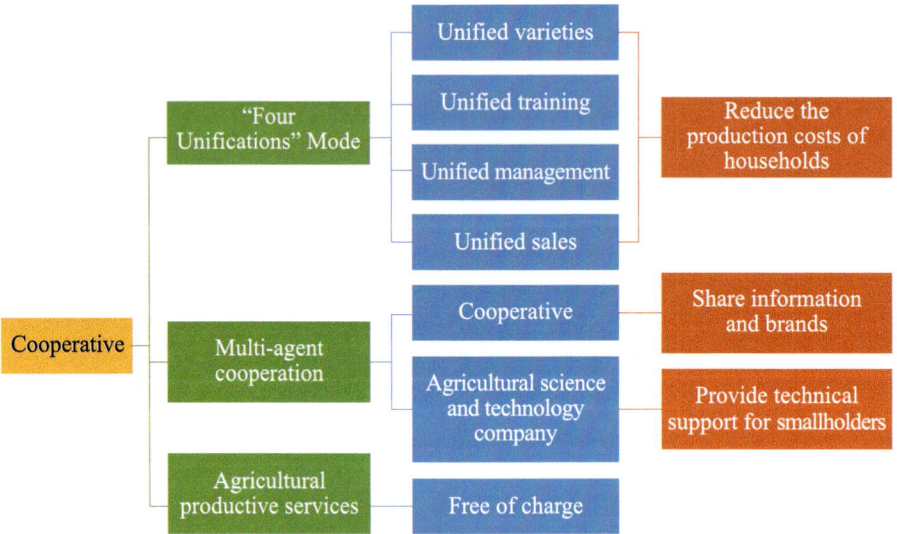

Figure 26   Development mode of Fenghuotai Apple Planting Professional Cooperative

(3) Effectiveness

In 2023, the cooperative provided 41 members with free agricultural services, including the supply of farming inputs, plowing and harvesting services, pest prevention and control training, packaging services, and product storage and sales support. It also officially established the "Biandangou Apple" brand. While developing its agro-industry chain, the cooperative has continuously expanded its planting area—from 50 mu in 2021 to 1,400 mu in 2023. This expansion has created more employment opportunities for local smallholders. The cooperative offers six medium to long-term jobs and provides up to 120 temporary positions during harvest season, with daily wages for temporary workers ranging from CNY 140 to 150.

7. Yonghe Taoyuan Gastrodia Elata Chinese Medicinal Materials Professional Cooperative in Cangxi

(1) Basic Information

Yonghe Taoyuan Gastrodia Elata Chinese Medicinal Materials Professional Cooperative was established on May 7, 2014, in Taoyuan Village, Yonghe Township, Cangxi County. The cooperative primarily engages in the cultivation, processing, and sale of Gastrodia elata, lilies, and other traditional Chinese medicinal materials(Figure 27), with a total investment of CNY 2 million. The cooperative comprises 101 member households, with the chairman holding a 27.5% share. In January 2013, Yang Min, the cooperative's founder, returned to his hometown to start a business. He introduced high-quality black Gastrodia elata from Yunnan and led efforts to establish the cooperative. The cooperative actively promoted Gastrodia elata planting techniques throughout the village, enabling villagers and neighboring communities to achieve prosperity together. The cooperative owns the registered trademarks "Cang Zhi Yuan" and "Gastrodia Girl." In 2023, it received project support, which was invested in production facilities, the purchase of processing and storage equipment, and member training programs.

Figure 27 Gastrodia elata seed breeding base and Gastrodia elata from Yonghe Taoyuan Gastrodia Elata Chinese Medicinal Materials Professional Cooperative

7. Yonghe Taoyuan Gastrodia Elata Chinese Medicinal Materials Professional Cooperative in Cangxi

(2) Main Practices

Firstly, providing technical support to smallholders. The cooperative offers comprehensive training in Gastrodia elata cultivation techniques. To date, nearly 1,000 person-times have participated in these training sessions, including 800 women person-times. This initiative has enabled every member household to develop at least one "Cultivation Expert", significantly enhancing their technical proficiency and self-reliance in Gastrodia elata farming(Figure 28).

Figure 28　Training at Yonghe Taoyuan Gastrodia Elata Chinese Medicinal Materials Professional Cooperative

Secondly, implementing a financial support mode. The cooperative addresses smallholders' financial constraints in Gastrodia elata cultivation by advancing funds, setting purchase prices, and unifying settlement with deductions. This approach has greatly stimulated enthusiasm for Gastrodia elata cultivation among the community, leading to a significant expansion in planting areas. The cooperative applies the "Five Unified" standardized management technique, which includes unified varieties, unified technical training, unified seasonal management, unified supply of agricultural inputs, unified branding. This ensures product consistency in quality and effectiveness while reducing production costs.

Thirdly, increasing smallholders' income in surrounding areas. Currently, the cooperative manages over 200 mu of Gastrodia elata planting. It employs 11 regular workers (including 2 from poverty-alleviated households) and provides over 1,200 temporary job opportunities annually, primarily to workers from poverty-alleviated households. In 2023, the cooperative distributed nearly CNY 180 thousand in wages to regular and short-term workers, enabling local smallholders to earn income through nearby employment. Using a "hub-and-spoke" approach, the cooperative has promoted the cultivation of Chinese medicinal materials in nine villages across the township, covering more than 2,000 mu. Over ten new farming entities, including family farms, enterprises, and large-scale farmers, have been engaged in cultivation efforts. For example, 100 mu of Huangjing base in Shiniu Village, 50 mu of Salvia base in Market Village, etc., forming a planting mode of "net cropping, understory intercropping, plants intercropping, kiwifruit and medicinal plants plants intercropping, grain and medicinal intercropping". These efforts support the cultivation of multiple Chinese medicinal materials, including Gastrodia elata, Salvia, Polygonatum, Paris polyphylla, Epimedium, and Poria. This diversified approach promotes the healthy development of the township's Chinese medicinal materials industry. Development mode of Yonghe Taoyuan Gastrodia Elata Chinese Medicinal Materials Cooperative is shown in Figure 29.

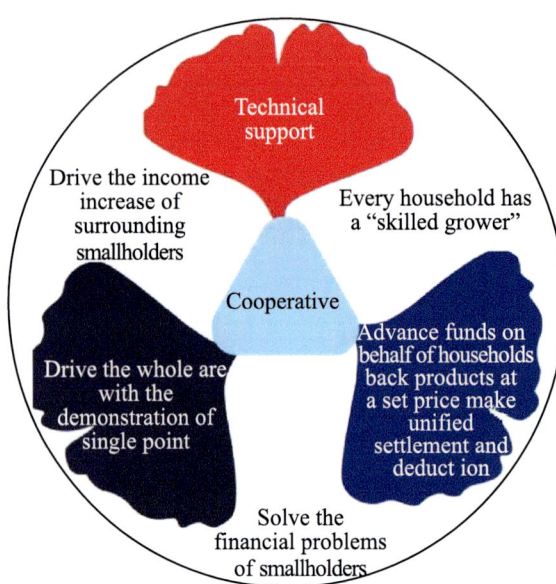

Figure 29　Development mode of Yonghe Taoyuan Gastrodia Elata Chinese Medicinal Materials Professional Cooperative

(3) Effectiveness

The cooperative has utilized project funds to continuously improve its production equipment, significantly enhancing production efficiency and laying a solid foundation for further expansion. As the cooperative's production scale and business operations expand, the demand for labor has also increased, providing more employment opportunities for surrounding smallholders and contributing to regional economic development and

7. Yonghe Taoyuan Gastrodia Elata Chinese Medicinal Materials Professional Cooperative in Cangxi

employment stability. With the introduction of new equipment, the cooperative has extended the industry chain by developing a variety of edible Gastrodia elata products, such as Gastrodia elata powder, dried Gastrodia elata slices, Gastrodia elata noodles, and fresh Gastrodia elata. Following a development strategy of "Cooperative + Base + Smallholders + Services + Products + Sales", the cooperative is committed to building an integrated operational mode encompassing Gastrodia elata cultivation, acquisition, processing, and sales. This approach promotes the standardization, intensification, and branding of the Chinese medicinal materials industry. In 2023, the cooperative achieved a total revenue of CNY 690,000.

8. Shoukouyan Planting Professional Cooperative in Xuanhan

(1) Basic Information

The Shoukouyan Planting Professional Cooperative was established on January 9, 2018, in Chongshi Village, Mingyue Township, Xuanhan County, located on the southern slopes of the Daba Mountains in the northeastern Sichuan Basin. The cooperative specializes in the cultivation, processing, and sale of trifoliate orange (Zhike)(Figure 30) and Sichuan pepper. It was established with an investment of CNY 5.16 million. The cooperative consists of 115 member households and manages 387.8 mu of land and CNY 2.45 million in capital. After land and funds were converted into shares, the chairman holds a 29.4% stake. In 2020, the cooperative received project funding, which was invested in the installation of irrigation pipelines for the park, management training, and the construction of drying facilities.

Figure 30   Trifoliate orange processing at Shoukouyan Planting Professional Cooperative

(2) Main Practices

Firstly, extending the agro-industry chain and building the brand. With project support, the cooperative has invested in modern processing equipment and established drying facilities(Figure 31) to enhance the processing capacity and quality of medicinal herbs. At the same time, the cooperative emphasizes brand development and product certification, strengthening the agro-industry chain and boosting brand awareness to increase market competitiveness. Currently, the cooperative has obtained one trademark registration certificate and one agricultural product brand.

Figure 31　Drying equipment at Shoukouyan Planting Professional Cooperative

Secondly, expanding production scale and creating job opportunities. In 2023, the cooperative interplanted Polygonatum (Huangjing) and Acorus calamus (Shichangpu) within its trifoliate orange fields, cultivating 416 mu of trifoliate orange, 100 mu of Polygonatum, and 100 mu of Acorus calamus. This scale expansion has generated higher economic returns for the cooperative while creating more employment opportunities for surrounding smallholders. Currently, the cooperative provides 10 long-term jobs and 30 temporary jobs. Development mode of Shoukouyan Planting Professional Cooperative is shown in Figure 32.

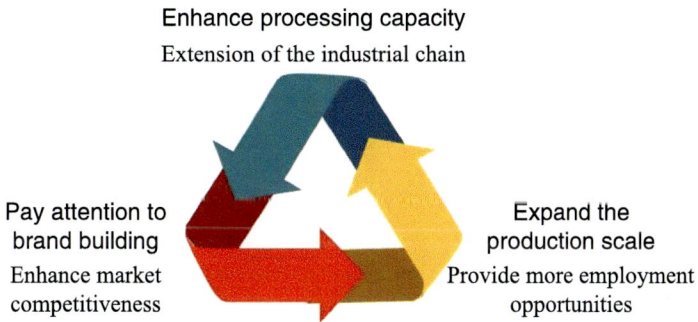

Figure 32　Development mode of Shoukouyan Planting Professional Cooperative

(3) Effectiveness

Since its establishment, the cooperative has ensured a guaranteed annual dividends of CNY 400/mu for its members, even during non-profitable years, ensuring stable incomes for its members. In 2024, the cooperative planed to initiate a secondary dividend distribution. The cooperative actively integrates and supports smallholders through training and technical guidance, improving benefit-sharing mechanisms. These efforts help retain added value from the industry in rural areas, benefiting local smallholders. The cooperative includes a significant number of smallholders and poverty-alleviated households, making meaningful contributions to rural revitalization.

9. Gongyi Tea Professional Cooperative in Xuzhou

(1) Basic Information

The Gongyi Tea Professional Cooperative was established in December 2011, located in Jianwan Village (Tiangong Mountain), Juexi Town, Xuzhou District. It primarily engages in tea cultivation, processing, and sales, agricultural machinery sales, agricultural tourism, and crop pest control services. The cooperative has an initial capital investment of CNY 5.15 million and has developed a 3,200 mu tea plantation base. The cooperative consists of 126 member households, including 39 poverty-alleviated households, 2 ethnic minority individuals, and 49 female members, covering 8 villages in Juexi Town.

In 2020, the cooperative was selected as a beneficiary of project support, receiving CNY 3.6 million in funding. In 2021, it was selected for a sub-project under the agricultural supermarket initiative, receiving another CNY 1.5 million support. The newly-built park of Gongyi Tea Professional Cooperative is shown in Figure 33.

Figure 33 The newly–built park of Gongyi Tea Professional Cooperative

(2) Main Practices

Firstly, establishing benefit linkages with smallholders. The cooperative signs agreements with smallholders to establish benefit linkages. It ensures product quality through enhanced quality awareness, technical guidance, and standardized production materials(Figure 34). If the smallholders' products do not meet quality standards, they are either rejected or purchased at lower prices for other uses. If the products meet the cooperative's standards, they are purchased at CNY 1.3 per kilogram above the market price. This approach aligns market demand directly with smallholders' production, achieving scientific, systematic, and professional agricultural production. The order-based mode not only boosts smallholders' enthusiasm but also resolves sales challenges, ensuring their income.

Figure 34　Products of Gongyi Tea Professional Cooperative

Secondly, promoting smallholders development through production services. The cooperative provides smallholders with free agricultural inputs, machinery, and outsourced plowing and harvesting services. In 2023, the Gongyi Tea Professional Cooperative provided agricultural input services to 18 households and agricultural production technical services to 124 households. These services significantly increased crop yields and quality, reduced losses caused by improper techniques or pests and diseases, lowered smallholders' production costs, and enhanced the market competitiveness of agricultural products. Moreover, the cooperative's production process requires substantial labor. As the cooperative's tea plantation expanded, it hired 84 temporary workers during peak tea-picking periods, providing additional income sources for local smallholders while alleviating labor shortages for the cooperative.

9. Gongyi Tea Professional Cooperative in Xuzhou

Figure 35　The newly-built workshops and equipment of Gongyi Tea Professional Cooperative

Thirdly, the cooperative offers post-harvest processing and sales services. It provides smallholders with free services such as processing, packaging, storage, transportation, and sales(Figure 35). In 2023, the cooperative processed and packaged products for 124 households, provided storage services for 82 households, transportation services for 67 households, and sales services for 124 households. It purchased 93,145 kg of fresh tea leaves from smallholders and leveraged its brand influence and market channels to achieve a total transaction volume of CNY 1.781 million through collection and sales on behalf of the smallholders.

By offering post-harvest services, the cooperative has also created long-term employment opportunities for smallholders. Smallholders participate in processing, packaging, and transporting agricultural products, forming a mutually beneficial and complementary relationship between the cooperative and the smallholders. This partnership fosters a win-win situation and promotes the sustainable development of rural industries. Gongyi Tea Professional Cooperative development mode is shown in Figure 36.

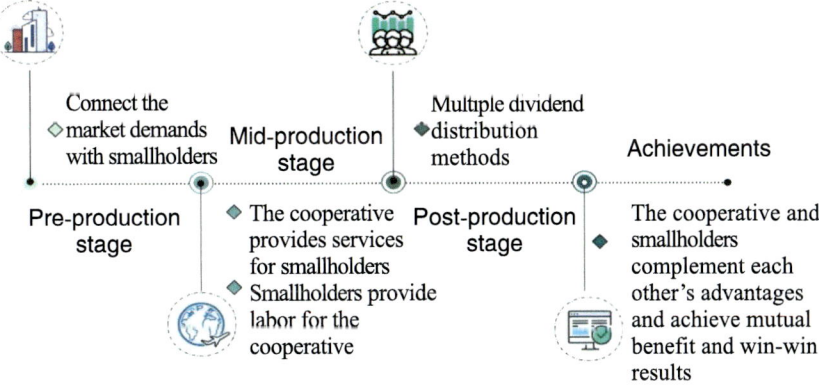

Figure 36　Gongyi Tea Professional Cooperative development mode

(3) Effectiveness

Through project support, the cooperative introduced 5 million new tea seedlings, including new varieties such as Fuxuan No. 9, 131, Wu Niuzao, and Golden Bud. It also registered trademarks such as "Ye Gu Chun" and "Xi Tan". In 2021, the cooperative was recognized as a "National Demonstration Cooperative," and in 2022, it passed the ISO 9001 quality certification. The cooperative enhanced its capacity through activities aimed at improving its operations and providing skills training to its members. This led to an increase in members' skills, production capacity, and income. Cooperative members directly benefited from labor income and profit-sharing. Thus, over 120 households directly benefited.

In 2023, the cooperative's operating income reached CNY 7.5 million, with a surplus of CNY 670 thousand. Of this surplus, CNY 400 thousand was allocated as dividends, with each household receiving an average of more than CNY 3,000. The cooperative also increased the operating income of both upstream and downstream businesses and created temporary employment opportunities for more than 2,200 women and disadvantaged groups in the mountainous areas. The cooperative helped local tea farmers increase both production and income, resulting in an additional income of CNY 1,200 per person for smallholders outside the cooperative.

10. Jiahe Planting Professional Cooperative in Xuanhan

(1) Basic Information

The Jiahe Planting Professional Cooperative was established on 28 November 2016, in Huali Village, Fankui Town, Xuanhan County. The cooperative primarily engages in services related to tea planting, processing, and sales, focusing on selenium-enriched green tea. It has a total investment of CNY 10.95 million(Figure 37). The cooperative has 306 member households, managing 1,000 mu of land and CNY 4.94 million in funds. After quantifying shares based on land and funds, the chairman holds a 19.6% stake. The cooperative's chairman and vice-chairman are brothers, with complementary backgrounds—one in construction and agricultural production technology, and the other financially well-resourced. Inspired by their experience in managing other projects, they decided to leverage the region's long-standing tea cultivation history and extensive production expertise. By integrating technology, capital, and farmers' interests, they consolidated and enhanced the local tea planting industry, aiming to increase smallholders' incomes and drive economic prosperity. In 2020, the cooperative received project support, which was utilized to purchase tea-picking machines, tea-rolling machines, de-enzyming machines, and to develop a WeChat mini-program.

Figure 37 Jiahe Planting Professional Cooperative base in Xuanhan

(2) Main Practices

Firstly, attracting new smallholders. The cooperative's growth has attracted young people from the village to return or stay in their hometown to work. With professional knowledge, they bring new vitality to the cooperative. The cooperative hired experts to provide specialized and systematic training for smallholders, improving their planting skills and processing levels. Jiahe Planting Professional Cooperative processing workshop in Xuanhan is shown in Figure 38.

Secondly, integrating the industry chain. By allowing farmers to invest capital as shareholders, the cooperative has raised substantial funds, ensuring strong financial backing for its development. It integrates the planting, processing, and sales of tea into a complete industry chain. This reduces smallholders' production costs and risks while increasing product value and market competitiveness.

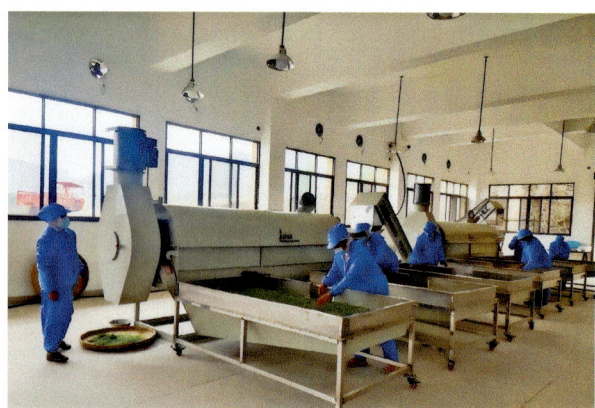

Figure 38 Jiahe Planting Professional Cooperative processing workshop in Xuanhan

Thirdly, expanding the market. The cooperative sells its tea to consumers outside the province through e-commerce platforms, opening new sales channels and boosting product awareness and reputation. It also supplies tea to local sales companies and the construction association, realizing multi-channel sales. Jiahe Planting Professional Cooperative development mode is shown in Figure 39.

(3) Effectiveness

Through specialized and systematic training, smallholders' planting and processing skills have improved, leading to a significant increase in both the quantity and quality of

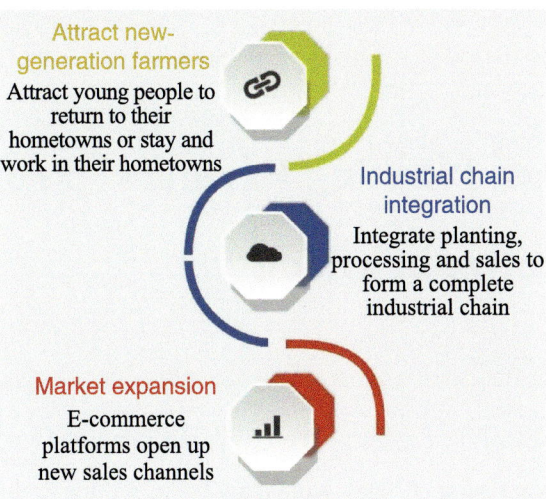

Figure 39　Jiahe Planting Professional Cooperative development mode

tea. As the tea industry grows, smallholders benefit from intercropping, labor opportunities, and profit-sharing, significantly increasing their incomes and improving their quality of life.

The cooperative's tea products have gained more recognition and favor from consumers through e-commerce platforms and multi-channel sales, strengthening its brand influence. The development of the cooperative has not only helped smallholders increase their incomes but also promoted the prosperity of the local rural economy. Furthermore, the cooperative has attracted returning talent, thereby providing human resources for rural revitalization.

11. Maoyuan Planting Farmers' Professional Cooperative in Yilong

(1) Basic Information

The Maoyuan Planting Farmers' Professional Cooperative was established on 2 January 2018 in Gaotanggou Village, Xinzheng Town, Yilong County, Nanchong City, Sichuan Province. The cooperative specializes in the cultivation, processing, transportation, and sales of edible mushrooms such as shiitake and black fungus(Figure 40). It has a total investment of CNY 5.5 million and consists of 130 member households. After converting funds into equity shares, the chairman holds a 0.6% share. In 2021, the cooperative received project support, which was invested in building mushroom production sheds, cold storage facilities, and drying rooms, as well as establishing e-commerce and promotional platforms.

Figure 40 Black fungus produced by Maoyuan Planting Farmers' Professional Cooperative

(2) Main Practices

Firstly, infrastructure development and resource integration. With project funding, the cooperative invested significantly in the construction of production facilities(Figure 41), processing and marketing infrastructure, service training, and product branding. It has built eight mushroom cultivation greenhouses covering 1,280 square meters, three cold storage units within a 250-square-meter cold-chain plant, a drying facility of 240 square meters, and one set of drying equipment. Additionally, it procured 6 sets of office equipment, including computers, photocopiers, and desks, laying a solid foundation for development.

The cooperative also consolidated land resources, established pollution-free planting bases, and promoted standardized planting techniques for high-quality varieties, increasing the productivity of rural land resources.

Figure 41　Base of Maoyuan Planting Farmers' Professional Cooperative

Secondly, developing circular agriculture and extending the industry chain. The cooperative has adopted a circular agricultural mode by using mulberry branches to produce mushroom bags for cultivating black fungus(Figure 42). The mushroom bags are then composted and used as fertilizer for mulberry trees, creating a closed-loop system for resource recycling. The market price for black fungus is estimated at CNY 60–70 per kilogram. This approach not only achieves resource recycling but also extends the industry chain, increasing the added value of agricultural products and upgrading the agricultural industry structure in the project area toward higher value-added production.

Figure 42　Mushroom cultivation greenhouse of Maoyuan Planting Farmers' Professional Cooperative

Thirdly, introducing technology and innovating products. By introducing new varieties and technologies, the cooperative has improved product quality, built its brand, and expanded its influence. It has cultivated a variety of mulberry-based edible mushrooms, including oyster mushrooms, black fungus, golden fungus, and shiitake, enriching its product range to meet market demands. The cooperative also prioritizes technical training to help smallholders enhance their planting skills, promoting the scale, standardization, and agro-industrialization of the mushroom industry. This effort provides local smallholders with more economic benefits and development opportunities.

Fourth, expanding markets and sales channels. The cooperative uses diversified sales channels, including e-commerce platforms, wholesale markets, and supermarkets, to broaden its market reach and enhance its competitiveness. It actively promotes its products and attracts customers to visit the cooperative's base for picking and purchasing, thereby increasing direct sales revenue. Operational mode of Maoyuan Planting Farmers' Professional Cooperative is shown in Figure 43.

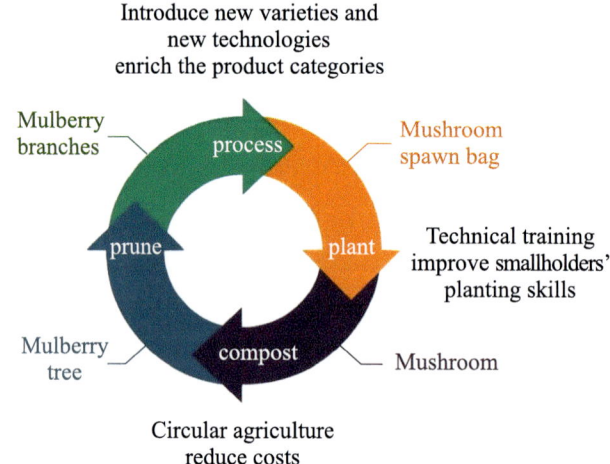

Figure 43   Operational mode of Maoyuan Planting Farmers' Professional Cooperative

(3) Effectiveness

The cooperative maximized benefits from measures such as improving production efficiency, extending the industry chain, technological innovation, and market expansion. By incorporating smallholders into its production system and encouraging their participation in base harvesting, the cooperative enhanced smallholders' sense of involvement and fulfillment, thus fostering a close connection between the smallholders and the cooperative. Additionally, by creating employment opportunities and providing land transfer fees, the cooperative directly contributed to increasing smallholders' incomes.

12. Zhonghe Village Yinong Breeding Demonstration Base in Yuanzhou

(1) Basic Information

Zhonghe Village in Yuanzhou District, Guyuan City, Ningxia, serves as a demonstration livestock park for the "separation of humans and livestock" cattle fattening initiative, aimed at strengthening the collective village economy through beef cattle farming. With support from rural revitalization and poverty alleviation funds, the Zhonghe Village Yinong Breeding Demonstration Base constructed three cattle barns(Figure 44). Following support from agricultural development projects, the base added four steel-structured cattle barns and built auxiliary facilities, including silage pits, feed storage rooms, sewage pools, power transmission lines, park roads, and perimeter walls(Figure 45).

Figure 44　Zhonghe Village Yinong Breeding Demonstration Base

(2) Main Practices

Zhonghe village collective has explored a "Household+Base" mode to develop the beef cattle farming industry, focusing on large-scale, standardized farming while continuously increasing product value. The base provides outsourced cattle rearing services for over 120 cattle on behalf of smallholders, adopting a mode where smallholders invest in calf purchases while the collective handles rearing and sales. The base implements a unified system of disease prevention and control, environmentally friendly manure treatment, and scientific management, employing standardized, mechanized, and scientific breeding methods to improve efficiency. Feeding more than 100 cattle take just one hour. Smallholders only pay for calves, with all subsequent rearing and sales managed by the village collective. Zhonghe Village Yinong Breeding Demonstration Base operational mode is shown in Figure 46.

Figure 45　Project-supported disinfection room and storage facility

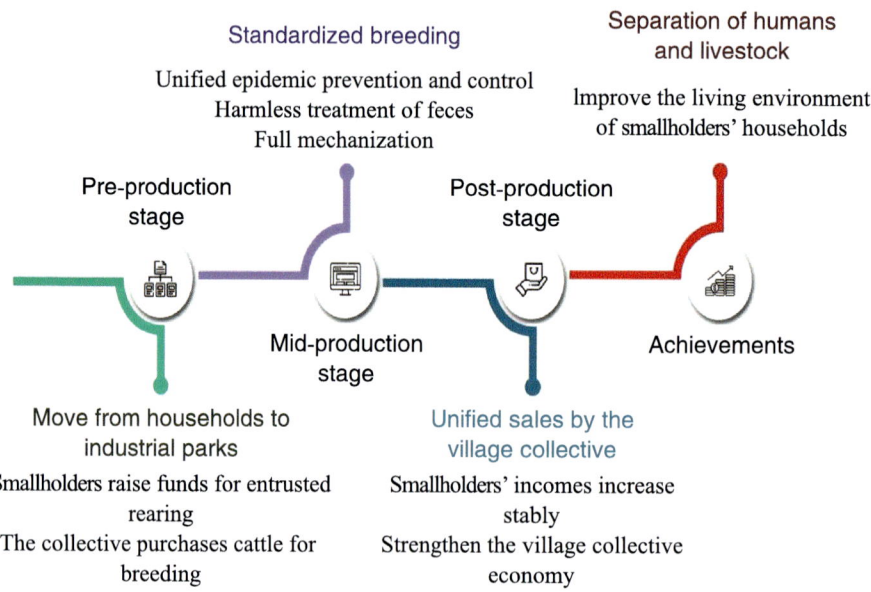

Figure 46　Zhonghe Village Yinong Breeding Demonstration Base operational mode

(3) Effectiveness

In 2024, the base employed 4 long-term workers and raised over 400 cattle, with approximately 300 cattle expected to be sold by year-end. The demonstration base signed rearing agreements with more than 40 surrounding smallholders, providing outsourced rearing services. Each smallholders receives an annual dividend of CNY 3,000, thereby helping smallholders achieve stable income growth.

13. Shanniuyuan Beef Cattle Science and Technology Breeding Professional Cooperative in Pengyang

(1) Basic Information

Shanniuyuan Beef Cattle Science and Technology Breeding Professional Cooperative was established on 1 November 2012, in Renhe Village, Gucheng Town, Pengyang County, Guyuan City. The cooperative primarily engages in cattle breeding and sales(Figure 47), as well as feed processing, with an initial capital investment of CNY 1 million. It consists of 50 member households who contribute land and funds to the cooperative. After converting land and funds into equity, the cooperative's director holds an 11.3% stake. In 2020, the cooperative received project support, investing the funds in feed harvesters, grass powder machines, and management training.

Figure 47 Cattle Farming at Shanniuyuan Beef Cattle Science and Technology Breeding Professional Cooperative

(2) Main Practices

Since the project's implementation, the cooperative has developed a "321" empowerment mechanism, 3 ("Three free services"): the cooperative provides free livestock farming technical guidance, free high-quality commercial sales channels for smallholders, and free distribution of fattening cattle to households that have exited poverty. 2 ("Two payments"): the cooperative pays labor wages and land transfer fees to participating smallholders. 1 ("One incentive"): the cooperative's initiatives aim to inspire self-reliance and motivate smallholders to pursue economic independence. Shanniuyuan Beef Cattle Science and Technology Breeding Professional Cooperative driving mode is shown in Figure 48.

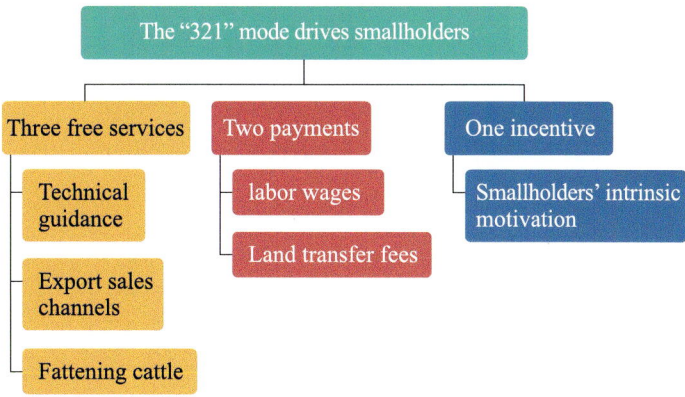

Figure 48 Shanniuyuan Beef Cattle Science and Technology Breeding Professional Cooperative driving mode

(3) Effectiveness

As an experimental demonstration base for the Feed Engineering Technology Research Center of Ningxia University, the cooperative has achieved professional recognition in feed formulation and cattle breeding. In 2023, the cooperative sold 80 cattle (Figure 49) at a price of CNY 14,000 each, provided free technical guidance to 60 households, and facilitated external sales for 10 households at no cost.

Figure 49 The cattle shed of Shanniuyuan Beef Cattle Science and Technology Breeding Professional Cooperative

14. Xiangyuan Village Mutton Sheep Breeding Base in Hongsibu

(1) Basic Information

Residents from nine townships in the Ningxia Hongsibu Immigration Development Zone formed Xiangyuan Village. These breeders primarily rely on corn farming and sheep herding for their livelihood. Villagers typically sell about 15 sheep per year, with a 10 kilogram lamb selling for CNY 700-800. After accounting for various costs such as electricity and taxes, the profit per sheep is about CNY 40. Following support from an agricultural development project, the village prioritized helping those who had not previously received financial aid, particularly former impoverished households, by providing sheep sheds to 30 households.

(2) Main Practices

Before receiving project support, more than 30 sheep were crowded into makeshift soil-built sheds with insufficient sunlight and limited space, resulting in poor quality and appearance of the sheep bred. After the project's implementation, each household received modern sheep sheds constructed with cement(Figure 50), with each sheep shed costing over CNY 30,000 to build. So far, 28 sheep sheds have been constructed in the village. The

Figure 50 Sheep sheds renovation in Hongsibu project area

village organizes breeding training classes for farmers, sharing breeding techniques and providing on-site vaccination services to ensure the healthy development of the village's livestock industry. Xiangyuan Village driving mode is shown in Figure 51.

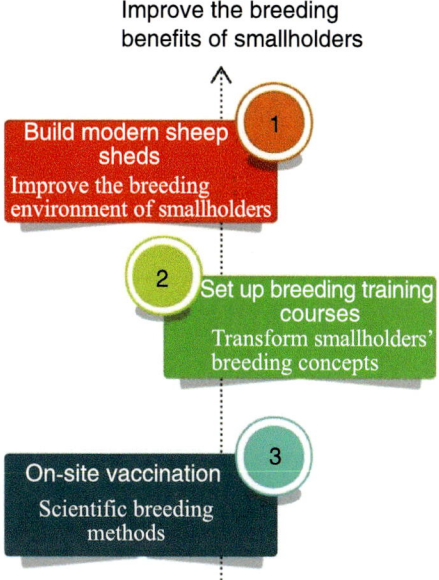

Figure 51　Xiangyuan Village driving mode

(3) Effectiveness

With the construction of modern sheep sheds, smallholders now rear over 40 sheep, using corn mixed with bran and soybean meal as feed. They sell the lambs when they reach 10–15 kg (at around three months old), fetching CNY 500–600 per lamb. Smallholders can sell lambs as needed to earn money, with annual breeding income reaching CNY 40,000. Some smallholders sell their sheep directly in the market, where they can sell for approximately CNY 2,000 each.

15. Shuitao Village Breeding Base in Hongsibu

(1) Basic Information

Shuitao Village has established a distinctive industry centered around Tan sheep farming, with pen-raising as the primary agricultural activity. Supported by project funding, the village constructed 19 sheep sheds. These new facilities were converted into rental spaces by the village collective, providing local breeders with sheep pens and feed storage sheds(Figure 52).

Figure 52　Feed storage sheds and sheep pens in Shuitao Village Breeding Base

(2) Main Practices

With financial support from the project, Shuitao Village built a new livestock farming facility, which was put into operation upon completion. The village rents out each shed to major livestock farmers at an annual fee of CNY 4,500 per shed. Guided by the Hongsibu Bureau of Agriculture and Rural Affairs, the village organized multiple technical training sessions, have brought livestock technicians and instructors to visit households and deliver on-site training. These sessions broadened breeders' perspectives, transformed traditional farming concepts, and improved their husbandry skills. The development mode of Shuitao

Village Breeding Base is shown in Figure 53.

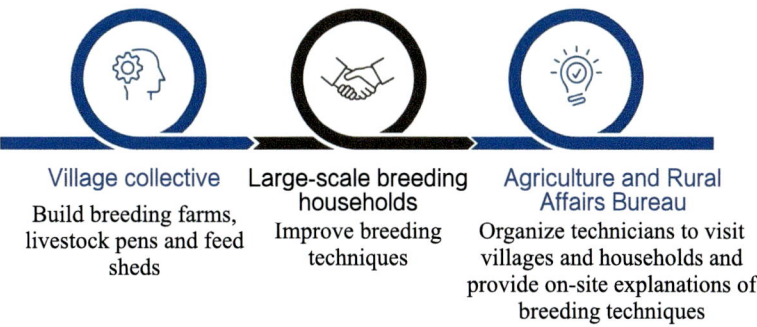

Figure 53　The development mode of Shuitao Village Breeding Base

(3) Effectiveness

The construction of livestock sheds and the provision of technical training have addressed many practical challenges faced by breeders in livestock farming. With training and guidance, smallholders became more confident and expanded their operations. Among the second batch of sheep sheds built, 10 households rented two sheds in total, while others rented one shed. The livestock scale has since grown to over 200 sheep per household.

16. Hongke Farmers' Breeding Professional Cooperative in Yuanzhou

(1) Basic Information

The Hongke Farmers' Breeding Professional Cooperative was officially established on 21 April 2009, in Pengbao Village, Pengbao Town, Yuanzhou District, Guyuan City. The cooperative primarily engages in poultry farming and the sale of feed grains(Figure 54), with a registered capital of CNY 15.18 million. It comprises 54 member households, who contribute land and labor as equity. After equity quantification, the cooperative chairman holds a 50.9% share. In 2021, the cooperative received project support, which enabled investments in infrastructure improvements such as drying yard hardening, feed corn drying facilities, and training services, thereby fostering significant development among local smallholders.

Figure 54　Chicks and eggs from Hongke Farmers' Breeding Professional Cooperative

(2) Main Practices

Firstly, comprehensive socialized services. The cooperative has established an integrated service system spanning pre-production to post-production. Its "Seven Unified" services include financial credit, technical training, chick supply, feed distribution, disease prevention, fresh egg sales, and manure management. This "home production, cooperative service" mode ensures consistency and efficiency. The chairperson plays a pivotal role by actively seeking training resources, not only takes the lead in training, but also arranges for members of the co-operative to participate in various types of training, participating in programs, and organizing at least three training sessions annually for members, enhancing their husbandry techniques and management skills.

Secondly, circular agriculture development chain. Utilizing project funding, the cooperative built a feed corn drying facility and partnered with entities such as the Xinxing Land Shareholding Cooperative and family farms to purchase and process corn into feed(Figure 55). The cooperative delivers 5,000 tons of processed feed annually to surrounding farmers. A manure fermentation pool further supports nearby farmers by transforming waste into organic fertilizer. This forms a circular agricultural mode encompassing corn planting → feed corn drying → healthy egg-laying hen farming → harmless manure treatment → field application. This approach minimizes chemical fertilizer use and pesticide dependency. Feeding hens with dried corn feed (moisture content: 14%–15%) has increased egg production by about 3% and reduced intestinal inflammation rates by 70%, cutting costs and boosting agricultural productivity and quality.

Figure 55　Corn drying yard at Hongke Farmers' Breeding Professional Cooperative

Thirdly, diverse profit-sharing mechanisms. The cooperative has established member accounts for equity-based profit distribution, ensuring members' benefits and improving households' economic returns. Additionally, it offers transaction-based dividends, including a rebate of CNY 0.03 Per kilogram for cooperative members' corn purchases and CNY 0.02 Per kilogram for external smallholders. These measures have boosted smallholders' confidence in poultry farming, enabling the cooperative to expand its egg-laying hen operations and driving surrounding smallholders toward prosperity through poultry farming. The development mode of Hongke Farmers' Breeding Professional Cooperative is shown in Figure 56.

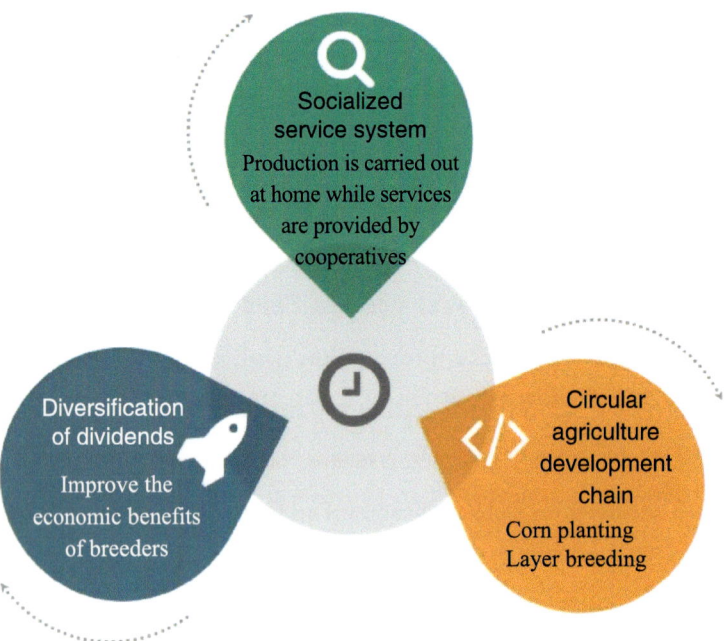

Figure 56　The development mode of Hongke Farmers' Breeding Professional Cooperative

(3) Effectiveness

After the project was implemented, the cooperative has achieved remarkable success. In 2023, it became the first cooperative in Ningxia listed as a "National Farmers' Cooperative Mode Case" by the Ministry of Agriculture and Rural Affairs. The cooperative's drying yard has resolved grain drying challenges for surrounding farmers, directly benefiting its 54 member households and indirectly supporting 114 farming households. Since receiving project support, the cooperative has provided free technical training and financial loan services to its members, with an average loan of CNY 75,000 per household in recent years.

17. Liupanshan Ecological Breeding Professional Cooperative in Yuanzhou

(1) Basic Information

Established on 10 October 2015, the Liupanshan Ecological Breeding Cooperative is located in Yanghe Village, Touying Town, Yuanzhou District, Guyuan City. The cooperative specializes in raising ecological poultry, including chickens(Figure 57), gray geese, turkeys, and native roosters, with a registered capital of CNY 700,000. Its primary goal is to lead mountainous rural residents in Yanghe Village toward free-range ecological chicken farming. Comprising 58 member households, the cooperative uses monetary contributions for equity, with the chairman holding a 57.1% stake after equity quantification. In 2020, project funding supported the cooperative's investments in farm construction and technical management training.

Figure 57 Ecological chickens raised by Liupanshan Ecological Breeding Professional Cooperative

(2) Main Practices

Firstly, enhancing infrastructure as a foundation for development. With project support, the cooperative improved the infrastructure of the farming area, including roads, water supply, electricity, and communication systems. These upgrades reduced transportation times, ensured water quality, enabled the use of agricultural machinery(Figure 58), and provided modern communication tools for accessing market information and conducting e-commerce. The cooperative also organized and standardized the farming zones by setting up isolation areas and equipping them with standardized shelters. This reduced the physical labor required from smallholders, centralized resources for farming, improved efficiency and biosecurity, and minimized risks. The cooperative further unified forage cultivation, harvesting, processing, and storage, reducing waste and economic burdens on smallholders, allowing them to focus on improving farming quality and efficiency.

Figure 58 Agricultural machinery used by Liupanshan Ecological Breeding Professional Cooperative

Secondly, training smallholders to enhance scientific farming skills. Collaborating with local agricultural extension centers, the cooperative established a three-tiered technical service network covering districts, towns, and villages. It offered training on ecological livestock farming, rural revitalization, rural civilization and cooperative management. Combining hands-on demonstrations and classroom instruction, the cooperative organized visits to exemplary agricultural sites within Ningxia, have allowed smallholders to directly observe modern farming techniques. These initiatives transformed smallholders' mindsets, enhanced technical skills, and increased confidence in adapting to market demands.

Thirdly, building sales networks to expand market access. The cooperative encouraged smallholders to collaborate, scale operations, and increase market share by signing supply contracts with buyers, branding effect. It promoted a unified sales strategy, avoiding price wars and ensuring maximum benefits for members. Two value chains were developed: conventional farming for markets in Ningxia, Qinghai, and Inner Mongolia, and ecological farming for quality-focused consumers through online sales and offline distribution. Brand certification efforts built consumer trust, while the cooperative maintained strict quality control over green poultry products, ensuring survival through quality and growth through credibility. These measures broadened market access, boosted smallholders' confidence, and motivated them to scale operations. Development mode of Liupanshan Ecological Breeding Professional Cooperative is shown in Figure 59.

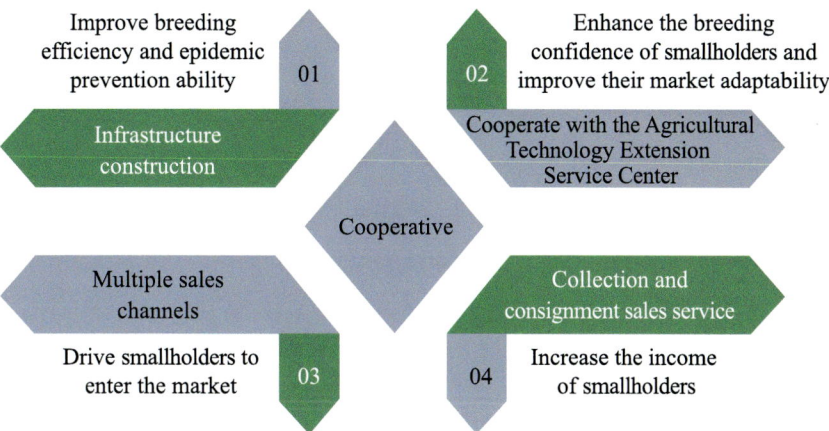

Figure 59　Development mode of Liupanshan Ecological Breeding Professional Cooperative

(3) Effectiveness

By expanding market channels, the cooperative significantly increased the price of ecological chickens. Smallholders previously sold chickens for CNY 60 each; now, the cooperative purchases them at an average price of CNY 70 each. Direct beneficiaries include 30 former poverty-stricken households (112 individuals), thereby collectively increasing their income by CNY 400,000, with an average per capita increase of about CNY 3,571. Additionally, the cooperative purchased corn from its members and surrounding growers at CNY 3,000 per ton, exceeding the market price by CNY 600 per ton, generating an additional income of CNY 96,000 for local growers.

18. Fengtai Breeding Farmers' Professional Cooperative in Yilong

(1) Basic Information

The Fengtai Breeding Farmers' Professional Cooperative was established on 13 June 2023 in Huilong Village, Dayin Town, Yilong County, with a total investment of CNY 1 million. The cooperative specializes in contract pig rearing, currently partnering with Wens Group for pig breeding. It operates a 200 mu forage base in Huilong Village(Figure 60), utilizing pig manure and biogas slurry from its pig farming for fertilization. Additionally, cooperative members have been mobilized to cultivate 300 mu of rapeseed, 300 mu of wheat, and 200 mu of beans. The cooperative encompasses over 100 farming households across Huilong, Chuanxing, Jianfeng, and Huashan Villages in Dayin Town, with poverty-alleviated households accounting for 32% of its members.

Figure 60　Base of the Fengtai Breeding Farmers' Professional Cooperative

(2) Main Practices

Firstly, providing free manure to smallholders. Chemical fertilizer expenses constitute a significant part of agricultural costs. The cooperative supplies dry manure, a high-quality organic fertilizer rich in nitrogen, phosphorus, potassium, and organic matter. By providing this fertilizer for free, smallholders can use it on fields, orchards, and vegetable plots, improving soil structure and fertility. This reduces smallholders' expenses on fertilizer, effectively lowering agricultural production costs.

Secondly, straw collection for feed processing(Figure 61). The cooperative has set up collection points to purchase straw from villagers, which is then transported back for processing. This practice increases smallholders' income and improves their livelihoods. Additionally, encouraging straw collection reduces open burning and random disposal, benefiting environmental protection, enhancing soil fertility, and boosts crop yields.

Figure 61　Agricultural machinery purchased by Fengtai Breeding Farmers' Professional Cooperative

Thirdly, using biogas slurry to fertilize forage crops. Biogas slurry, rich in nitrogen, phosphorus, potassium, trace elements, and organic matter, improves soil structure, enhances moisture and nutrient retention, and promotes aeration, aiding pasture root growth. Consequently, pesticide use and production costs decrease. The resulting high-quality forage provides a reliable feed source for pig farming, reducing reliance on external feed and further lowering costs. Moreover, better forage improves pork quality and taste, increasing market competitiveness and profitability(Figure 62). The mode of Fengtai Breeding Farmers' Professional Cooperative is shown in Figure 63.

Figure 62　Forage harvesting of Fengtai Breeding Farmers' Professional Cooperative

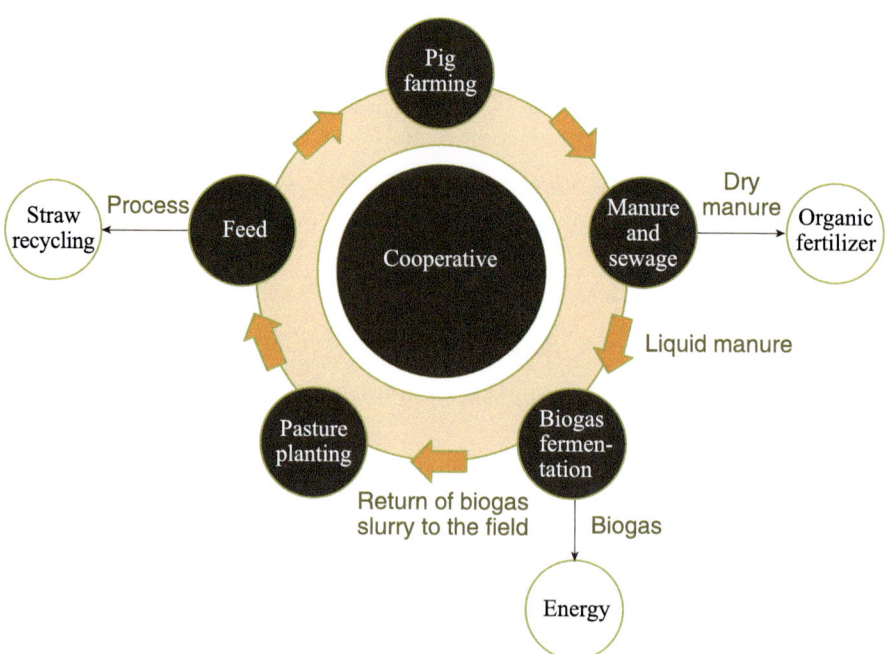

Figure 63　The mode of Fengtai Breeding Farmers' Professional Cooperative

(3) Effectiveness

The cooperative raises two batches of pigs annually, with approximately 3,000 pigs per batch. Wens Group purchases these pigs at around CNY 300 per head, while offering piglets, feed, veterinary drugs, and technical services at a cost of CNY 130 per head. Thereby, this integrated approach reduces rearing costs and enhances smallholders' incomes. Additionally, the cooperative employs a dry-wet separation system for manure, with liquid waste treated via biogas fermentation. This sustainable system creates a circular farming mode, improving resource efficiency and reducing environmental impact.

19. Jiangxin Ecological Breeding Professional Cooperative in Xuanhan

(1) Basic Information

Established on January 14, 2021, Jiangxin Ecological Breeding Professional Cooperative is located in Huali Village, Fankui Town, Xuanhan County. The cooperative specializes in poultry farming and the primary processing of agricultural products, with a total investment of CNY 5 million. Situated at an average altitude of over 1,300 meters, the cooperative provides an ideal natural environment for rearing hybrid Tibetan pigs. The cooperative comprises 100 member households, with contributions of land and capital. After equity quantification, the director holds a 40.6% stake. However, the cooperative faced significant challenges in its early stages due to the high costs required for constructing breeding facilities, processing plants, cold storage, and other infrastructure. In 2021, it was included in a government-supported project, enabling investments in essential facilities such as breeding pens(Figure 64), cold storage, drying rooms, production, and processing equipment, as well as promotional activities.

Figure 64　Black pig farming at Jiangxin Ecological Breeding Professional Cooperative

(2) Main Practices

Firstly, processing and marketing pig meat. The cooperative diversifies its product offerings by selling fresh Tibetan pork and producing specialty Sichuan-style sausages and cured meats. These products are marketed in local agricultural markets. Additionally, the cooperative purchases piglets and provides guidance on breeding and management techniques to smallholders. It then buys back mature pigs for processing into market-ready products. This mode has positively impacted over 20 surrounding households.

Secondly, profit-sharing to ensure smallholders income. Operating under the mode of "Cooperative + Smallholders + Base," the cooperative integrates member contributions of forests and cash into its operations. It manages a 1,000-square-meter breeding facility and over 20,000 mu (approximately 3,300 acres) of forest for free-range pig farming, with a current stock of 2,500 pigs and annual sales of 1,500 pigs. Smallholders benefit from profit-sharing arrangements, receiving a guaranteed minimum dividend of CNY 2,180 per share and an additional dividend of CNY 500 per share annually. Jiangxin Ecological Breeding Professional Cooperative's operational mode is shown in Figure 65.

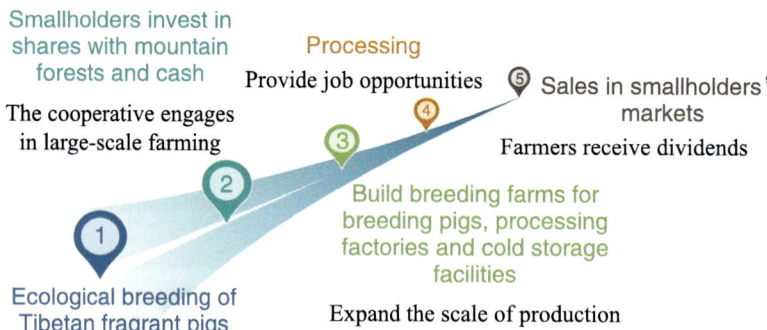

Figure 65　Jiangxin Ecological Breeding Professional Cooperative's operational mode

(3) Effectiveness

With project support, the cooperative has achieved significant progress. By 2023, in addition to selling some of the pork in the form of fresh meat, most of the pork is baked and sold in the form of waxy products, generating profits of CNY 650,000. The cooperative has created over 30 jobs, with labor payments exceeding CNY 700,000 annually. These positions primarily benefit local smallholders, including 50% from previously impoverished households and approximately 75% women, thereby addressing the needs of vulnerable rural groups.

20. Shunying Silkworm Breeding Professional Cooperative in Xuzhou

(1) Basic Information

The Shunying Silkworm Breeding Professional Cooperative was established on 2 July 2019, in Aiguo Group, Tangkan Village, Heshi Town, Xuzhou District. The cooperative focuses on mulberry cultivation, silkworm breeding(Figure 66), mulberry branch mushroom production, and silk quilt manufacturing, with a total investment of CNY 2 million. It has 102 member households, with the chairman holding a 15% share after fund equity conversion. In 2022, the cooperative was approved for project funding, receiving CNY 2.2 million in financial support. This funding was primarily used to purchase production and processing equipment, promote the cooperative, and provide skills training for its members. The cooperative has signed supply and purchase agreements with Sichuan Yibin Xuzhou Tian Can Silk Co., Ltd., and Xichang Silkworm Breeding Farm. These partners are responsible for acquiring and selling the cooperative's mushrooms and silkworm seeds.

Figure 66 The silkworm shed of Shunying Silkworm Breeding Professional Cooperative

(2) Main Practices

Firstly, enhancing production facilities. The cooperative used agricultural development project funds to build a 200-square-meter mulberry branch mushroom cultivation room(Figure 67) and upgrade 1,000-square-meter of silkworm feeding facilities. It purchased one agricultural vehicle, one small three-wheeler, two rotary tillers, eight mulberry branch cutters, 20 sprayers, and eight disinfection machines. Additionally, it constructed a 100-square-meter mechanical cold storage unit and renovated a 30-square-meter drying room.

Figure 67　Mulberry branch mushroom production of Shunying Silkworm Breeding Professional Cooperative

Secondly, promoting green production. The cooperative planted mulberry trees to increase regional vegetation coverage, implemented measures to reduce chemical fertilizers and pesticides, and adopted circular farming practices to combat agricultural non-point source pollution. This effort improved the local ecological environment. Techniques such as soil mulching with straw and applying organic fertilizers enhanced soil properties, improving its water retention, nutrient-holding, and erosion control capabilities. Shunying Silkworm Breeding Professional Cooperative base is shown in Figure 68.

Figure 68　Shunying Silkworm Breeding Professional Cooperative base

Thirdly, expanding operations to increase profitability. Supported by new technologies and varieties, the cooperative helped its members increase their income. Post-project implementation, professional training for farmers and technical support from experts significantly improved the skills and earnings of women participants. The cooperative sought to move beyond the lower levels of the agro-industry chain by processing silkworm cocoon products, developing mulberry branch mushrooms, and offering tourism services. These initiatives enhanced the cooperative's profitability while creating more jobs and increasing work opportunities for members and surrounding smallholders(Figure 69). Shunying Silkworm Breeding Professional Cooperative mode is shown in Figure 70.

Figure 69　Harvest of Shunying Silkworm Breeding Professional Cooperative

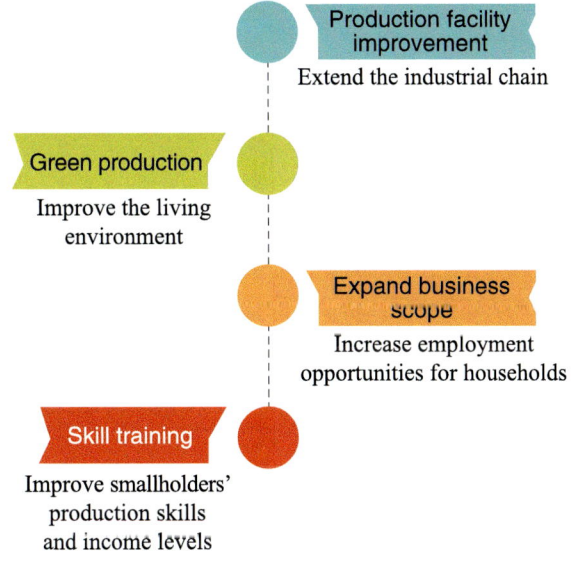

Figure 70　Shunying Silkworm Breeding Professional Cooperative mode

(3) Effectiveness

In 2023, the cooperative produced 20,000 kilogram of silkworm cocoons and 20,000 kilograms of mulberry branch mushrooms, generating CNY 2.4 million in sales revenue and CNY 200,000 in surplus. Over 100 member households benefited directly through wages, guaranteed dividends, and profit-sharing, earning CNY 240,000 in labor income and CNY 40,000 in dividends, averaging CNY 2,800 per household. Households that had previously been in poverty received additional dividends. The cooperative increased its revenue by collaborating with upstream and downstream enterprises, creating over 3,800 temporary jobs for women and disadvantaged groups in mountainous areas. It boosted local smallholders' productivity and income, raising non-member smallholders' earnings by CNY 800 per person.

21. Jinyongfeng Agricultural Machinery Service Professional Cooperative in Cangxi

(1) Basic Information

Established on 29 November 2013, Jinyongfeng Agricultural Machinery Service Professional Cooperative is located in Qiaozi Village, Yongning Town, Cangxi County, with a total capital of CNY 2.108 million. The cooperative focuses on green rice production and agricultural machinery services, consisting of 150 member households. Members contribute funds to the cooperative, which are converted into equity shares; the director holds a 43.1% stake. The cooperative employs a "Four Standardized Services" mode: standardized operational scheduling, quality standards, pricing, and maintenance, which significantly improves service efficiency and quality. In 2022, with project support, the cooperative invested in production facilities and processing equipment, further enhancing its operational capacity(Figure 71).

Figure 71　Processing equipment of Jinyongfeng Agricultural Machinery Service Professional Cooperative

(2) Main Practices

Firstly, provision of machinery and processing services. The cooperative has introduced advanced agricultural machinery(Figure 72), as well as grain processing and packaging production lines, to enhance its service capacity and the quality of agricultural product processing, providing smallholders with a more efficient and convenient service. It has established an 800-mu high-quality rice cultivation base and has provided mechanized operations for 1,200 mu under entrusted management. Additionally, it undertakes 1,300 mu of contract farming and cross-regional farming services. These efforts improve the socialized agricultural service capacity while increasing product value through integrated processing equipment.

Figure 72 Agricultural machinery at Jinyongfeng Agricultural Machinery Service Professional Cooperative

Secondly, training in operations, management, and techniques. The cooperative offers training in farm management, planting techniques, and machinery operation to improve members' and smallholders' technical skills. Publicity and market promotion efforts further expand its sales channels, boosting cooperative profitability and smallholders' incomes. Together, these measures support income growth for members, including previously impoverished households.

Thirdly, transition from traditional to modern farming. With the adoption of advanced machinery, the cooperative has facilitated a shift from traditional to modern farming. This has resulted in a yield increase of 50 kilogram per mu for rice, a labor cost saving of CNY 300 per mu, and an overall net profit increase of over CNY 400 per mu. Through its "Cooperative + Base + Smallholders" mode, it combines dispersed farmer guidance with centralized management, reducing production costs and enhancing the quality and value of agricultural products. Jinyongfeng Agricultural Machinery Service Professional

Cooperative's operational mode is shown in Figure 73.

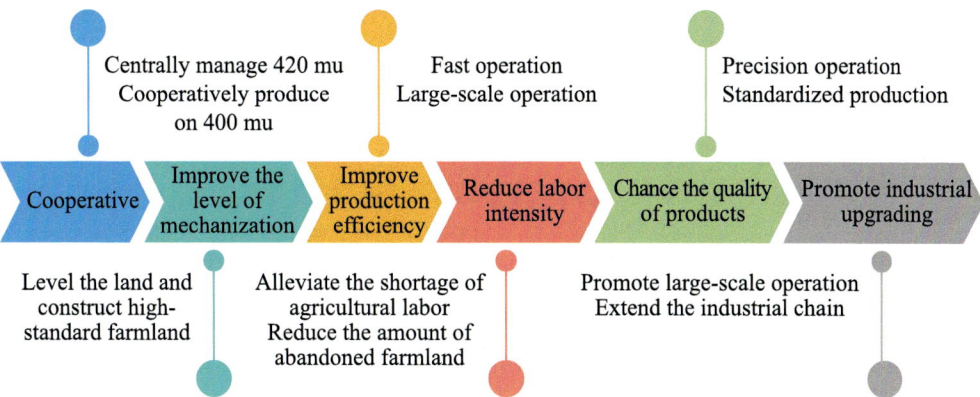

Figure 73　Jinyongfeng Agricultural Machinery Service Professional Cooperative's operational mode

(3) Effectiveness

Over several years of development, the cooperative has achieved significant results. Annual profits reached CNY 274,000, with a total revenue of CNY 3.755 million. The average annual dividend for members was CNY 1,586 per household, with previously impoverished members earning as much as CNY 1,764 annually. This demonstrates the cooperative's vital role in increasing smallholders' incomes and promoting poverty alleviation.

22. Wuzhong Haizhifeng Planting Farmers' Professional Cooperative in Litong

(1) Basic Information

The Haizhifeng Planting Farmers' Professional Cooperative was established on 31 July 2023, in Haizijing Village, Biandangou Town, Litong District, Wuzhong City, Ningxia Hui Autonomous Region, with an initial capital investment of CNY 100,000. While primarily focused on corn cultivation, the cooperative also offers planting, fertilization, and management services to surrounding villages. Consisting of 51 member households, the cooperative accepted cash investments for equity, with the director holding a 1.4% stake. Additionally, the village collective contributed land for a 30% equity stake. In 2023, the cooperative received project support, enabling the purchase of tractors, seeders, and rotary tillers(Figure 74).

Figure 74 Agricultural machinery at Wuzhong Haizhifeng Planting Farmers' Professional Cooperative

22. Wuzhong Haizhifeng Planting Farmers' Professional Cooperative in Litong

(2) Main Practices

Firstly, enhancing production facilities and equipment. The cooperative has laid a strong foundation for its development by upgrading and expanding its infrastructure, including a 360-square-meter machinery storage facility and acquiring 11 pieces of agricultural equipment. The mechanized fertilization process has doubled fertilizer efficiency. To manage and maintain the 3,600 mu of farmland equipped with an advanced water-efficient irrigation system, the cooperative employs its machinery to provide agricultural resources, equipment, and management services to local smallholders, thereby offering a CNY 10/mu service discount within the village(Figure 75).

Figure 75   Farm machinery services at Wuzhong Haizhifeng Planting Farmers' Professional Cooperative

Secondly, implementing the "Five Unified" service mode. As a result of Litong District's efficient water use initiatives, most Haizijing Village smallholders have leased out their land. The cooperative, through collective village management, has adopted a large-scale farming approach, standardizing production, training, irrigation, fertilization, and harvesting. It offers technical and training services to smallholders, enhancing their agricultural skills and enabling them to supply high-quality silage corn to the market. Post-harvest, the cooperative expands its sales channels, supplying silage corn to local smallholders and livestock facilities established by the village collectives, thus gradually building brand recognition. Mode of economic stimulation at Wuzhong Haizhifeng

Planting Farmers' Professional Cooperative is shown in Figure 76.

Figure 76　Mode of economic stimulation at Wuzhong Haizhifeng Planting Farmers' Professional Cooperative

(3) Effectiveness

Through improving its infrastructure and equipment, the cooperative has significantly enhanced its ability to provide socialized services, enabling cost reductions of CNY 150 per mu and increases revenue by over 20% through unified purchasing, sales, packaging, and processing methods. The cooperative expects that by 2025 it will cover an agricaltural machinery operation service area of 3,000 mu, generating an additional income of CNY 150,000 through its machinery services.

23. Yongqi Planting and Breeding Farmers' Professional Cooperative in Yilong

(1) Basic Information

Established on October 18, 2011, Yongqi Planting and Breeding Farmers' Professional Cooperative is located in Group Five, Xiangtan Village, Shuangsheng Town, Yilong County, Nanchong City. The cooperative primarily focuses on grain and oilseed cultivation(Figure 77), processing, and sales, with a capital of CNY 6.3 million. In 2022, the cooperative received project support to invest in medium-sized steel-frame greenhouses, new wheel tractors, grain dryers, primary grain sorting equipment, and grain processing machinery.

Figure 77　Vegetable cultivation at Yongqi Planting and Breeding Farmers' Professional Cooperative

(2) Main Practices

Firstly, upgrading facilities and equipment. Prior to receiving project support, the cooperative had constructed basic cold shelters, which did not meet standards. With the aid received, it built 66 compliant cold shelters and procured a series of agricultural machines, including large tractors, transplanters, sowing and harvesting machinery, laser leveling machines, crop protection drones, drying equipment, and storage facilities. These advancements have significantly improved agricultural production efficiency and standardization, reduced costs and enhanced output effectiveness.

Secondly, staggering product market entry and improving marketing. By utilizing greenhouses for rotational cropping, the cooperative staggers the market entry of agricultural products. It combines online and offline sale strategies to expand distribution channels to markets and institutional buyers, adopting a low-margin, high-volume approach to enhance market competitiveness. The cooperative has successfully registered its "Yongqi" rice trademark, increasing brand recognition and value through brand effectiveness, achieving annual rice sales of 500 tons with a production value of CNY 2.8 million, enhancing product market recognition and added value.

Thirdly, enhancing social services. Operating under a "Company + Cooperative + Base + Smallholders" mode, the cooperative cultivates 6,280 mu of quality rice, corn, wheat, rapeseed, vegetables, and fruits, alongside 35 mu of aquaculture, generating annual sales of nearly CNY 20 million and profits of CNY 1.1 million. Employing a contract farming and social service mode has facilitated income growth for 89 formerly impoverished households, with an average increase of over CNY 3,000 per household. The cooperative supplies over 300 tons of production materials to more than 5,000 farming households, provides mechanization services for 2,300 trips, processes and sells over 500 tons of members' products, and conducts over 2,000 training, exchange, and consultation sessions. Economic stimulation mode of Yongqi Planting and Breeding Farmers' Professional Cooperative is shown in Figure 78.

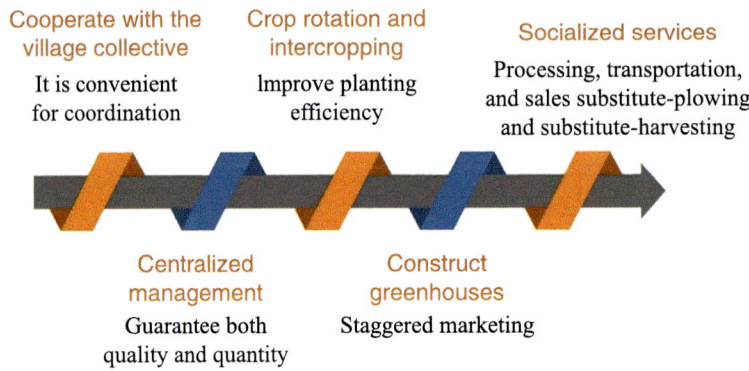

Figure 78 Economic stimulation mode of Yongqi Planting and Breeding Farmers' Professional Cooperative

(3) Effectiveness

Firstly, significant economic benefits. The cooperative has demonstrated its diverse operational capacities and market adaptability with annual sales close to CNY 20 million, profits of CNY 1.1 million, and a cultivated area of 6,280 mu(Figure 79) alongside 35 mu of aquaculture.

Figure 79 Base of Yongqi Planting and Breeding Farmers' Professional Cooperative

Secondly, wider beneficiary base. Beyond boosting the income of 89 formerly impoverished households, the cooperative aids over 5,000 farming households with production materials and services, providing over 2,000 technical training, exchange, and consultation sessions to enhance smallholders' production skills and market awareness. Looking forward, the cooperative plans to strengthen its grain and oilseed base, enhance marketing and promotion efforts, with the goal of achieving an average annual dividend of CNY 200,000 for its members.

24. Chushannonggu Planting and Breeding Professional Cooperative in Guangan

(1) Basic Information

Established on 11 December 2017, Chushannonggu Planting and Breeding Professional Cooperative is located in Huatan Village, Pengjia Township, Guang'an District, with an initial investment of CNY 1 million. The cooperative focuses on climate-smart agricultural practices to synergize agriculture and tourism, promoting green sustainable development. Comprising 55 member households, the cooperative's financial equity arrangement allocates a 5% stake to the chairman. In 2021, it received project funding to invest in multi-span greenhouses(Figure 80), smart monitoring systems, refrigerated transport, and retail facilities.

Figure 80   Greenhouses of Chushannonggu Planting and Breeding Professional Cooperative

(2) Main Practices

Firstly, standardized management. The cooperative emphasizes robust internal management improving regulations, employment practices, and reward and penalty mechanisms to safeguard smallholders' rights, particularly protecting the interests of previously registered impoverished households. Unified management and training of both members and non-members ensure the reduction of fertilizer and pesticide use. The cooperative focuses on technological innovation, fostering sustainable agriculture. By collaborating with research institutions, the cooperative integrates advanced technology, providing training for smallholders to enhance agricultural proficiency, improve product quality, and establish a distinctive agricultural brand. The cooperative's standardized management has enhanced the market competitiveness of its agricultural products, improved smallholders' skills, and safeguarded their rights.

Secondly, developing a "Shared Farm" mode. The cooperative integrates agriculture with tourism, offering activities such as fruit picking, research activities, and animal interaction. Visitors can enjoy hands-on experiences like harvesting, learning agricultural knowledge, and interacting with animals during their visit. This "ecological farm" initiative aims to stimulate resource utilization and entrepreneurship among smallholders, increasing their incomes. By transforming online "virtual farms" into real "shared farms", the cooperative employs smallholders to tend crops for customers who cannot visit, offering them additional income.

Thirdly, establishing the "115 city distribution" group purchase Apps(Figure 81). As a pilot for farm-supermarket connections, the cooperative adopts a time-sensitive delivery mode, promising morning orders by 11 a.m. and afternoon orders by 5 p.m. Customers place orders via an online platform(Figure 82), and cooperative members handle deliveries. Fresh product from the cooperative's base are quickly delivered to supermarkets and then to dining tables, reducing distribution steps, lowering logistics costs, and creating more service jobs. The driving mode of the Chushannonggu Planting and Breeding Professional Cooperative is shown in Figure 83.

Figure 81　The "115 city distribution" and group-buying supermarkets established by the Chushannonggu Planting and Breeding Professional Cooperative

Figure 82　The online shopping mini-program of the Chushannonggu Planting and Breeding Professional Cooperative

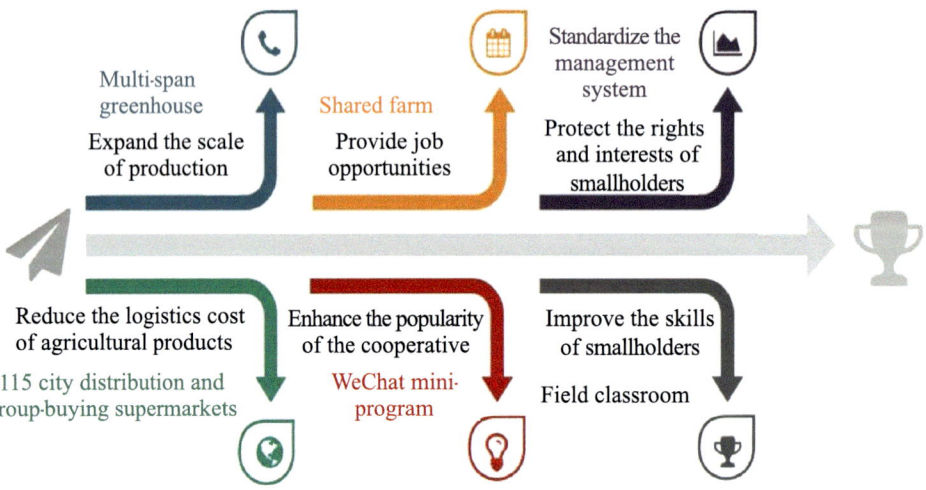

Figure 83　The driving mode of the Chushannonggu Planting and Breeding Professional Cooperative

(3) Effectiveness

Firstly, economic benefits. The cooperative members, including major shareholders, smallholders, formerly impoverished households, minorities, and women, directly benefit with average dividends of CNY 2,137 per member. Former impoverished members receive higher dividends averaging CNY 2,653, reflecting increased income and improved living conditions.

Secondly, boosting agro-industry development and upgrading. Prior to project enablement, the cooperative focused on vegetable production, the project support allowed the cooperative to diversify into "farm-supermarket" operations, expanding business and consumers client bases and boosting revenue. The "shared farm" project offers urban residents farming experiences while providing local smallholders with employment and income, spurring regional agricultural industry development, and promoting the adjustment of the agro-industry structure.

Thirdly, stimulating local economic development. The cooperative's development supports related sectors like construction, equipment manufacturing, packaging, and logistics. It indirectly energizes housing, dining, retails, entertainment, and finance sectors, contributing to local economic growth.

Fourthly, contributing to rural revitalization. Attracting 12 university graduates to return and innovate in agriculture over five years, the cooperative is at the forefront of modernizing local agriculture, and become a mode for new-generation smallholders, The establishment and operation of the cooperative have improved the living conditions of local smallholders and increased their income levels, playing a positive role in facilitating the smooth implementation of the rural revitalization strategy. By promoting the development of the local economy, the cooperative has alleviated social problems such as those of left-behind children and enhanced the sense of happiness and fulfillment among local residents.

25. Yueyinong Agronomic Professional Cooperative in Yinchuan

(1) Basic Information

Yueyinong Agronomic Professional Cooperative was established on 10 August 2020 in Yueyahu Village, Yueyahu Township, Xingqing District, Yinchuan City. The cooperative primarily focuses on the cultivation and sale of vegetables and fruits(Figure 84), with a total investment of CNY 1 million. It has 70 member households, who contribute capital to the cooperative. After share quantification, the chairman holds a 2.8% stake. In 2021, the cooperative received project support, which was invested in constructing large-span greenhouse facilities and sorting centers.

Figure 84   Tomato cultivation at Yueyinong Agronomic Professional Cooperative

(2) Main Practices

Firstly, leasing greenhouses and providing employment. The cooperative currently operates 21 greenhouses, primarily cultivating mushrooms, fruits, and vegetables. Through partnerships with three companies, it leases these greenhouses under formal agreements, whereby the companies manage the greenhouses and pay rent. Cooperative members work in these greenhouses, earning wages for their labor(Figure 85).

Figure 85　Cooperative's greenhouses and agricultural machinery

Secondly, promoting agri-tourism integration for increased revenue. The cooperative is located on the south side of the main entrance of Huangsha Ancient Ferry Scenic Area, a national AAAA-level tourist attraction. It is the only way for tourists to enter and exit, with the scenic area receiving 200,000 visitors annually. The cooperative leverages its strategic location to integrate tourism with greenhouse picking. Through establishing Ningxia hot air balloon low-altitude ecotourism development company(Figure 86), the cooperative offers tourists the opportunity to engage in picking activities and purchase produce during their visits. The development of an eco-friendly, pesticide-free picking garden optimizes the planting structure, enhances overall economic benefits, provides additional jobs, and supports local agri-tourism, thereby increasing smallholders' incomes. Mode of economic stimulation at Yueyinong Agronomic Professional Cooperative is shown in Figure 87.

Figure 86　Ningxia hot air balloon low-altitude ecotourism development company

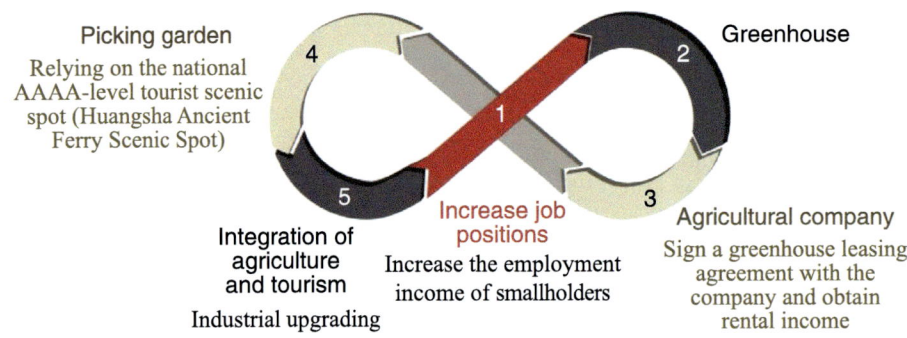

Figure 87　Mode of economic stimulation at Yueyinong Agronomic Professional Cooperative

(3) Effectiveness

By 2023, the cooperative's greenhouse operations created over 300 employment opportunities for villagers and nearby smallholders. Cultivating cherry tomatoes on 5 mu yielded sales of CNY 100,000, from which CNY 57,000 was distributed as secondary dividends to members. The cooperative's successful operations have not only improved local smallholders' living standards but also fostered rural tourism development, enhancing the attractiveness of rural areas.

Acknowledgements

The Institute of Agricultural Resources and Regional Planning of the Chinese Academy of Agricultural Sciences (IARRP, CAAS) undertook the International Fund for Agricultural Development (IFAD) loan project on advantageous and distinctive industries, titled "Institutional Arrangements, Agro-industrial Choices and Value Chain Construction for Promoting Smallholders' Development." The research was led by Researcher Yin Changbin from IARRP, CAAS, who was responsible for the overall design of the project, determining the research plan, organizing and implementing surveys. The expert team members included Researcher Lu Kaiyu from the Institute of Agricultural Economics and Development of the Chinese Academy of Agricultural Sciences (IAED, CAAS), Researcher Yi Xiaoyan, Associate Researcher Ren Jing, Associate Researcher Li Fuduo, and Assistant Researcher Yang Xiaomei from IARRP, CAAS; The postdoctoral researcher Zheng Yuyu, assistant Zhao Yufan, Dr. Yin Yanshu, Dr. Yang Zihong, and Master Zhou Lijun participated in the research.

The research was guided and assisted by the Steering Committee. The research team would like to thank the relevant leaders of the National Project Office(NPO, Department of Farmland Construction and Management of MARA) for their support, and thank Mr. Sun Yinhong, Director of the China Office of the International Fund for Agricultural Development, and Ms.Shi Yinyin, project supervisor and evaluator, for their recognition and suggestions.

The research team conducted multiple surveys in various project areas of Sichuan and Ningxia. We would like to extend our gratitude to Tang Jie, Liu Hongbing, Liang Fan, Zhang Qi, Wei Wei, Wu Hao, Wu Kunyue, Yuan Fang, Zhao Tao, Zeng Jihong, Lan Guangming, Deng Dequan, Liu Hailong, Ma Shaojun, Yong Yanxia, Hao Dandong, Liang Shengfan, and Wang Fangzhi from the provincial (autonomous region) project offices and county (city, district) project offices for their strong support and assistance!

In addition, the research team would like to thank the experts who provided valuable suggestions, including Professor Kong Xiangzhi and Professor Zhong Zhen from Renmin University of China, Researcher Jiang Changyun from the National Academy of Macroeconomics of China, Researcher Nie Fengying from the Institute of Agricultural Information of Chinese Academy of Agricultural Sciences, Associate Researcher Shao Ke from the Management Cadre College of the Ministry of Agriculture and Rural Affairs, Associate Researcher Zhang Shu from the Institute of Agricultural Economics and Development of Chinese Academy of Agricultural Sciences, Teacher Tan Xiaoyun from the former Rural Economic Management Station of the Ningxia Hui Autonomous Region, and A Mu Bu Chu from the Institute of Agricultural Information and Rural Economy at the Sichuan Academy of Agricultural Sciences.

It should be noted that the research process of the project refers to many literature materials, which can be listed as far as possible in the text, but there may be some negligence or omission. If there are any deficiencies in the book, the research team kindly ask readers to criticize and correct!

Editorial Committee
December 2024, Beijing

Attachment 1: Investigation Questionnaire

Investigation Questionnaire of Professional Cooperatives

I. Basic Information and Operation Management of Cooperatives

Number	Question	Option/unit, check the corresponding number of the multiple choice question with a "square", fill in the corresponding space with the value of the fill-in-the-blank question.	2023
1	When the cooperative signed a business plan with IFAD	_____Year	
2	The Fund from IFAD	_____10,000 yuan	
3	Self-funding	_____10,000 yuan	
4	Purpose of business plan funds (multiple options allowed)	1=Direct conversion of equity; 2=Infrastructure construction; 3=Extending the industrial chain such as processing equipment; 4=Strengthening member training, technical guidance, etc.; 5=Increasing the publicity of the cooperative, brand promotion; 6=Expanding sales channels; 7=Other, please explain	
5	Registered name of the cooperative		
6	Year of registration of the cooperative	_____Year	
7	Registered address		
8	Registered capital	10,000 yuan	
9	Registration type	1=Planting; 2=Breeding; 3=Processing; 4=Sales; 5=Integrated production, processing and sales; 6=Agricultural machinery service; 7=Financial service; 8=Land trusteeship service; 9=Other, please explain	

			(continue)
Number	Question	Option/unit, check the corresponding number of the multiple choice question with a "square", fill in the corresponding space with the value of the fill-in-the-blank question.	2023
10	Name of the president/ chairman of the cooperative		
11	Age of cooperative president/ chairman	_____Year	
12	Gender of the president/ chairman of the cooperative	1= Male; 2= Female	
13	The educational level of the president/ chairman	1= Primary school; 2= Junior high school; 3= Senior high school; 4= College degree or above	
14	Whether the president/ chairman runs his own business	1=Yes ; 2=No	
15	Shareholding ratio of president/ chairman	_____%	
16	Number of members of the Council	_____Number	
17	Number of small farmers in the Council	_____Number	
18	Number of women in the Council	_____Number	
19	Whether the cooperative has a full-time accountant	1= Yes; 2= No	
20	Total number of members in the cooperative (including board of directors and members)	_____Number	
21	Among them: the number of members	_____Number	
22	Number of young members (18-45)	_____Number	
23	Number of member households	_____Number	
24	Members of the community used to be registered households	_____Number	

Attachment 1: Investigation Questionnaire

(continue)

Number	Question	Option/unit, check the corresponding number of the multiple choice question with a "square", fill in the corresponding space with the value of the fill-in-the-blank question.	2023
25	The frequency of the cooperative meeting with members	_____Per year	
26	Number of times the cooperative held board meetings	_____Per year	
27	Number of times the board of supervisors of the cooperative has been held	_____Per year	
28	Method for members to join the cooperative (multiple options available)	1=Land; 2=Labor force; 3=Capital; 4=Technology; 5=Agricultural machinery; 6=Other, please explain	
29	If the land is invested in the community, is it quantified?	1=Yes; 2=No	
30	If the capital is invested in the community, is it quantified?	1=Yes; 2=No	
31	What is the dividend method of the cooperative?	1=Guaranteed dividend (i.e., land transfer fee); 2=Profit dividend (second dividend); 3=Other, please explain	
32	What is the basis for the second dividend?	1=Dividend according to trading volume; 2=Dividend according to shares; 3=Dividend according to trading volume and shares combined	
33	What is the profit in 2023?	_____10,000 yuan	
34	What is the profit in 2022?	_____10,000 yuan	
35	Will there be a second dividend in 2023?	1=Yes; 2=No	
36	If so, what is the total amount of the second dividend?	_____10,000 yuan	

(continue)

Number	Question	Option/unit, check the corresponding number of the multiple choice question with a "square", fill in the corresponding space with the value of the fill-in-the-blank question.	2023
37	What is the proportion of the second dividend amount to the profit?	_____%	
38	How much can each member get on average?	_____Yuan	
	Fixed assets of cooperatives		
39	What is the net fixed assets for the fiscal year 2022?	_____10,000 yuan	
40	What is the net fixed assets for fiscal year 2023?	_____10,000 yuan	
	Cooperative capacity building		
41	Does the cooperative establish a management system?	1=Yes; 2=No	
42	Do the board members participate in the training related to the development of cooperatives?	1=Yes; 2=No	
43	Introduce new varieties	_____Number	
44	Investment in new varieties	_____Number	
45	Introduce new technologies	_____Number	
46	Cost of new technology	_____Yuan	
47	Whether it is a mode cooperative	1= Yes; 2= No	
48	If yes, the demonstration level is	1= National level; 2= Provincial level; 3= Municipal level; 4= County level	
49	Whether to operate agricultural products processing	1= Yes; 2= No	
50	Do you have your own agricultural brand	1= Yes; 2= No	

Attachment 1: Investigation Questionnaire

(continue)

Number	Question	Option/unit, check the corresponding number of the multiple choice question with a "square", fill in the corresponding space with the value of the fill-in-the-blank question.	2023
51	Agricultural products "Three Products and One Standard" through several items (can choose more)	1= Pollution-free agricultural products; 2= Green agricultural products; 3=Organic agricultural products; 4= Agricultural geographical indications	
52	Whether the trademark registration certificate has been obtained?	1= Yes; 2= No	
53	Is there joint development with other cooperatives?	1=Yes; 2=No	
54	Is there joint development with other family farms?	1= Yes; 2= No	
55	Whether to develop jointly with agricultural enterprises?	1= Yes; 2= No	
56	Cooperation between cooperatives and sales partners	1=Order contract; 2=Verbal agreement; 3=Other	
57	How many jobs does the cooperative provide?	_____Number	
58	Among them: how many people are in the original poor households/ registered households?	_____Number	
59	Women	_____Number	
60	Middle-aged and young people (18-45 years)	_____Number	
61	How many people (1 year or more) are provided for medium-and long-term positions?	_____Number	
62	Provide the number of temporary workers in the post	_____Number	

(continue)

Number	Question	Option/unit, check the corresponding number of the multiple choice question with a "square", fill in the corresponding space with the value of the fill-in-the-blank question.	2023
63	How much does the cooperative need for daily operation expenses? It does not include expansion investment, but only daily personnel expenses, management fees and so on	_____10,000 yuan per year	
64	Does the cooperative have a loan at present?	1= Yes; 2= No	
65	Loan channels? (Multiple options allowed)	1= Rural credit cooperatives; 2= Commercial banks; 3= Other, please explain	
66	The purpose of obtaining financial services (loans)?	1= Purchase agricultural machinery; 2= Construction of storage and other factories; 3=Purchase of good seeds; 4= Purchase of office equipment; 5= Recruitment of professional technical personnel of the cooperative; 6= Other, please explain	
67	What measures should cooperatives take to address climate change? (Multiple options allowed)	1=Water-saving irrigation/water and fertilizer integration; 2=Organic fertilizer replacement of chemical fertilizer; 3=Green biological pesticide; 4=Straw returning to the field; 5=Other, please explain	
68	Do cooperatives with agricultural production bases buy agricultural (commercial) insurance?	1= Yes, _____yuan/mu; 2= No	
69	How many natural disasters has the cooperative suffered in the past five years?	_____Number of time	
70	What are the types of natural disasters?	1= Flood; 2= Drought; 3= Frost; 4= Other, please explain	
71	How much area was affected?	_____Mu	

Attachment 1: Investigation Questionnaire

(continue)

Number	Question	Option/unit, check the corresponding number of the multiple choice question with a "square", fill in the corresponding space with the value of the fill-in-the-blank question.	2023
72	What is the proportion of production loss?	_____%	
73	What are the ways to help you resume production? (Multiple choices)	1= Local government emergency response; 2= Insurance company compensation; 3= Assistance from enterprises/cooperatives; 4= Other, please explain	
74	How many pest and disease disasters have you encountered in the cooperative in the past five years?	_____number of time	
75	What is the type of pest and disease disaster?	Please specify_____	
76	How much area was affected?	_____Mu	
77	What is the proportion of production loss?	_____%	
78	What are the ways to help you resume production? (Multiple choices)	1= Local government emergency response; 2= Insurance company compensation; 3= Assistance from enterprises/cooperatives; 4= Other, please explain	
79	What changes have the commercial plans supported by IFAD brought to cooperatives? (in order of importance)	A. The financial problem has been solved; B. Strengthened technical guidance; C. Increased the confidence of cooperatives to grow; D. Strengthened industrial chain management, brand awareness, publicity, etc; E. Helped small farmers to increase their income; F. Other, please indicate	
80	Satisfaction with support for business plans	1=Very satisfied; 2=Relatively satisfied; 3=Average satisfied; 4=Relatively dissatisfied; 5=Very dissatisfied	

II. Production, Purchase, Processing, Sales and Service of Cooperatives

Year	Product type 1.Grain crops; 2. Oil crops; 3. Greenhouse vegetables; 4. Outdoor vegetables; 5. Fruits; 6. Seedlings and flowers; 7. Medicinal herbs; 8. Livestock breeding; 9. Under-forest breeding or scattered breeding on wasteland; 10. Others	Product name List them one by one according to the raw material product name, such as citrus, cattle, sheep, etc	Self-production scale: planting or breeding/ (mu or head)	Self-production output/kg	Number of acquisitions/ kg	Purchase cost/ (yuan/kg)	Number of farmers acquired/ household	Among them: ① Poor households/ household	② Farmers in this cooperative/ household	Sales price of unprocessed agricultural products sold by cooperatives/ (yuan/kg)	Cooperative unprocessed sales channels 1= Free market; 2= Enterprise orders; 3= Farm-supermarket connection; 4= E-commerce; 5= Other, please explain	The quantity of processed products (kg) here refers to the agricultural products before processing	Processing cost/ (yuan/kg)
2023													

Attachment 1: Investigation Questionnaire

(continue)

Processed products /kg	Sales price of processed products / (yuan/kg)	After processing, sales channels 1= Free market; 2= Enterprise order; 3= Farm-supermarket connection; 4= E-commerce; 5= Other, please explain	If it is sold online, what percentage of the total sales volume is sold/%	Total sales amount/ (10,000 yuan)	Among them: ① Self-produced sales/ (10,000 yuan)	② Sales of cooperative members (sales on behalf of the cooperative) /(10,000 yuan)	Changes in sales compared with the previous year (1=Decrease; 2= Unchanged; 3= Increase)				
2023											

Number	Questions and options	Agricultural services (seed, fertilizer, pesticide, feed and other agency sales)	Agency farming and harvesting (including agricultural machinery services and trusteeship)	Agricultural production technology (including technical training and guidance on prevention and control of epidemic prevention)	Product processing, packaging and so on (including primary processing, packaging and deep processing)	Product accumulation	Product transportation	Product sales (including consignment and orders)	Finance loan
1	Whether to provide the services to members	1= Yes; 2= No	1= Yes; 2= No	1= Yes ;2= No	1= Yes ;2= No	1= Yes; 2= No	1= Yes; 2= No		
2	How many members have used the services provided by the project in the past 12 months?								
3	How many members have used the services provided by the project since its implementation?								
4	Is the service charged?	1= Yes; 2= No	1= Yes ;2= No	1= Yes; 2= No	1= Yes; 2= No	1= Yes; 2= No	1= Yes; 2= No		

Investigation Questionnaire for Smallholders

I. Basic Information of Household

Smallholders types: 1. Beneficiaries of public infrastructure and climate smart agriculture in the project area; 2. Beneficiaries of the construction of Ningxia base in the project area; 3. Beneficiaries of the cooperative supported in the project area; 4. Non-project households (Please select the corresponding farmers types and check them, multiple selections are allowed)

1. Household members (from the respondent, first adult, then child, if separated from children, do not count as one family)

Code	A1	A2	A3	A4	A5	A6	A7	A8	A9	A10
Number	Full name	Gender: 1= Male; 2= Female	Identity: 1=Householder; 2=Spouse of the householder; 3=Children/wife/ husband-in-law; 4=Grandchild (female); 5=Parents/In-laws/ parents-in-law; 6=Other, please explain	Age (one full year of life)	Marriage Status: 1= Married; 2= Unmarried; 3=Widowed; 4=Divorced	Ethnicity: 1= Han nationality; 2=Minority nationality	Education level: 0=Never attended school; 1=Primary school; 2=Middle school; 3=High school; 4=University and above	Health status: 1= Good; 2= Mild disability, able to work; 3=Moderate to severe disability, unable to work	Whether engaged in non-agricultural work: 1=Yes; 2=No	If so, what is the main occupation? 1= Working outside; 2=Working in a company; 3=Individual business; 4=Village cadre; 5=Public institution; 6=Civil servant; 7=Other, please explain
1										
2										
3										
4										
5										

2. Basic information about smallholder household operation

	Indicator content	Option/unit	2023
1	Whether your family was formerly registered as a registered household	1= Yes; 0= No	
2	What position do you hold in the village?	1= Village chief; 2= Village secretary; 3= Other cadres of the village committee; 4= Ordinary villagers	
3	Whether women in the family participate in village activities? (such as voting)	1= Yes; 0= No	
4	The main person who does housework at home is (single choice):	1= Father (husband); 2= Mother (wife); 3= Son (son-in-law); 4= Daughter (daughter-in-law); 5= Other	
5	Mother (wife) has the right to decide on major family matters such as buying a house, taking out a loan, running a business and sending children to school	1=90% or more; 2=50%-90%; 3=30%-50%; 4=Below 30%	
6	Who controls household income?	1= Father (husband); 2= Mother (wife); 3= Each manages their own income	
7	Household disposable income? (Including agricultural operation, individual business, wage income, property income and transfer income)	This year _____ 10, 000 yuan; last year _____ 10, 000 yuan	
8	Among them: net income from agricultural operations	This year _____ 10, 000 yuan; last year _____ 10, 000 yuan	
9	Net income from wages	This year _____ 10, 000 yuan; last year _____ 10, 000 yuan	
10	Floor area of family housing (excluding yard)	_____ Square meter	
11	House type	1= Bungalow; 2= Apartment building; 3= Adobe house	
12	Housing construction time	_____ Year	
13	Whether there will be repairs in 2020-2023?	1=Yes; 2=No	

Attachment 1: Investigation Questionnaire

(continue)

	Indicator content	Option/unit	2023
14	Does the house have a separate bathroom?	1= Yes; 2= No	
15	Your toilet type is	1= Flush toilet; 2= Dry toilet; 3= Other	
16	Main sources of domestic water (single choice)	1= Tap water; 2= Well water; 3= Mountain spring water; 4= River water; 5= Rainwater; 6=Other	
17	In addition to electricity, whether other energy sources (lighting, cooking, etc.) are used in household life	1= Solar energy; 2= Gas; 3= Biogas; 4= Firewood; 5= Coal; 6= Other	
18	Have you bought agricultural machinery in the past two years?	1= Yes; 2= No	
19	If so, how much did it cost?	_____ 10,000 yuan	
20	Have you bought a car in the past two years?	1= Yes; 2= No	
21	If so, how much did it cost?	_____ 10,000 yuan	
22	Main uses of car purchase	1= Living convenience; 2= Freight; 3= Passenger car	
23	Annual household living expenses	_____Yuan	
24	Among them: food expenditure	_____Yuan	
25	Annual family interpersonal expenses	_____Yuan	
26	How much farmland do you have?	_____Mu	
27	Types of livestock owned by families	Cattle / (head/cow)	Sheep /(head/ number)	Pig /(head/ number)	Poultry/ birds
28	Number of shipments				
29	How far is your home from the nearest market?	_____Minutes (time required for general transportation)	
30	Has the infrastructure or transportation in the market been rebuilt or repaired in the last two years?	1=Yes; 2=No	
31	Has your time in the market been shortened by infrastructure improvements over the past two years?	1= Yes; 2= No	
32	Do you process some of your products in a processing facility?	1= Yes;0= No (If "no", skip 33 to 37)	

(continue)

	Indicator content	Option/unit	2023
33	The processing channels of agricultural products produced by you (multiple options allowed)	1= Self-processing; 2= Nearby processing plant; 3= Cooperative	
34	Is the processing facility practical?	1=Very practical; 2=A little practical; 3= A little impractical; 4= Very impractical	
35	How far (how long) is it to the processing facility?	_____Minutes (time)	
36	Has the time spent at this processing facility decreased in the last two years?	1= Yes; 2= No	
37	Has the channel of using processing facilities increased in the past two years?	1= Yes; 2= No	
38	Does the family hold financial products such as stocks, funds, national bonds, trust products, foreign exchange products?	1= Yes; 2= No	
39	Does your family have a loan or debt?	1= Yes; 2= No	
40	If so, how much?	_____10,000 yuan	
41	The source of the loan or borrowing is (multiple options allowed)	1= Government interest subsidy loan; 2= Personal credit or property mortgage loan; 3= Private loan; 4= Borrowing from relatives and friends; 5= Other, please explain	
42	Who decides where the loan is to be used?	1= Father (husband); 2= Mother (wife); 3= Other	
43	Who pays the loan or the loan at home?	1= Father (husband); 2= Mother (wife); 3= Children; 4= Others	
44	Is there an improvement in diet and nutrition?	1=Improved greatly; 2=Improved somewhat; 3=No change; 4=Worse than before	
45	How many natural disasters have you experienced in the past five years?	_____Time	
46	What is the type of natural disaster?	1=Flood; 2= Drought; 4= Frost; 4= Other, please explain	

Attachment 1: Investigation Questionnaire

(continue)

	Indicator content	Option/unit	2023
47	How much area was affected?	_____Mu	
48	What are the ways to help you resume production? (Multiple choices)	1= Local government emergency response; 2= Insurance company compensation; 3=Assistance from enterprises/cooperatives; 4= Other, please explain	
49	How many serious pests and diseases have you encountered in your home in the past five years?	_____Time	
50	What are the types of pests and diseases?	Please specify_____	
51	How much area was affected?	_____Mu	
52	What are the ways to help you resume production? (Multiple choices)	1= Local government emergency response; 2= Insurance company compensation; 3=Assistance from enterprises/cooperatives; 4= Other, please explain	
53	What is your relationship with the nearby cooperatives?	1=Working; 2=Selling agricultural products to the cooperative; 3=Using the services provided by the cooperative (such as agricultural services, farming and harvesting on behalf of others); 4= No relationship at all	
54	Does your family join a cooperative?	1= Yes; 2= No	
55	Are you a member of the board of directors of the cooperative?	1= Yes; 2= No	
56	Have you ever attended a general meeting?	1= Yes; 2= No	
57	What is the way to join a cooperative? (Multiple options allowed)	1=Land; 2=Labor force; 3=Capital; 4=Technology; 5=Agricultural machinery; 6=Other, please explain	
58	How much of the shares do you own in the cooperative?	_____Yuan	
59	How much dividend do you get each year?	_____Yuan	
60	How many times have you attended cooperative training?	_____Time	

II. Adoption and Sales of Environmentally Friendly Technologies for Agricultural Production (if both planting and breeding are available, both Table (1) and Table (2) need to be filled in)

1. Crop cultivation (fill in according to the production season of each crop, such as corn in the first half of the year and wheat in the second half of the year)

Year	Crop type (1. Food crops; 2. Oil crops; 3. Facility vegetables; 4. Open field vegetables; 5. Fruits; 6. Seedlings and flowers; 7. Medicinal herbs; 8. Others, please specify [variety code and write down the specific crop)	Planting area/ mu	Whether to use new varieties 1=Yes; 2=No	Irrigation method 1= Flood irrigation; 2= Integrated water and fertilizer; 3= Drip irrigation	Fertilizer input/ (kg/mu)	What is the basis for fertilizer input? 1= Based on experience; 2= See the manual; 3= Advice from agricultural sales personnel; 4= Advice from agricultural technology extension personnel	Organic fertilizer input/ (kg/mu)	Type of organic fertilizer1= Composted farm fertilizer; 2= Commercial organic fertilizer	What is the basis for organic fertilizer input? 1= Based on experience; 2= See the manual; 3= Advice from agricultural sales personnel; 4= Advice from agricultural technology extension personnel	Whether the organic fertilizer used is provided by the cooperative 1=Yes; 2=No
2023	For example: 1-Corn									
	1-Wheat									
	2-Rapeseed									
	3-Tomatoes									
	4-Carotene									
	5-Citrus									

Attachment 1: Investigation Questionnaire

Year	Crop type (1. Food crops; 2. Oil crops; 3. Facility vegetables; 4. Open field vegetables; 5. Fruits; 6. Seedlings and flowers; 7. Medicinal herbs; 8. Others, please specify [variety code and write down the specific crop)	If so, is the price cheaper than the market price 1=Yes; 2=No	Pesticide use basis 1= By experience; 2= See the instructions; 3= Order of agricultural sales personnel; 4= Advice of agricultural technology extension personnel	The treatment of mulch film after use is 1= Stay in the field; 2= Pick it up and throw it to a special recycling station; 3= Companies will collect it	The treatment methods of crop straw are 1=Shredding and returning to the field;2=Using as feed;3=Using as fuel; 4=Using as substrate for edible mushroom; 5=Local burning	Change in crop yield compared with last year 1= Increase; 2= Decrease; 3= No change	Reasons for increased production 1= Favorable weather; 2= Variety improvement; 3= Production management technology improvement	Reasons for decreased production 1= Natural disasters; 2= Pests and diseases; 3= Other	Whether sales have changed from last year 1= Increase; 2= Decrease; 3= No change	Sales channel 1= Cooperative distribution; 2= Vendor acquisition; 3= Retail
2023	For example: 1-Corn									
	1-Wheat									
	2-Rapeseed									
	3-Tomatoes									
	4-Carotene									
	5-Citrus									

2. Animal husbandry

Year	Breeding type (specify the code and specific name) 1= Livestock breeding in pens; 2= Under forest or scattered breeding on wasteland	Whether to buy a new variety 1=Yes; 2=No	Feed purchase source: 1=Free market; 2=Cooperative distribution; 3=Cooperation with other enterprises; 4=Other, please explain	Whether the manure is composted into fertilizer or commercial organic fertilizer 1=Yes; 2=No	If not, how is the manure disposed of 1= Direct discharge; 2= Sold to enterprises; 3= Given free or paid to farmers	Whether the feces is separated wet or dry 1=Yes; 2=No	If so, the treatment of urine is 1= Direct discharge; 2= Sewage tank storage 3= Sedimentation tank treatment and discharge; 4= Discharge into biogas tank; 5= Oxidation pond treatment; 6=Other, please explain	Dry manure method (multiple options) 1= Compost fermentation and return to field; 2= Sell to cooperative; 3= Sell to enterprise; 4= Other, please explain	The disposal methods of diseased livestock and poultry are 1= Sold to buyers; 2= Thrown into rivers or seas; 3= Buried deeply; 4= Incinerated; 5= Decomposed in decomposition pools;6= Other	Sales channels (multiple options) 1= Self-retail; 2= Sales through cooperatives; 3= Order contract; 4= E-commerce; 5= Buyer; 6= Other	Whether the output has changed from last year 1= Increase; 2= Decrease; 3= Unchanged
2023	For example: 1-Cow										
	2-Sheep										
	3-Pigs										
	4-Chickens										

Attachment 1: Investigation Questionnaire

III. Participation Degree of Farmers in the Project and Technology Adoption and Satisfaction (farmers in non-project areas do not answer)

Code	Content	Have you benefited from the following construction projects? 1=Yes; 2=No (if not, do not score)		Are you satisfied with these projects? (1-5, 5 is the most satisfied)	
	1. Infrastructure construction (irrigation and drainage system, water source project, safe drinking water for human and livestock, power supply system, village roads, infrastructure operation and maintenance)				
1	Flood and drainage system (including ditches)				
2	Agricultural water supply projects (mountain ponds, reservoirs, river dams, etc.)				
3	Human and animal safe drinking water projects (water pipes, purification equipment, etc.)				
4	Power grid circuit				
5	Village roads				
	2. Construction of climate smart production bases	Whether the facility is used or relevant training has been received: 1=Yes; 2=No	Do you think these practices work? 1= Yes; 2= No	Will you continue to use it? 1=Yes; 2=No	Are you satisfied with these projects? (1-5, 5 is the most satisfied)
6	Land leveling (slope to terraces, etc.)				
7	Greenhouse for planting facilities/breeding greenhouses				
8	Integrated water and fertilizer facilities				
9	Drip irrigation facilities				
	3. Agricultural productive services	Whether the facility is used or relevant training has been received: 1=Yes; 2=No	Do you think these practices work? 1=Yes; 2= No	Will you continue to use it? 1=Yes; 2=No	Are you satisfied with these projects? (1-5, 5 is the most satisfied)

(continue)

Code	Content	Have you benefited from the following construction projects? 1=Yes; 2=No (if not, do not score)	Are you satisfied with these projects? (1-5, 5 is the most satisfied)
10	Agricultural materials procurement services (seeds, fertilizers, pesticides, feed, etc.)		
11	Soil testing and formula fertilization		
12	Green pest control		
13	Replace chemical fertilizers with organic fertilizers		
14	Agency farming and harvesting (including agricultural machinery services and trusteeship)		
15	Conservation tillage such as fallow rotation, intercropping, interplanting, deep plowing and deep turning		
16	Return straw to the field or comprehensive utilization		
17	Waste film treatment		
18	Feed ratio for breeding		
19	Prevention and control of animal and poultry diseases		
20	Animal and poultry manure treatment		
21	Product processing, packaging (including primary processing, packaging and deep processing)		
22	Product accumulation		
23	Product transportation		
24	Product sales (including consignment and orders)		

Attachment 2: Investigation Photos

1. Investigate the construction and production of cooperatives in Nanchong City, Dazhou City and Guang'an City, Sichuan in July 2022

2. Investigate the construction and production of cooperatives and bases in Guyuan City, Ningxia, Guangyuan City and Nanchong City, Sichuan in September 2023

3. Household survey of beneficiary households in Guyuan City, Ningxia in November 2023

4. Special research on the agro-industry development and promotion of smallholders

in Yibin City, Sichuan and the Cooperatives in Hongsibu District, Ningxia in May 2024

5. Special research on cooperatives and beneficiary smallholders in Ningxia and Sichuan projects areas in October 2024

291

Attachment 2: Investigation Photos

293

Attachment 2: Investigation Photos

图书在版编目（CIP）数据

带动小农户发展的制度安排、产业选择和价值链建设研究：基于国际农业发展基金贷款优势特色产业发展示范项目 / 尹昌斌等编著 . -- 北京：中国农业科学技术出版社, 2024.12. -- ISBN 978-7-5116-7237-7

Ⅰ . F320

中国国家版本馆 CIP 数据核字第 2025NY7730 号

责任编辑　周伟平　崔改泵
责任校对　李向荣
责任印制　姜义伟　王思文

出 版 者	中国农业科学技术出版社
	北京市中关村南大街 12 号　邮编：100081
电　　话	（010）82106638（编辑室）（010）82106624（发行部）
	（010）82109709（读者服务部）
网　　址	https://castp.caas.cn
经 销 者	各地新华书店
印 刷 者	北京建宏印刷有限公司
开　　本	185 mm×260 mm　1/16
印　　张	19.25
字　　数	398 千字
版　　次	2024 年 12 月第 1 版　2024 年 12 月第 1 次印刷
定　　价	120.00 元

版权所有·侵权必究